D0042315

BEN-GURION

Ben-Gurion

Father of Modern Israel

————◆◀◆▶◆————

ANITA SHAPIRA

Translated from the Hebrew

by Anthony Berris

Yale

UNIVERSITY

PRESS

New Haven and London

Frontispiece: Ben-Gurion in 1971.

Yale University Press books may be purchased in quantity for educational,
business, or promotional use. For information, please e-mail
sales.press@yale.edu (U.S. office) or sales@yaleup.co.uk (U.K. office).

Set in Janson Oldstyle type by Integrated Publishing Solutions.
Printed in the United States of America.

Library of Congress Cataloging-in-Publication Data
Shapira, Anita.
Ben-Gurion : father of modern Israel / Anita Shapira ; translated from the
Hebrew by Anthony Berris.
pages   cm — (Jewish lives)
Includes bibliographical references and index.
ISBN 978-0-300-18045-9 (alk. paper)
1. Ben-Gurion, David, 1886–1973.   2. Prime ministers—Israel—Biography.
I. Berris, Anthony, translator.   II. Title.
DS125.3.B37S53713   2014
956.9405'2092—dc23
[B]   2014010381

A catalogue record for this book is available from the British Library.

This paper meets the requirements of ANSI/NISO Z39.48-1992
(Permanence of Paper).

10 9 8 7 6 5 4 3 2 1

CONTENTS

Preface, vii

1. Plonsk, 1

2. "I Found the Homeland Landscape," 17

3. Exile and Return, 43

4. Labor Leader, 62

5. From Labor Leader to National Leader, 82

6. Days of Hope, Days of Despair, 102

7. On the Verge of Statehood, 135

8. "We Hereby Declare . . . ," 154

9. Helmsman of the State, 174

10. Ben-Gurion Against Ben-Gurion, 203

CONTENTS

11. Decline, 232

Epilogue, 242

Notes, 247

Acknowledgments, 257

Index, 259

PREFACE

PAULA BEN-GURION STOOD at the entrance to the wooden cottage in Sdeh Boker, blocking the door. "What do you want?" she barked at me.

"I have an interview with Mr. Ben-Gurion," I replied, embarrassed.

She moved aside to let me pass. "Don't tire him!" she ordered.

I was working on my first research project, which dealt with the Hashomer (Watchman) organization. I wanted to clarify a point regarding the clash between former Hashomer members and Ben-Gurion, then general secretary of the Histadrut labor organization. So I wrote to the retired leader, asking to meet him and discuss this question. I was a completely unknown scholar, a young woman of no consequence. Nevertheless Ben-Gurion replied in his own writing, on a page from his enumerated notebooks with sheets of carbon paper between the pages.

He agreed to meet, and even consented to see me on whatever day was convenient for me. I brought my husband and toddler son, and we drove south from Tel Aviv in our small Fiat 600. It took us at least three hours to reach Sdeh Boker over bumpy roads. My son enjoyed chasing birds in the fields, and my husband chased him.

When I crossed the threshold of the famous cottage, Ben-Gurion received me very graciously. He opened his diary to the year in question and talked at length about the Hashomer case. I was overwhelmed by the grand old man. I stayed with him for more than two hours. Then my family and I started the long drive home. It was only when we reached Tel Aviv that I realized that he had not answered my question.

Since then I have researched many subjects, and Ben-Gurion, a central figure in Zionist history, has been a constant presence in my work, but I have not written directly about him before. He was the second most important figure in my biography of Berl Katznelson, his friend and colleague in leadership. He was the person who clashed with the Haganah general command during the War of Independence, who brutally dismissed Yigal Allon—the golden boy, the best field commander in the war—all topics I devoted books to. Only in a few articles did I give him first place, such as one I wrote about his attitude toward the Bible and its role in Israeli culture. So it seems time to finally make him the central figure, here in this biography.

Ben-Gurion attracted many writers and biographers, during his lifetime and after; they include historians, journalists, admirers, and antagonists. As while he lived, so ever after he cast a larger-than-life shadow, and many of these writers could not rid themselves of their sympathy or hatred, old grudges or adulation. Most prominent among his biographers are Michael Bar-Zohar and Shabtai Teveth, whose works I read very carefully and made use of in my own study. Other historians wrote about specific issues in his career, such as his decision to launch the Sinai Campaign, his relationships with intellectuals, his attitude toward the Diaspora, and so on. I have read these works, of course, and made use of them elsewhere, but here I relied mostly on my own past studies. I did much new research into the period after 1948, which Teveth did not cover and Bar-Zohar dealt with only partially. I was given access not only to Ben-Gurion's archive in Sdeh Boker, which is online, but also to his files in the archives of the Israel Defense Forces, where I found many interesting documents, especially letters.

While Ben-Gurion's public persona has been the subject of many works, I have tried to sketch his private persona, as well as the long process of his development into a national leader and one of the most significant figures of the twentieth century. Ben-Gurion tended not to display his feelings, and tracing his inner self is difficult. I hope this work will add a page with a different perspective to the large collection of works dealing with his achievements, failures, and role in history.

BEN-GURION

1

Plonsk

In 1962, a woman from the town of Plonsk, Poland, who had emigrated to Palestine went back for a visit. On returning to Israel she sent a letter to Prime Minister David Ben-Gurion, also born in Plonsk, describing what she had found: "the destruction of Jewish Plonsk," as Ben-Gurion put it in his reply.[1] Only three of the town's Jews remained. The magnificent synagogue and the three Jewish religious schools were completely destroyed, and the cemetery was uprooted. The market was still there, but no Jews displayed their merchandise. With much pain and restrained nostalgia, Ben-Gurion inquired what had become of his father's house and whether the garden behind it still existed. The rupture between "now" and "then" caused by World War II, the Holocaust, and the subsequent communist regime was total. An entire world had been made extinct and existed now only in memories and images.

In his later life Ben-Gurion used to glorify the memory of

his hometown. In his recollections, this small, humble place of some eight thousand souls, of whom five thousand were Jews, became "the most progressive Hebrew city in Poland."[2]

Plonsk sat on a minor road off the highway between Warsaw and Gdansk. Although it was only sixty-five kilometers from Warsaw, the journey to the capital took over three hours. In the early 1900s the railway had not yet reached Plonsk, and there was no paved road to the town. It had no running water, and sewage flowed in the streets. The winds of the Haskala (Jewish enlightenment) were blowing in Plonsk, but as might be expected in such a backward place, most of its Jews were piously observant, and progress was only relative. There were three Jewish religious schools and numerous heders (Jewish elementary schools), including both traditional schools and progressive, relatively modern institutions that nevertheless did not teach Russian or mathematics, despite the Russian authorities' demand that the children also be taught secular subjects. The town did not have a *gymnasium* (high school). Plonsk resembled many other shtetls under the tsarist empire's rule, and despite the ideological storms raging all around, it remained largely conservative, tranquil, and removed from the revolutionary fervor that characterized the Pale of Settlement in Ukraine and White Russia.

David Ben-Gurion was born in Plonsk in 1886, the fourth son of Sheindel and Avigdor Green. Nothing in his origins, his birthplace, or his education hinted at future greatness. The Greens had no notable lineage, no important rabbis or religious arbiters in their history, which they could trace only as far back as the grandparents on both sides. Ben-Gurion's paternal grandfather was a writer of requests, petitions, and letters for the Polish peasants who came to town on market day and sought to take cases to the local court. Avigdor Green inherited this occupation from his father. His son referred to him as a "lawyer," although he was more of a pettifogger *(Winkeladvokat)* who sat on the corner outside the courthouse. The family was on a fairly sound financial footing thanks to Sheindel's dowry: two wooden houses with a garden behind them on a large plot of land. These houses were on the outskirts of the town, on Goat Alley (whose name attests to its character) next to the priest's house. The family lived in one and rented out the other, and this rent plus Avigdor's income enabled them to live reasonably well.

The most distinguished family in Plonsk was the Zemachs, who were proud of their lineage. Shlomo Zemach and Ben-Gurion were friends from their youth, but there was a big difference between them: the Zemach family genealogy reached back to the seventeenth century, and among its forebears were some eminent Torah scholars. They were wealthy and aristocratic. Shlomo was a tall, handsome young man and a good student in the religious school. Zemach senior was a proud, well-respected Jew, not pleased by his son's friendship with the son of Avigdor Green; there were murmurings in the town about Green because he had exchanged the traditional ultra-Orthodox garb of the long black *kapota* (coat) for a short European jacket, he had a penchant for cards, and he was a Mitnaged (opponent of Hasidism), whereas most Plonsk Jews were followers of the Rabbi of Gur. On one occasion Zemach senior even slapped Shlomo for visiting the Green house. But the youngsters' friendship was firm, and Zemach was forced to accept his son's connection with the dubious Greens.

The Jews of Plonsk were largely Hasidim who were artisans, apprentices, carpenters, cobblers, and small merchants. Above them was a sparse middle class of homeowners, most of whom were "enlightened" (tolerant of modernity and open to Haskala influences such as secular education); these included many Mitnagdim. At the top of the socioeconomic ladder stood a few rich, aristocratic families, also disciples of the Rabbi of Gur. The Greens were a relatively "modern" middle-class family.

They joined the Hibbat Zion (Lovers of Zion) movement when it arose in the 1880s, and, following the dramatic appearance of Theodor Herzl, became loyal Zionists. Avigdor Green was a member of Hibbat Zion, and he imparted his beliefs to his eldest son, Abraham, and his youngest, David.

Plonsk did have its political disputes. Some Hasidim, for example, made the life of another Hasid a misery because he was a Zionist, and the father of a young man who intended to emigrate to Palestine hid his clothes, preventing him from leaving the house. But it seems such events were rare, which is why people mentioned them in their memoirs. The intergenerational struggles that typified the first generation of religious backsliders, the soul-wrenching deliberations that recur in the literary descriptions of the time, are absent from the accounts of Ben-Gurion and his friends in Plonsk. There the process of modernization was gentler and less traumatic than that experienced by many of Ben-Gurion's contemporaries. At the time, Pale of Settlement Jewry was torn between the autonomism of Simon Dubnow, which strove for Jewish cultural autonomy in Eastern Europe; the Jewish socialism of the Bund (founded in 1897, the same year as the First Zionist Congress); Russian social democracy; Zionism; and territorialism, a movement that sought a possible territory for the Jews outside Palestine. These stormy ideological struggles barely touched the Jewish youth of Plonsk. There the youngsters deliberated over remaining in Poland and somehow acquiring a higher education, emigrating to the United States, or becoming a Zionist and going to Palestine.

Ben-Gurion attended a heder and then a Jewish religious school, which he left after his bar-mitzvah. Talmudic disputation did not appeal to him, or perhaps he lacked the talent for this type of study. He wanted a higher education, but was unable to obtain a matriculation certificate, either because of the quota by which Russian gymnasia limited the number of Jewish students, or because he could not afford it. Since Plonsk had no gymnasium, attending one meant moving to Warsaw. Like many Jewish youngsters in this situation, he tried to prepare for the admission examinations by studying on his own.

Meanwhile, unbeknownst to his son, Avigdor Green wrote a letter to Theodor Herzl, the leader of the Zionist movement— a letter Ben-Gurion only became aware of some fifty years later, when it was found in the Central Zionist Archives in Jerusalem. In high-flown, archaic Hebrew, Green explained to the man considered "the King of the Jews" that he had a talented, diligent son who wanted to study but was unable to do so. He would like to send the boy to study in Vienna, Herzl's city, and he sought the advice of the president of the Zionist Organization, and also his financial aid, "for I am unable to support my son, the apple of my eye."[3] The letter reveals the naïveté of the advocate from Plonsk who imagined that he would receive a reply to his letter. But it was also the first expression of the father's belief that his son possessed extraordinary talents.

The years between 1899 and 1904 are shrouded in mist. Ben-Gurion left school but stayed in Plonsk. He apparently learned Russian, read a great deal, and probably helped his father write petitions and requests outside the courthouse. He still wore the traditional *kapota*. The one ray of light in his life was his activity in Ezra, an organization of Jewish religious school students (the intellectual and social elite of Plonsk), which he founded along with Shlomo Fuchs and Shlomo Zemach after the three decided to speak Hebrew.

Ben-Gurion recalled learning Hebrew from his grandfather at age three. His grandfather would sit him on his lap, point at different body parts, and say what they were in Hebrew; then the child repeated the names after him. He moved on to various household objects, and continued until the boy began chattering in Hebrew. The three friends' decision to speak Hebrew was quite courageous: although it was the language of the Torah, nobody spoke it at that time.

Written Hebrew was different; modern Hebrew literature was widely read. In fact, its language captivated enlightened Jews. Ben-Gurion always mentioned the first Hebrew novel, Abraham Mapu's *Ahavat Zion* (Love of Zion), as one of the factors that led him to Zionism, just as *Uncle Tom's Cabin* made him a socialist, while Tolstoy's *Resurrection* had such a powerful effect on him that for a while he became a vegetarian. Young David Green read a great deal of Hebrew literature and poetry. The youngsters at the Jewish religious school used to hide Hebrew literature inside their Gemara books, but Ben-Gurion had no need of these stratagems since his father allowed him to read as much Hebrew literature as he wanted. He read Mordecai Feuerberg, Micha Yosef Berdyczewski, and Ahad Ha'am, and knew Hayim Nachman Bialik's poems, which he loved, by heart. He also loved Judah Leib Gordon's and Saul Tchernichovsky's poetry. He read the best of Russian literature: Tolstoy, Dostoevsky, and Turgenev. In later interviews he stressed that he never learned Polish since he had always known he would emigrate to Palestine and saw no point in learning a language he considered provincial. There is some doubt whether this assertion is true, for he needed Polish to communicate with the peasants who attended the courthouse. Most likely his repudiation of Polish was intended to underscore both his fervent desire to emigrate to Palestine and his connection to Russian, which the Yishuv (the Jewish community in Palestine) considered more prestigious than Polish.

In any event, written Hebrew was accepted by the *maskilim* (enlightened, educated Jews) as part of the revival of original Hebrew culture, in the spirit of national movements seeking to return to their nation's ancient roots or invent a genealogy for themselves. But Hebrew was not a spoken language, even in

Palestine. Eliezer Ben-Yehuda, compiler of the modern Hebrew dictionary, was well known for speaking Hebrew to his son from the day he was born. But until the Herzliya Gymnasium in Tel Aviv adopted Hebrew as the language of instruction, and a generation of Hebrew-speaking graduates emerged, spoken Hebrew was a rarity. When Ben Gurion met the Zionist leader Nachum Sokolov, editor of the Hebrew-language newspaper *Hatzfira* and future Zionist Organization president, in Warsaw around 1904 and addressed him in Hebrew, Sokolov could reply only in broken Hebrew.

Thus the decision by the three boys in Plonsk to speak only Hebrew among themselves and teach it to their families was a real cultural and political statement. As it turned out, they were so successful that conversing in Hebrew became the hallmark of Zionist youth in Plonsk. The Ezra association also set a goal of disseminating Hebrew education among the poorer youth, the social stratum of apprentices who had barely acquired a little education. The boys devoted themselves enthusiastically to this endeavor, and the local artisans responded by allowing their apprentices to study for an hour and a half a day. It appears that the influence of the Russian "Go to the People" movement was at work here: if the Russians can volunteer in order to advance the people, then so can we! The members of Ezra tried to register as a recognized Zionist association and pay the Shekel membership dues, but their application was rejected because of their age—Ben-Gurion, the youngest of the three, was fourteen at the time, and Fuchs, the oldest, was sixteen.

In 1903, the Kishinev pogrom rocked the entire Jewish world, but there were no reverberations in tranquil Plonsk. What did shock our three youngsters was Herzl's proposal at the Sixth Zionist Congress that same year to establish Jewish settlement in East Africa, known as "the Uganda Program." Driven by a sense of urgency over the distress of Jews in the Pale of Settlement, Herzl sought a "night shelter" for them until they could settle in Palestine, where the Turks were doing everything in their power to prevent such settlement. The proposal caused an uproar at the congress. Its opponents, most of whom were Zionists from Eastern Europe where Jewish tradition and culture were still firmly rooted, threatened to split the Zionist Organization. To Ben-Gurion and his friends the proposal seemed a betrayal of Zion. One hot summer day, as they were drying themselves in the sun after a swim in the River Plonka and talking about momentous issues, they decided that the most appropriate response to the Uganda Program was to emigrate to Palestine.

Yet there was still a long road to travel between decision and action. Shlomo Fuchs was the first to leave Plonsk, but instead of going to Palestine he went to London and thence to New York, like millions of other young Jews seeking to free themselves of the stifling atmosphere of a small, remote town where there was no chance of advancement. Fuchs and Ben-Gurion corresponded at length and in great detail, and through these letters we can reconstruct the young Ben-Gurion's mindset during those years. Fuchs kept Ben-Gurion's letters for almost fifty years until, almost miraculously, they came into the possession of the editor of Ben-Gurion's papers. When asked why he had kept the letters so long, Fuchs replied that they had always known Ben-Gurion was destined for greatness. We shall never know if this was the wisdom of hindsight or genuine precognition. In any event, these letters provide contemporaneous testimony of Ben-Gurion's history from 1904 on.

He was a sensitive, emotional boy, very attached to his friends. His mother died in childbirth when he was eleven and his father remarried, but Ben-Gurion never called his stepmother "mother" and did not feel close to her. The loss of his mother caused him pain that never healed; she dwelt in the mind of the child, the youth, and even the adult as an irreplaceable source of love, devotion, and emotional affinity, for whose loss there was no reparation. David, known as Duvche, was a sickly child, so his mother left her older children for a time and took him to the country where he could recuperate in the healthy air, eating nutritious country food. This episode was etched in the child's mind as a precious memory of unparalleled devotion. "It seems to me that she was one of a kind," he wrote to one of his friends whose mother had died; "she had eleven children [most of whom died in infancy] yet she cared for me as if I were her only son. It is hard for me to describe such abundant love. And it is hard for me to forget being orphaned as a child."[4] On every occasion when Ben-Gurion, as prime minister of Israel, wanted to console a friend on the death of his or her mother, he always mentioned the loss of his own mother. In a letter to Golda Meir following her mother's death, he wrote that a mother "is the most intimate of things, second to none," and with her passing "something unparalleled in love, loyalty, the most intimate bond, is cruelly torn from the soul, the heart, and will eternally be a precious, irreplaceable treasure."[5] He would give his age at his mother's death as younger than it really was—"My mother died when I was ten"—to underscore the misery of the little boy bereft of motherly love.

His idealization of his mother and clinging to her memory suggest that although Avigdor was a devoted father and Duvche his favorite son, relations in the house on Goat Alley were not warm, and the boy lacked love and affection. He first discovered the thrill of love for a member of the opposite sex at twelve, but this seems to have been just worship from afar. It is unclear whether the object of this first love was Rachel Nelkin, the town beauty, for whom he developed real feelings several years later, or another girl. Plonsk Jewish society was very conservative, and attachments between the sexes were usually expressed solely by an exchange of yearning glances.

Ben-Gurion's relations with his Ezra friends seem to have gone deeper, as suggested by his emotional, revealing letters to

Fuchs. He was unabashedly sentimental and tried his hand at writing poetry, but in light of his friends' criticism quickly realized he would not gain fame as a poet. He showed an interest in philosophy and believed he had a future as a philosopher. He lectured at Ezra on Baruch Spinoza, hotly disputing the philosopher's concept of the Chosen People—a subject he returned to in his old age. Among the Zionist thinkers he respected Ahad Ha'am as a pure-minded writer and an important critic, but his heart lay with Micha Yosef Berdyczewski, Ahad Ha'am's sworn adversary and the man who introduced Nietzschean ideas into the Jewish milieu. Shlomo Zemach later wrote: "We, the young people of Plonsk, would walk down Ploczk Street with the Nietzschean phrases we learned from Berdyczewski on our lips, and pondered life as death and death as life, not understanding much about it, yet taking in something of it."[6] The new Hebrew literature and poetry were full of vitalistic ideas that fired the youths and led them to embrace Zionism as an expression of the desire to breathe the instinct of life and will-power into the Jewish people and change their image.

In 1904 Herzl died. It was a terrible blow. The man who by the force of his will and energy had created the Jewish people's national movement and the tools to implement its aspirations, and defined its objective—a Jewish state in Palestine—was suddenly no more. It was as if a comet had flashed into being, burned for less than a decade, then was suddenly extinguished, leaving no one in Jewish public life who might be his successor. Ben-Gurion's letter to Fuchs following Herzl's death reflects the depth of the emotion roused by the leader's passing and hints at young David Green's opinion of the qualities a leader should have. "There will never be another man as wonderful as he who combined the heroism of the Maccabeans with the stratagems of David, the courage of Rabbi Akiva who died with the word 'One' on his lips and the humility of Hillel, the beauty of Rabbi Yehuda Hanassi, and the fiery love of Rabbi Yehuda

Halevi." Courage, cunning, self-sacrifice, humility, and love of the nation—these were the traits he enumerated. Then he added: "The desire to strive for the rebirth delegated to us by the man with the will of the gods will burn within us until completion of the great task, for which the great leader sacrificed his illustrious life."[7] The typically Nietzschean expression he used, "the man with the will of the gods," alludes to a leader's most notable quality—willpower—linking it to the legacy Herzl has supposedly left young people: the task of navigating the ship of Zionism to a safe harbor. And indeed, accepting the mission of realizing Zionism as a personal undertaking was one of the qualities characterizing the people of the Second Aliya (wave of immigration), which began that year.

However, despite the dramatic decision to emigrate made on the bank of the River Plonka, and even after Herzl's death, David Green was in no hurry. He wanted first to acquire a higher education and a diploma in engineering or a similar field. He had his sights set on the Warsaw Mechanical-Technical School, founded by Jewish philanthropist Hyppolite Wawelberg in order to enable Jews to study. But to be accepted he had to study Russian and mathematics, and instruction in these subjects in Plonsk was not at the required level. It is also probable that his father could not continue supporting him. So at eighteen David Green left home for the first time and traveled to the big city, Warsaw. For young Jews, leaving their parents' home was a traumatic experience that entailed leaving behind everything that "home" symbolized—faith, tradition, parental authority—and standing on one's own two feet without financial support. This crisis usually occurred at a younger age, but Ben-Gurion lived at home until he was eighteen, even though there was no good reason why he did not leave earlier, except possibly his attachment to Rachel Nelkin.

Moving to Warsaw did not mean leaving the tight-knit Jewish society he was used to. In Jewish Warsaw he was surrounded

Ben-Gurion as a youth in Warsaw, beginning
of the twentieth century (Courtesy of the
Lavon Institute for Labor Movement
Research)

by familiar scenes, so much that he was not particularly impressed by the city. He did exchange his *kapota* for a student's
short jacket and peaked cap. Nonetheless, whenever he went
back home for a visit he would revert to traditional attire—
suggesting that his parting from traditional society was not
traumatic, but also not complete. He found a teaching position
in Warsaw and was able to support himself. He studied dili-
gently, and although he tried several times to get into Wawelberg's school, he was unsuccessful. In the meantime the quota

applied in this school, which was originally intended for Jewish students, became more stringent, so that only those who had graduated from gymnasium stood any chance of getting in. Each time one of his attempts failed, the idea of going to Palestine resurfaced, but he still harbored hopes of acquiring an education first. He explained his stubborn persistence by saying he wanted "to work in a broad framework in our land," but did not say what this meant.[8]

Meanwhile Plonsk was in a furor: Shlomo Zemach, the Jewish school's most diligent and outstanding student, had taken some money his father had in the house, fled his home, and used the funds for passage to Palestine. He stopped off in Warsaw, where he could get information on illegal border crossings and catch a train to the Austrian border, and saw Ben-Gurion. Zemach senior soon followed on his heels. Ben-Gurion loved describing a fictional scene in which the father came to his room in Warsaw and pleaded with him to reveal his son's whereabouts, even kneeling and hugging Ben-Gurion's knees. Ben-Gurion's imagination portrayed this proud, distinguished man who opposed his son's friendship with the son of the *Winkeladvokat* being forced to abase himself. But in a letter to Fuchs he described what actually happened: Zemach came to Ben-Gurion's room, and during a courteous conversation tried to get him to reveal Shlomo's whereabouts. Ben-Gurion claimed that Shlomo had already left, and after a further exchange Zemach gave up and returned to Plonsk.

Shlomo Zemach immigrated to Palestine at the end of 1904, one of the first in the wave known as the Second Aliya. Like the other immigrants from Plonsk he was driven not by the pogroms or by existential anxiety, but by the belief that the Jewish people's rebirth would be brought about by returning to their homeland, where they would live a natural life and till the soil. Zemach's immigration had a snowball effect; he was followed by quite a few young people from distinguished

Plonsk families and also from poorer ones. The fact that Shlomo Zemach was the hero of the hour in Plonsk was probably not exactly music to David's ears, for there was a persistent, though covert, rivalry between him and his handsome friend. However, he had not yet decided when he would go to Palestine.

In January the Russian Revolution of 1905 began in Warsaw. Ben-Gurion was not involved in the strikes and demonstrations that took place, but during these events the Polish Poalei Zion (Workers of Zion) party was founded in Warsaw. It held its first conference in the home of Yitzhak Tabenkin, Ben-Gurion's future friend and political adversary. Ben-Gurion attended the founding conference and joined the party. It was the first time he had shown any interest in politics. Poalei Zion combined Zionism and Marxist Socialism according to the doctrine of Ber Borochov, a young genius who successfully united internationalism and nationalism, the coming world revolution, and the redemption of the Jewish nation.

It is doubtful that Ben-Gurion was acquainted with the Marxist formulas that Poalei Zion adopted. As far as we know he did not read radical Russian polemical literature as did other young, left-leaning Jews, nor was he familiar with the accepted political style. But he quickly learned the socialist jargon and became a superb debater, even though his grasp of Marxism was probably very shallow. He accepted as self-evident the class war concept, the moral superiority of the revolutionaries and the revolution as opposed to the ruling classes, and the socialist image of the future. But with respect to the realization of Zionism, it is doubtful that he accepted Borochov's perception that historical necessity led the Jews, with ironclad logic, to Palestine of all places. Some fifty years later he claimed that before immigrating to Palestine he had not read even one of Borochov's articles. He was probably prepared to accept Borochov's concept that, because the Diaspora Jews would not be allowed to join the proletariat due to opposition among local populations, they were doomed to be crushed in the future titanic struggle between capitalists and proletariat. Beyond that, however, his perception of Zionism was based not on necessity but on Berdyczewski's concept of will.

Suddenly life had direction and content. He exchanged his student garb for a revolutionary side-buttoned Russian shirt and peaked cap, and he let his hair grow long. He attended meetings, traveled to distribute propaganda materials, and enjoyed the thrill of risking being caught for revolutionary activity. And he was indeed caught and arrested. The first time, his party comrades managed to bribe an official to give them the forbidden material that had been found on him, and he was released due to lack of evidence. On the second occasion his father came to his rescue and persuaded a police officer to let him go.

Revolutionary radicalization brought the Bund to Plonsk, where its members preached their Jewish-Socialist ideology among the Jewish workers and the poorer Jews. Ben-Gurion returned to Plonsk in his new character of a Zionist-Socialist activist and embarked on an all-out war against the Bund, which advocated that the Jews remain in Russia and take part in the coming general revolution, which would end their misery. The residents of Plonsk enjoyed seeing their favorite son Duvche tearing a Bundist outside agitator to pieces in debates. Meanwhile, there was fear of a pogrom, and David Green proudly sported a pistol and organized the apprentices to join Poalei Zion and for self-defense. He instructed his Ezra friends in the use of weapons. Arms belonging to the Jews were cached in Avigdor Green's house and miraculously not discovered in a police search. In the spirit of revolutionary foment David successfully organized an apprentices' strike for a twelve-hour day—a change that was eventually willingly accepted by their artisan employers.

In contrast with the quietness of the previous years, the

almost frenetic activity of the new member of Poalei Zion was particularly notable. Ben-Gurion's energy, which was to become his hallmark, had apparently lain dormant and unexploited until he discovered political activity. He had found his vocation.

In the summer of 1906 Shlomo Zemach, who had reconciled with his father, returned to Plonsk for a visit. On his journey back to Palestine he was joined by several Plonsk Jews, including the wife of Simcha Aizik, the Hasid who had been hounded because of his Zionism and was already in Palestine, and Aizik's beautiful stepdaughter Rachel Nelkin, whom David Green loved. Ben-Gurion joined them, having concluded that there was nothing more to look forward to in the Russian Empire. As a Poalei Zion activist, he would be better off in Palestine. His father supported his wishes and even paid for his passage. The parting celebration, held in Rachel Nelkin's home, concluded with the singing of "The Oath," the moving Yiddish anthem of Poalei Zion that had been composed for the Sixth Zionist Congress and spread rapidly throughout the Pale of Settlement and beyond. The immigrants traveled by coach to the railway station at Modlin Fortress, and from there set out for Warsaw, Odessa, and thence by sea to Jaffa. Rachel's and David's feelings for each other were evident, so the girl's mother made sure to sleep between them aboard ship to avoid gossip.

2

―――――◆◆◆◆◆◆――――――

"I Found the Homeland Landscape"

BEN-GURION'S GRAVE stands on a cliff overlooking the ancient desert landscape of Wadi Zin. As he instructed, his tombstone is inscribed simply with the dates of his birth and death and the words: "Immigrated to Palestine in 1906." When asked what were the three most decisive events in his life, he always included his immigration to Palestine. It symbolized a form of rebirth that soon led him to change his name and adopt a new identity: no longer David Green, son of Avigdor, but David Ben-Gurion, scion of a leader of the Great Revolt against Rome, a courageous fighter described in Flavius Josephus's *The War of the Jews Against the Romans*. When he arrived in Palestine, Ben-Gurion asked his father to keep the letters he would send. When he began publishing articles, he cut them out and pasted them in special notebooks for safekeeping. These actions reflected a feeling that was widespread among people at the time: that they were making history that should be documented.

Ben-Gurion left Plonsk at the end of July 1906 and landed on 6 September in Jaffa, where he was greeted by the usual tumult of this port town. Strapping Arab boatmen rowed out to the ships anchored offshore, loaded the passengers and their belongings onto their boats, and brought them ashore. For many immigrants this was a terrifying encounter. The foreign boatmen seemed menacing, the sea was rough, and the small boats bobbing on the waves seemed about to capsize. But the short trip ended well, and after passing through the Ottoman bureaucracy, Ben-Gurion reached the port gate.

Passing through the gate, he was free to wander as he wished. The contrast with the stifling Russian regime was stark. The atmosphere of Palestine breathed an almost anarchic sense of freedom, in which the dreams of Jewish independence could take shape. Ben-Gurion was thrilled by displays of the nascent Jewish entity: shop signs in Hebrew, people speaking Hebrew in the street, a Jewish boy riding a horse, a Jewish girl riding a donkey. "These are sights of the rebirth!" he exulted.[1] He was unimpressed by Jaffa: the dusty streets, the narrow alleys—perhaps even the Arab residents, whom he does not mention. Together with a group of immigrants he quickly left the town for Petach Tikva, the oldest Jewish *moshava* (colony). The landscape, along with his first encounter with a Jewish village in Palestine, intoxicated him; his childhood dreams were coming true. The nocturnal sounds of howling jackals and braying asses brought to life the biblical verses that mentioned these animals.

At first Ben-Gurion exalted village life and work in the fields. Later, he liked to glorify the title of agricultural worker. Even long after, in the first census taken following the establishment of the state, under "profession" he wrote "agricultural worker." But it was hard work, and he contracted malaria that recurred every few weeks. Quinine, the drug used to combat it, did not help; he often ran a fever of forty degrees Celsius. Living in crowded quarters with only meager food did not improve his health.

The people of the Second Aliya came to Palestine as individuals. They were not members of organizations that could have helped them settle there and had no social resources to cushion the hardships of the place. Ben-Gurion and his companions—young people far from home and family for the first time in their lives—lived under harsh conditions, feeling terribly lonely.

These immigrants' deepest desire was to build the country, and physical labor in the fields was the only way to do so, contended the members of Hapoel Hatzair (The Young Worker), a party that rejected Marxism and instead made its goal the "conquering of all the labor occupations in Palestine by the Jewish worker." Only by returning to primal labor, to direct communion with nature and farming, would the Jewish people undergo the metamorphosis necessary to reshape their image. Only thus would a broad class of Jewish agricultural workers be formed to become the foundation of the Jewish national entity. A worker's ability to cope with a hard day of tedious agricultural labor in a foreign, hostile climate was therefore the ultimate test. With painful sarcasm, the writer Yosef Haim Brenner described the unfounded dreams of the Jewish intellectual who wanted to till the soil of the homeland but swiftly realized that he had neither the physical nor the mental ability for it.

This was the great crisis of the Second Aliya young people, and the reason many of them left the country—Ben-Gurion estimated the figure at ninety percent. Every ship that anchored in Jaffa Port carrying new immigrants was met by people wanting to return to Russia or Galicia, or go on to London or New York. For many new immigrants, the traumatic encounter with those who were departing—and who justified their decision with stories of the hard reality of Palestine that could thwart any idealist—was a formative experience and formed a common trope in the literature of the period.

Ben-Gurion was careful not to cast aspersions on the country. He scrupulously painted an apparently balanced, unromantic, yet not hostile picture: "In general, potential immigrants to Palestine usually think about and remember only the romance of the country, its beauty, its future, memories of its grand past and the magic of its antiquities, and disregard the real Palestine with its simple, rough, everyday life," he wrote to his father. Instead of their lofty dreams "they find an intimate, naked, prosaic reality—a limited village life and work . . . hard, exhausting work," and then comes the crisis. "On a scorching summer day to stand hoeing the *hamra* [hard earth] . . . the sweat flows, the hands are covered in blisters and bruises, and it is as if all your limbs are falling apart," he wrote.[2] His love Rachel Nelkin failed this test, but Ben-Gurion was preoccupied with his own difficulties and did not find the energy to console and make things easier for her. She found another soulmate, Yechezkel Beit-Halakhmi, who helped her through her difficulties, and they were married within a year. Ben-Gurion did not write his father about this, either because of the characteristic reserve of the period—people did not discuss intimate matters, certainly not with their parents—or because it was too painful for him. For many years he tried to get Rachel back, and kept a warm place in his heart for her to the end of his life. Initially he stayed close to his friends from Plonsk, especially Shlomo Zemach, who provided comfort that ameliorated the loneliness of a twenty-year-old who found it hard to make friends with strangers. But they drifted apart after a few months.

His true consolation was party activity, which he was drawn into almost immediately. On 2 October 1906, less than a month after he landed, Ben-Gurion traveled from Petach Tikva to Jaffa to attend the founding conference of Poalei Zion in Palestine.

He was elected conference chairman and also to the committee that formulated the party platform at a meeting in Ramla. Party activity offered a legitimate break from physical labor as well as an arena where he felt he was doing something important, and succeeding, which boosted his sense of self-worth. The founders of the Palestine party came from Poalei Zion in Russia and sought an organizational structure suitable to the type of political activity they were used to there. Political work in Russia was built around a party, which required a platform, a leadership, and an organ.

Hapoel Hatzair, the first party founded in Palestine, was local and had no mother party in the Diaspora. Populist in nature along the lines of the Russian "Go to the People" movement, it had no detailed platform, but simply focused on Jewish workers in general, and agricultural workers in particular. It considered cultural activity extremely important, and making Hebrew the national language was its top priority. Its journal, *Hapoel Hatzair*, was of very high quality, reflecting its somewhat elitist character as the party of the Jewish intelligentsia in Palestine; the members were not only workers but also teachers and writers. Most of the country's intellectuals leaned toward this party, which despised Marxism and refused to define itself as socialist, even though its orientation toward the worker was no different from that of Poalei Zion. Neither was its members' lifestyle.

Ben-Gurion saw no essential differences between the two parties, and later contended that the only difference was in their names. But there were in fact two main sources of disagreement between them. Poalei Zion in Palestine was divided between Hebraists, who wanted to make Hebrew the spoken language, and Yiddishists, who favored Yiddish. It was also just a branch of the party in Russia, which soon founded the World Federation of Poalei Zion, with branches in other countries as well. The two issues of the local party's independence and of

Hebrew's precedence over Yiddish were bones of contention between Poalei Zion and Hapoel Hatzair, and also within the local Poalei Zion party itself. Ben-Gurion insisted both that Hebrew be the national language and that the Palestine party be independent. He addressed the Jaffa conference in Hebrew, even though most of his audience did not understand him; some even left the hall.

Even though the majority of the Poalei Zion membership (which numbered only a few score) were "Rostovists"—brash young men from Russia with no Jewish, Yiddish, or Hebrew background, who spoke only Russian and for whom Zionism was secondary to socialism—Ben-Gurion was elected to the committee that formulated what went down in history as "the Ramla Platform." Exactly how this brand-new immigrant, not blessed with any notable qualities, was elected to two important positions is unclear. In the view of Ben-Gurion biographer Shabtai Teveth, it was due to string-pulling by Israel Shochat. Shochat, a man of great personal charm, excelled at behind-the-scenes maneuvering in small conspiratorial groups. He was looking for someone to strengthen the Palestinocentrist trends in Poalei Zion (in order to give priority to Palestinian interests over those of Diaspora communities), who was also familiar with Socialist-Borochovist jargon and had a gift for oratory, which Shochat lacked. Ben-Gurion fit this profile. In accordance with the Russian movement's tradition of conspiracy, the platform drafting committee convened in a remote *khan* (inn) in Ramla, a town without a single Jew. They had yet to internalize the fact that secret meetings were completely unnecessary in Palestine.

In the history of the Palestine labor movement the creation of the Ramla Platform is an uncharacteristic and actually negligible event that likely would never be mentioned in movement history if Ben-Gurion's name had not been connected with it. The Ramla Platform was purely Marxist, in the Borochov style.

It opens with a sentence extracted from the Communist Manifesto, amended to suit Zionism: "The history of all hitherto existing society is the history of class and national struggles."[3] The word "national" was added to legitimize the struggle of the Jewish national movement. Borochov described a spontaneous process that would drive the impoverished, unemployed Jewish proletariat in the Diaspora to Palestine, then subject to what he perceived as a feudal Ottoman regime. A bourgeois society would slowly be built and capitalism would develop, followed by class war, revolution, and the era of socialism. Meanwhile the workers' party would struggle to democratize the regime and for workers' rights—though it would have no responsibility to build the economy. Since immigration would occur quite on its own, neither Zionist propaganda nor efforts to organize immigration would be necessary. Nevertheless the committee recognized the need to assist immigrants by setting up an "information bureau" to direct them to places of work. The party had debated whether to participate in the Zionist Congress, since it represented the scorned Jewish bourgeoisie. The Ramla Platform recognized the need to take part in the congress for the benefit of the workers, but as a counterbalance it also requested membership in the International Socialist Congress, even though it did not accept parties without a national homeland.

The basic Borochovist premises did not pass the test of Palestinian reality. First, young people came out of nationalist motives, not as a result of unprompted processes. Second, most of the Second Aliya immigrants settled in the towns and had no intention of changing their lifestyle to become proletarians. Third, there was hardly any industry in Palestine. Poalei Zion's target audience was a small minority of several thousand young men and women who were drawn to Palestine by Zionist idealism; it was this group that created the mythology of the Second Aliya. Finally, the Second Aliya workers were willing to undertake economic and social initiatives without waiting for the advent of socialism.

Poalei Zion was not a great success, but for Ben-Gurion it represented an important experience, as well as his first attempt at appearing before a Palestinian audience. He even hoped to be elected as a delegate to the Eighth Zionist Congress in The Hague, where he might meet his friend Fuchs, who had joined Poalei Zion in America. But these hopes were dashed when Yitzhak Ben-Zvi reached Palestine in 1907. Ben-Zvi (who later became president of the State of Israel) was a member of the movement in Russia and had a revolutionary background that included incarceration and exile. He was Borochov's friend and fully conversant with the intricacies of socialist theory. A few years Ben-Gurion's senior, he was a warm, kind, courteous, convivial man who never quarreled with anyone. Ben-Gurion, by contrast, lacked both warmth and the ability to communicate with people; in the harsh circumstances of the Second Aliya period, his difficulty in forming personal relationships was a great disadvantage. On his arrival, Ben-Zvi, who was considered the party's senior member, took over the top position. Ben-Gurion failed by a large margin to be elected as a delegate. Disappointed, affronted, and exhausted, he decided to abandon intense political activity. Presumably this was why he decided to move from Judea to Galilee.

Galilee has a special place in Second Aliya mythology. The old orchard-based moshavot in Judea were already well established when the new pioneers arrived. They employed hundreds of Arab workers in seasonal work. Many farmers refused to hire Jews as agricultural laborers. They claimed that doing this work would demean the Jews in the eyes of the Arabs; that Jews did not work as well as Arabs; and that the new pioneers were insolent, demanded respect, and were not religiously observant. They thought that Jewish workers would endanger both the physical and economic security of the moshavot. To the workers, the farmers were traitors driven by selfish economic motives who were hindering the establishment of a working Jewish community.

By contrast, the new moshavot of Galilee were based on field crops. The relative wealth of the Judean moshavot, which had enjoyed the generous support of the French philanthropist Baron Edmond de Rothschild, was nonexistent in Galilee, and the standard of living there was very low. The farmers and their families worked their land themselves, employing one annual worker who lived with the family and shared their food.

Ben-Gurion moved to Galilee in October 1907 and found work at the Sejera moshava in Lower Galilee. "After Judea, Sejera was almost what Petach Tikva was for me after Plonsk and Warsaw. There I found the Palestine I had dreamed about," he wrote in his memoirs. "In Sejera I found the homeland landscape I had yearned for so much."[4] The beauty of the mountainous Galilean landscape stunned the Second Aliya immigrants who had come from the flat countries of Eastern Europe. In a letter to his father Ben-Gurion waxed lyrical about the amazing light that enabled him to see from afar majestic, snow-covered Mount Hermon. Sejera itself captivated him. He worked at the moshava, plowing, guiding the oxen along the furrow while his mind was occupied with other matters. It was not as fatiguing as hoeing rows of fruit trees, and in the evening he had time for reading, writing, or public activity. Moreover, the cooler Galilee climate was easier to tolerate, and malaria was less common. In Ben-Gurion's self-created mythology, Sejera was a magical place that justified bestowing on himself the title "agricultural worker." He often recounted his experiences there as seminal events in the life of a worker in Palestine, referring to the three years or so he spent there. But according to Shabtai Teveth's calculations, he was there only thirteen months.

Like many of the Second Aliya pioneers, Ben-Gurion's youthful restlessness sent him wandering all over the country, going from one workplace to another, searching for something intangible that would bring tranquility and happiness. For the young men, enforced bachelorhood was distressing and painful. There were few young women, even fewer who were pretty. And how could a worker even think about a serious relationship with a woman when he could barely make a living? Starting a family was out of the question. As Shlomo Zemach put it, "We were a group of hundreds of young men and six or seven young women, and we did not visit whores."[5] It was customary to pack up one's few belongings and walk from place to place. Thus, for example, Ben-Gurion walked from Judea to Sejera with Zemach for three days. Between his arrival in Sejera in the fall of 1907 and his journey to Saloniki in 1911, he worked in Zikhron Ya'akov, which he called the most beautiful of the moshavot; went back to Plonsk to report for duty in the Russian army—otherwise his father would have had to pay a fine—then deserted and returned to Palestine; worked on the editorial board of *Ha'akhdut*, his party's new journal in Jerusalem; revisited his family in Poland; and went to Vienna for the World Federation of Poalei Zion conference and saw the wonders of the city, the first big European capital he had visited. Clearly he did not spend a great deal of time working in agriculture.

Despite this seminal experience in Sejera, and even though he called it the crowning glory of his participation in the Second Aliya, at the end of 1909 Ben-Gurion informed his father that he did not see his future in agriculture. "I myself have no inclination or desire to be a farmer." His stated reason was ideological: "I hate the possession of land that binds the owner to it, and I love freedom with all my heart, the freedom of body and mind."[6] This statement is worthy of a proud socialist, but it conceals a simpler motive: he had had enough of agricultural work. Shlomo Zemach contended that Ben-Gurion was miserable doing this work, and did it poorly. And indeed, many prominent Second Aliya personalities abandoned agriculture.

Those who could became editors or teachers, or took up any other profession that freed them from backbreaking labor in the burning sun. Ben-Gurion was no exception, but more than others he turned his past in Sejera into his calling card.

In that same letter to his father he hinted that what interested him was political activity and explained that to prepare himself for this he needed to travel to Istanbul to study law. A few months later he told his father that he intended to dedicate his life to working on behalf of the Jewish worker in Palestine. If he could, he would do so as a lawyer; and if not, as an agricultural worker. "This is the essence of my life, and I shall devote myself to it under any conditions."[7]

Sejera was divided into a colony (moshava) on a hillside, and a farm established by the Jewish Colonization Association (JCA) on the summit of the hill. Ben-Gurion worked for a farmer in the moshava. The farm employed quite a few members of Poalei Zion, among them Manya Wilbushewitch, a well-known revolutionary from Russia who fled to Palestine and was captivated by it (she later married Israel Shochat). She managed to persuade the Sejera farm manager to set up a "collective" whose members organized their own work, without a manager, and shared their pay. Twenty pioneers, mostly Poalei Zion members, joined the collective, which was connected with Bar-Giora, a clandestine organization that had been founded by Israel Shochat at the Poalei Zion conference in September 1908 to serve as the nucleus of a Jewish self-defense force in Palestine. The collective included a number of Bar-Giora members, for whom it provided a way to make a living while hiding their organization within it. Ben-Zvi was invited to join Bar-Giora; Ben-Gurion was not.

After the Young Turks' revolution of 1908 under the banner of freedom and a constitution, the authority of the Turkish government in Palestine was seriously weakened, exposing the latent tensions between Arabs and Jews. During the Purim festival in 1908 there was a clash between Arabs and Jews in Jaffa. During Passover of 1909 the Poalei Zion conference was held in Sejera, and a Jewish photographer on his way there was attacked and robbed. He shot his assailant, and there followed a suspenseful few days of waiting to see whether the man would die. When he did, it was clear that the Arabs would seek to avenge him, and the Sejera conference was held amid great tension. In his memoirs Ben-Gurion described how one worker was killed in an Arab ambush, and how, during another attack, he and two other Jews went out to drive off the attackers, and one of his comrades was killed. In yet another incident, he was attacked on the road from Sejera to Yavne'el by an Arab shepherd who struggled with him and tried to take his Browning pistol. The robber got away with the basket containing Ben-Gurion's few possessions, but Ben-Gurion held on to the pistol.

These clashes arose out of the Jews' attempts not only to work at Sejera, but also to replace the Arab guards there. Employing Arab guards on a Jewish farm was equivalent to paying protection, since the guards were also the thieves. Aside from this humiliation, the pioneers aspired to defend themselves and their property as befitted the tradition they had brought from Russia, where Jewish self-defense had emerged following the 1903 Kishinev pogrom. Ben-Gurion recalled how he and his comrades enthused like children when they were given weapons, and how he himself became a guard. The romance of using arms to protect life and property plays a starring role in his portrayal of confrontations with the Arabs from the villages surrounding Sejera. It seems that the purpose of this description of heroism was to alleviate the pain and insult he experienced at the Sejera conference. At its end, the members of Bar-Giora and other workers invited by Shochat and Ben-Zvi gathered to found the Hashomer (The Watchman) organization, intended to take over guard duties from the Arabs to the extent that the farmers would let them. They even hatched grandiose plans to settle in border villages, in the manner of Cossack villages in Ukraine that combined agriculture and military operations.

Hashomer was not a clandestine organization, but like Bar-Giora it was conspiratorial, with a core leadership that rejected the authority of both the party and "civilian" public bodies. Although he was a member of Poalei Zion and an active guard, Ben-Gurion was not invited to join Hashomer. His good friends Rachel Yanait (later Ben-Zvi) and Ben-Zvi never explained how the relatively senior Ben-Gurion, who worked in agriculture and even bore arms, was not chosen, whereas they, two teachers new to Palestine, were. Shochat needed a connection with the party, which he already had via the easygoing Ben-Zvi, and it is possible that he did not want another "intellectual" in Hashomer. Its members were all simple, uneducated, yet dedicated people who accepted Shochat's authority as if he were a sort of rabbi or Cossack *ataman* (chief). Ben-Gurion did not fit into this setup. To Ben-Gurion, being excluded from Hashomer was an unforgettable, unforgivable insult, and ever after he bore a grudge against all kinds of military or underground organizations that did not accept the authority of civil institutions. Many years later, in 1957, Israel Shochat wrote to him personally and invited him to attend a ceremony commemorating Hashomer's fiftieth anniversary. As a belated apology he added: "That you were not a member is, in our opinion, just an accident."[8]

This exclusion from Hashomer was one reason why Ben-Gurion incorporated his clashes with the Arabs at Sejera, as well as the attack on the road between Sejera and Yavne'el in which he retained his pistol (the symbol of self-defense) into his self-mythologizing. The message was: even though he was not a member of Hashomer, he knew how to use a weapon and had shown great courage.

In 1907, despite Ben-Gurion's opposition, the party had decided to publish a Yiddish journal, to be called *Der Anfang* (The Beginning). In an attempt at conciliation, Ben-Zvi suggested that Ben-Gurion write for it in Hebrew. Ben-Gurion angrily refused and went to Galilee instead. *Der Anfang* was a failure and published only two or three issues. In 1910 the party leaders decided to publish a Hebrew weekly in Jerusalem, where they were located, to be called *Ha'akhdut* (Unity). The editors were meant to be experienced party loyalists, including Jacob Zerubavel, who had just arrived from Russia, other personalities from abroad, and, of course, Ben-Zvi and his future wife Rachel Yanait.

Ben-Gurion was not invited to join the editorial board. After a few weeks, however, when it became clear that no editors from abroad were coming, an approach was made to him, then working in Zikhron Ya'akov. In his memoirs Ben-Gurion played down his pleasure at this invitation, claiming that he was surprised and did not understand why they approached him, who had never written or edited anything in his life. We can assume that he was invited because his Hebrew was fluent, unlike that of other editorial board members whose articles he had to translate from Russian and Yiddish, and also because he was the only one who had been an agricultural worker and could credibly address the problems of labor, as befitted a workers' paper. In any case joining the editorial board was a big improvement in his life; it released him from digging holes in the soil of Zikhron Ya'akov and marked the end of his engagement with physical labor.

Ben-Gurion's work at *Ha'akhdut* did not make a great impression on either his colleagues or the public. His articles were tedious and written in a didactic style with a great deal of data and very little soul. Although he worked with the writer Yosef Haim Brenner, there was no chemistry between them. He stayed in contact with Ben-Zvi and kept his distance from the Marxist Zerubavel, who annoyed him as well as Brenner by trying to insert his nationalist rhetoric into their articles to make them more to his liking. All in all, Ben-Gurion's presence at *Ha'akhdut* was barely significant.

Meanwhile, he hatched with Ben-Zvi a plan to go to Istanbul to study law. For a while after the Young Turks' revolution, the Ottoman Empire seemed to be moving toward democracy. In a parliamentary regime, the people's elected representatives are important, and Ben-Gurion's idea was to study law in order to organize the Jews of the Ottoman Empire into a political force that would be represented in the Turkish parliament. Poalei Zion had a far-reaching political vision. The idea of Hashomer as the nucleus of a Jewish defense force, for example, could only have come from within its ranks, not from other circles in the Yishuv. Another example was its alignment with the world Jewish labor and world socialist movements.

At the same time, there was something rather pompous— not to say ludicrous—in Poalei Zion's interminable preoccupation with ideological matters encompassing the whole world, at a time when it had fewer than two hundred members. Inhabiting the ill-defined territory between visionary political concepts and groundless pretensions was characteristic of both Hashomer and Poalei Zion. In the same way, Ben-Gurion and Ben-Zvi's venture trod the fine line separating the lofty from the pathetic. They did not try to seriously examine its feasibility in advance. If they failed to blaze a trail for their party to the Jewish masses in Turkey and the Balkans, they thought, perhaps they would at least be able to get Jews from Palestine into parliament, where they could counterbalance the anti-Zionist propaganda disseminated by the Arab representatives. In any event, acquiring an Ottoman legal education seemed to them a very efficient path toward large-scale political activity—the kind Ben-Gurion dreamed of.

To enter a university in Istanbul, Ben-Gurion had to surmount several hurdles. First, he did not have a matriculation certificate. Ben-Zvi used his revolutionary contacts in Poltava to obtain a forged certificate for his friend, solving that problem. Second, Ben-Gurion spoke neither Turkish nor Arabic. He therefore went first to Saloniki to learn Turkish. He chose Saloniki because there were many Jewish workers there (the port was closed on Saturdays, in fact), and Poalei Zion hoped to organize these workers and lead them to socialist and Zionist awareness. The Jews of Saloniki, however, spoke Ladino, not Turkish, and the lingua franca was Greek, so Ben-Gurion was unable to set up a channel of communication with them—another example of the doubtful feasibility of Poalei Zion's grand plans. Many years later, Ben-Gurion described one workers' meeting: "I spoke Russian, Vlachov [a local activist] translated it into Turkish, and then Joseph Strumsa (my Turkish teacher) translated that into Ladino. The Jewish workers spoke in Ladino, which Strumsa translated into Turkish, and Vlachov then translated for me into Russian."[9]

The third hurdle was financial. Ben-Gurion wanted to devote himself full time to his studies, without needing to work, which meant that his father would have to cover his tuition and living expenses in Saloniki and later Istanbul. When Ben-Gurion had first started working in Petach Tikva, Avigdor heard that his son was going hungry, so he sent ten rubles to tide him over. Proud young Ben-Gurion, having just left home to survive on his own, returned the money, asserting that he could live from his work. This poor man's pride rapidly dissipated, and he no longer hesitated to ask his father to pay off the debts he had accumulated in Palestine, his travel expenses for a visit home, and more. Now he wanted his father to pay for his studies. Ben-Gurion knew that Avigdor had financial difficulties; he had to support two sons who could not make a living and two daughters. Fortunately his older daughter Rivka married a wealthy husband, and the younger daughter, Feigeleh (Zipporah), whom

Ben-Gurion was very close to, received a scholarship to study in Berlin, all of which eased the father's situation somewhat.

Ben-Gurion thereupon informed his father that if he did not pay for his studies, his entire life's hopes would be dashed. He demanded that his father support him, promising to study assiduously. Aware of his son's talents, Avigdor—like any Jewish father—wanted him to acquire a higher education. Still, supporting his son imposed an onerous burden. Ben-Gurion's constant complaints about delays in getting money, which frequently sounded like threats to break off relations with his father, reveal Avigdor's difficulty in finding the monthly stipend, on the one hand, and Ben-Gurion's insensitivity to his father's hardships on the other. Once Ben-Gurion had made up his mind that this was the task he had to focus on, he saw all the attendant difficulties as an unjustified annoyance that should be disregarded.

At last he received the passage money from his father, sailed for Saloniki in early November 1911, and found lodgings with an observant Jewish family who could not understand how it was that this young Jew did not speak Ladino. He studied Turkish intensively and discovered a previously unknown talent, astounding his teacher by how rapidly he grasped the language. After only three months he could read a Turkish newspaper, and a month later he swapped roles with his teacher; instead of the teacher teaching him Turkish, Ben-Gurion taught him Hebrew and turned him into a Zionist. He complained that he was lonely, for his only socializing was with his teacher. He corresponded with his *Ha'akhdut* colleagues, asking them to send him the paper, his only source of information on what was happening in Palestine, but delayed sending them articles from Saloniki, claiming that he needed first to understand the local situation and could only do that after learning to read the Turkish newspapers. His letters to his father were mainly about

money, but after a few months he began describing his scho-
lastic success. By contrast with his discouraging experience at
school, he was now capable of sitting for an entire day, dili-
gently learning.

He tried lecturing to a workers' group on socialism, the
national question, and Poalei Zion; which language he used is
unclear, since they knew no Turkish and he no Ladino. He
tried unsuccessfully to establish contact with local socialists.
He wallowed in self-pity, complaining that he felt isolated from
any work he liked, that letters from his father and others were
long in coming, and that he was lonely and homesick. Nevertheless he prepared for and passed the matriculation examinations in Turkish, the threshold requirement for acceptance into
a Turkish university. In a letter to his father he made a point of
saying that the gymnasium principal who examined him could
not believe that only eight months earlier he had not known
any Turkish at all and had said he would be happy if he had
more students like Ben-Gurion.

The last hurdle he had to jump on his way to university was
obtaining a passport, which he needed to enroll. Being a Russian army deserter, he did not have one and had to employ a
complicated ruse to obtain Turkish citizenship while simultaneously enrolling at the university; otherwise he would be conscripted into the Turkish army. All these efforts cost time and
money, which his father was late in sending, almost making him
miss the enrollment deadline.

The academic year began in October 1912. That same
month the First Balkan War broke out between the Ottoman
Empire and Bulgaria, Serbia, Greece, and Montenegro. The
Russian press reported on the persecution of Christians in Istanbul, but Ben-Gurion was amazed by the peace and tranquility in the capital and the disciplined conduct of the Turkish
army as it marched through the city on its way to the front
without disturbing public order. The law students were in no

hurry to enlist and lectures continued, but before long academic life was disrupted by the Turkish army's military failures against Bulgaria and by the wounded soldiers who filled the university buildings. After only a month as a student, Ben-Gurion decided to return to Palestine and stay there until the political situation became clearer. He was stunned by Turkey's defeats on the battlefield and its loss of almost all its territory in Europe. Asian Turkey still existed, but for how long? He remained in Palestine until early March 1913, when the political situation stabilized, then returned to Istanbul with Ben-Zvi.

The university did not reopen until the end of May, and in the meantime Ben-Gurion was sunk in depression because the money from his father had not arrived. He felt lonely and frustrated. Although he shared a small room with Ben-Zvi, his letters to his father do not mention either him or Shochat and his wife Manya, who were also studying in Istanbul. Ben-Zvi found work teaching and supported himself. Not so Ben-Gurion. Despite the increasing hardships of his family in Poland, he did not even think of looking for work. When his sister Rivka, backed by their father, suggested he return home, even if that meant enlisting in the Russian army—if only to stop being as miserable and sick as his letters claimed he was—he was profoundly insulted. "The objective I have set myself is a matter of life for me in the simplest sense of those three words, and only one thing can prevent me from attaining that objective—death," he wrote his father in tones of great pathos, insisting that for him returning home was a form of moral suicide.[10] He was so angry with his sister that he demanded that Avigdor tell her not to do him any favors, including sending money. His resolute determination, however, was accompanied by still another request for money from his father.

Despite his tight finances, his illnesses, and his intensive studies, he still found the time and money to travel to Vienna to attend the World Poalei Zion Conference and the Zionist

Congress. In the fall he sat for his first-year university examinations, then sent his father a detailed account of his high grades, comparing them with the lower ones achieved by his friends. In this way he compensated his father for the sacrifices he demanded from him. In December 1913 his second year began, and the cycle of poverty, illness, and complaints was renewed. "It seems that both of us made a terrible mistake: you took on something that is beyond your powers, and I agreed to live under circumstances likely to sap my physical and moral strength," he wrote his father.[11] In January he suffered a bout of malaria and was hospitalized. When he recovered he went to visit his sister in Lodz to recuperate. He returned to Istanbul at the end of April and immediately began preparing for examinations. This time, too, he passed with high grades, and again made sure his father knew it, while emphasizing how much better he had done than his friends. He planned to spend the summer of 1914 in Palestine. En route aboard a Russian ship the returning Palestinians heard that war had broken out between Russia and Germany; World War I had begun.

Ben-Gurion never finished his law studies in Istanbul; he barely completed two years, and was absent most of that time. He continued to experience the disquiet that had accompanied him on his wanderings in Palestine. His financial hardship and health problems were not unusual; the friends who studied with him were also poor, perhaps even poorer than he was. His trips to Poland were meant to ease his loneliness, enable him to recuperate, and allow him to eat home-cooked food, which he missed badly, and also to make sure that Avigdor's efforts to help him complete his studies were the primary family mission. Although he never received a lawyer's diploma, he did adopt a formalist, legalistic mode of thinking that was alien to his Second Aliya comrades. From then on, he broadened his education as an autodidact, by incessant reading.

Ben-Gurion and Ben-Zvi disembarked in Jaffa sporting

thick mustaches, red fezzes, and Turkish-style suits. This Ottoman look reflected their belief that the future of Jewish Palestine depended on the attitude of Turkey, so the correct policy
was to gain Turkey's trust in its Jewish subjects. This position
was soon severely tested. With the outbreak of war, Turkey ab-
rogated the Capitulations, agreements with the Great Powers
that impinged on the Ottoman Empire's sovereignty by granting foreign consuls jurisdiction over their own countries' subjects. Overnight the Jews, most of whom were Russian citizens,
became subject to the arbitrariness of the Turkish authorities.
Openly hostile toward the Jewish national idea, these authorities saw Zionism as yet another subversive movement aided by
foreign powers, like the Christians in Lebanon or the Armenians in Asia Minor, that threatened the empire's integrity.

Zionist symbols such as Hebrew signs in Tel Aviv, bank-
notes issued by the Anglo-Palestine Bank that replaced the
Turkish currency, and Jewish National Fund stamps on documents were strictly prohibited. Attempts by Jews to establish a
pro-Turkish militia were stamped out. After Turkey's entry into
the war on the side of the Central Powers in October 1914, the
citizens of enemy nations such as Russia were required to either become "Ottomanized" or leave the country. Becoming an
Ottoman citizen entailed paying a tax, but the biggest problem
was that Ottoman citizens were subject to conscription. Conditions in the Turkish army—ranging from sanitation and discipline to the attitude toward minorities—were harsh, so many
rejected this option.

The cruelty of the Ottoman regime became evident when,
some two months after Turkey's entry into the war, the commander of the Fourth Army, Jamal Pasha, ordered the deportation of all foreign subjects from Jaffa and Tel Aviv. The order
was executed arbitrarily, with children separated from their parents, wives from husbands, and baggage from its owners. Those
captured were put onto an Italian vessel anchored in Jaffa and

sent to Alexandria. This brutal expulsion led to protests by the German and American consuls in Istanbul. For the American consul, Henry Morgenthau, defending the Yishuv was a personal mission, and his intervention brought American vessels bearing donations from American Jewry, thanks to which the Yishuv was able to survive the hardships of the war. Still, many preferred exile in Alexandria or elsewhere over being subject to Jamal Pasha's callousness.

Amid the wartime confusion, with people deliberating whether to stay in Palestine or go into exile, to Ottomanize or not, Poalei Zion passed a firm resolution to remain in Palestine and to Ottomanize, a decision Ben-Gurion and Ben-Zvi fervently supported. In later years, Ben-Gurion's admirers praised his vision—his extraordinary gift for separating the wheat from the chaff and perceiving the essential reality that would guide his decisions as events unfolded. But there were quite a few exceptions to this generalization, and one of them was Ben-Gurion's attitude toward the Ottoman Empire and the future of Palestine within it. In fact, while living in Turkey he could have seen that "the sick man on the Bosphorus" was terminally ill. Turkey's failure in the Balkan War signaled its military and political weakness. The corruption of the bureaucracy and the students' unwillingness to enlist in the army were sure signs that there was something rotten in the empire. Jamal Pasha's general cruelty and specific actions—the hanging of Arab leaders in Damascus, the exile of Yishuv leaders, abuse during the expulsion from Jaffa—as well as Turkish officials' hostility toward the Jews should have shown Ben-Gurion that Zionism's only hope was to get rid of the imperial government in Palestine.

This fact was clear to quite a few Zionists who breached Zionist Organization discipline and sided with the Entente Powers. As an international organization whose members lived on both sides of the divide, and out of concern for the Yishuv, the Zionist Organization declared neutrality and moved from

Poalei Zion members receiving Ottoman citizenship in 1915. Ben-Gurion is seated in the center of the photo, with Yitzhak Ben-Zvi to his left. (Courtesy of the Lavon Institute for Labor Movement Research, P17511)

Berlin to Denmark, far from the turmoil of the war. Nevertheless Dr. Chaim Weizmann, a Zionist activist and prominent chemist in Manchester, England, began forming a pro-Zionist lobby among British government circles. Writer and Zionist activist Vladimir (Ze'ev) Jabotinsky worked to create the Jewish Legion in the British army, made up of Russian-Jewish immigrants in Britain, in hopes of inspiring some kind of British commitment to Zionism. Joseph Trumpeldor, a former officer in the tsarist army and a pioneer in the colony of Migdal, formed the Zion Mule Corps in Egypt and fought with the British in the Gallipoli debacle.

The Jews had two legitimate reasons for not siding with

the Entente Powers. First, it was not yet clear which side would win the war. Second, a shift to the enemy could lead to harsh Turkish reprisals against the Yishuv; the Turks' persecution of the Armenians was a warning sign. On top of this, to Ben-Gurion and his comrades the spectacle of thousands of Jews leaving the country in wartime threatened the loss of the Jewish foothold in Palestine that had been gained with great effort since 1882. They therefore decided to remain at all costs.

It seems, however, that their main reason for preferring the Turks was that despite all the Ottoman Empire's shortcomings, they were impressed by its might and did not believe that its rule over Palestine could be supplanted by another force. This belief seems to have been a result of their lack of familiarity with the West. Both Ben-Gurion and Ben-Zvi had come from the less developed regions of the Russian Empire and had never been to Western Europe. Ben-Gurion had made a short visit to Vienna and Krakow under Austrian rule, and was impressed by their exquisite objects and well-organized public order, which contrasted with his homeland. But he did not speak English and had not been exposed to Anglo-American culture. He learned French, but it is doubtful that he read books in that language. The West was alien to him, so he placed his trust in the Central Powers. Add to this the Russian Jews' hostility toward tsarist Russia, the unwelcoming homeland that had undermined their security, impaired their livelihoods, and wounded their human dignity, and the desire to support its enemies appears perfectly natural.

Poalei Zion's bet on the Turkish horse was a total loss. In 1915, after the mass deportation was stopped by foreign diplomats, Jamal Pasha adopted a new policy of deporting anyone connected with Zionist activity. Teachers at Tel Aviv's Herzliya Gymnasium, Hashomer leaders, editors of journals and newspapers, and party activists were all deported or left on their own. Ben-Gurion and Ben-Zvi, whose names appeared on the list of delegates to the Zionist Congress, were both sentenced to deportation. The order read "permanently." Their pleadings, the petitions they wrote, their displays of loyalty, their activity on behalf of Ottomanization, the red fezzes they wore, made no difference.

After receiving the order Ben-Gurion ran into Yahya Effendi, an Arab fellow student in Istanbul. When told about the deportation, he said, "As your friend I'm sorry, but as an Arab, I'm glad." This was Ben-Gurion's first encounter with Arab nationalism. Until then the Jews assumed that their clashes with the Arabs were no different from internal Arab conflicts such as Bedouin incursions into villages, robbery, and neighbors' disputes over land, pasture, or water. Now an educated Arab made it clear to him that opposition to the Jews derived from deeper motives and included Arab intellectuals.

At the end of March 1915, Ben-Gurion and Ben-Zvi, lacking papers, were taken aboard an Italian vessel bound for Alexandria. When the ship docked in Egypt they were arrested by the British as enemy citizens with no papers. They were released through the intercession of the American consul, and a few weeks later boarded a ship for New York. They reached the city on 17 May 1915, and were allowed to land as immigrants even though they had no documents. The only New York address Ben-Gurion had was that of the Poalei Zion office, and he went straight there. Thus began his activity in the United States.

In describing a leader's emergence, there is usually a tendency to discern future greatness, or at least the signs of it, in an earlier period. This is not so with Ben-Gurion. The Second Aliya was the time when the Palestine labor movement was formed, with its particular ideology combining belief in global reform with the salvation of the Jewish people, the first ideas of cooperative settlement, the importance of the village and agriculture as opposed to the city (symbol of capitalist decadence), and the sense of responsibility for the fate of the Jewish people. The few thousand idealists who made inverting the pyramid of Jewish professions and the move to manual labor the basis of the Zionist revolution in Palestine, sanctified Hebrew and demanded that it become the spoken language and culture of the new society, and created an ethos of simplicity, integrity, and dedication to their particular vision of Zionism produced a culture that took root in the Yishuv and shaped the Zionist pioneering movement for many decades.

Ben-Gurion played only a marginal role in these developments; the history of the Second Aliya can be recounted without mentioning his name. He was a mid-level activist in a party whose members were no different from other idealists, but whose ideology was not relevant to the society around them. In the semi-anarchic reality of Jewish Palestine of the time, no structures were built that were suited to Ben-Gurion's activity. The parties were less important than the agricultural workers' associations, and cultural work was more important than its political counterpart. The anvil on which Ben-Gurion's talents could be forged had yet to be created.

3

---◆◇◆---

Exile and Return

POALEI ZION IN PALESTINE gave "the two Bens"—Ben-Gurion and Ben-Zvi—the mission of organizing Hechalutz in America, a movement of young Jews willing to immigrate to Palestine, work there, and protect the Jews with arms. This mission had no basis in reality. There were over one million Jews in New York, mostly first-generation immigrants from Eastern Europe, and a small number of second- and even third-generation immigrants from Central Europe. But the former were preoccupied with their livelihood, their children's education, and finding their way in the new world, while the latter, already established, were focused primarily on being accepted in mainstream American society. To them, a display of Jewish nationalism was an obstacle to achieving this acceptance. Immigrants from Eastern Europe spoke Yiddish, and many belonged to various socialist groups. Zionists were few and far between. When Ben-Gurion met the Plonskites who had come to America, he was disappointed to find a vacuous, materialistic group of people who seemed preoccupied solely with improving their own living conditions. All in all, America was not holding its breath awaiting the Zionist message of Ben-Gurion and his comrades.

The Poalei Zion organization in New York that welcomed them agreed to help in their mission of establishing the Hechalutz movement, though without expecting much success. It organized tours for them throughout the United States, in large and small Jewish communities, and they delivered speeches in Yiddish. Ben-Zvi was better known to the public than Ben-Gurion, who was completely unknown. Ben-Gurion frequently complained about the inadequacies of the local party machines that set up the assemblies, where supporters were supposed to sign a letter committing themselves to Hechalutz. But the truth was that he did not know how to create an intimate, exciting atmosphere. He delivered his logical, well-organized talks in a calm tone, without creating the enthusiasm necessary to spark a mass movement. His meetings did not attract large crowds; more than once he faced almost empty halls. Even those who did come to hear him generally had no intention of enlisting. Only a few agreed to commit to going to Palestine when the time came. The two Bens' concerted efforts yielded no more than one hundred and fifty volunteers for Hechalutz.

The working-class American-Jewish public that Ben-Gurion encountered during the war years belonged to various leftist groups: trade unions, the Bund, Poalei Zion, and the broad readership of the daily *Forverts,* edited by the legendary Abraham "Abe" Cahan. In an attempt to reach beyond the proletarian class to the wider American-Jewish public, Ben-Gurion conceived the idea of organizing a general Jewish congress. But this proposal lacked a concrete objective. Moreover, it was opposed by groups like the American Jewish Committee (AJC), which saw it as a display of Jewish nationalism, something it feared like the plague.

This first attempt to mobilize American Jewry for a Jewish Palestine took place under unfavorable circumstances. America had not yet joined the war and remained neutral. Like the Germans and the Irish, the Jews fervently supported neutrality. Although they admired the liberal Western powers, which had granted rights to Jews, they despised their ally, tsarist Russia, which was doing everything in its power to oppress and humiliate its Jewish subjects. Second, the Jewish Socialists were pacifists, as was the Socialist International, which announced that it would not participate in the bloodshed. Ben-Gurion and Ben-Zvi supported this line, which was accepted by their movement and by the majority of American Jews. But such a policy could not inspire adherence to Zionism, for it implied continued Turkish rule in Palestine, which in turn meant that Zionism had few prospects.

Ben-Gurion first gained fame in the United States with the publication there of the Yizkor Book, which had originally been published in Palestine in Hebrew in 1911. A Yiddish version of the book—a mixture of literary pieces and eulogies for fallen Hashomer members, full of pathos—was edited by Ben-Zvi and his colleagues on the editorial board of *Ha'akhdut*, Zerubavel and Alexander Heshin, who had also found refuge in America. The Yiddish edition was successful and aroused some support for Zionism among thousands of Jews who were willing to put down money for it. But Ben-Gurion was not satisfied. He wanted to publish an enlarged, amended edition, at the center of which would be an expanded, enhanced version of the memoir of Judea and Galilee that he had published in the first edition. By this ploy Ben-Gurion managed to write himself into the Hashomer myth, despite having been rejected by that organization. He published the expanded book in a coffee-table format under his and Heshin's names only.

In 1958, at a nostalgic gathering in Kinneret, Ben-Gurion recalled that the typesetters who worked on the book would purify themselves before starting work by washing their hands. When they finished the typesetting, they claimed that the Holy Spirit had departed from them. Whatever the reason, the new book was hugely successful and enabled Ben-Gurion to make a name for himself among American Jewry. It also uncovered a latent Zionist fervor in the masses, which evidently had been waiting for the right spark to ignite it. The heroism of the Second Aliya and of Hashomer stirred the imagination of thousands of Jews impressed by the devotion of these young people and their willingness to sacrifice themselves. The excitement reached beyond the Yiddish-speaking public. Justice Louis Brandeis received one of the first copies, and his fellow members of the German-Jewish elite read it with enthusiasm. The book was also well received in France and Germany, and in 1918 was published in Germany, translated by the young Gershom Scholem and with a preface by Martin Buber.

This success delighted the Poalei Zion leadership. In addition to the publicity the book generated, it also produced a handsome income that made up for the failures of the American campaigns. As a result the party leaders agreed to pay Ben-Gurion and Ben-Zvi a monthly salary to write a comprehensive book about Palestine. A third of this book, *The Land of Israel Past and Present*, was written by Ben-Zvi, and Ben-Gurion wrote the rest. Swept up in the preliminary research, he worked day and night at the New York Public Library on Forty-second Street, immersing himself in dozens of books on the subject. A young woman volunteered to assist him by copying the passages he needed.

The young woman was Pauline Munweis, who had come by herself to America from Minsk in Russia a few years earlier. In New York she studied nursing, and Ben-Gurion met her at the home of a Jewish doctor where she lived and worked, a meeting place for party activists. Paula, as Ben-Gurion called her, was an appealing, bespectacled young woman, extremely

Just married: Ben Gurion and Paula, 1917 (Collection of Ben-Gurion House, Tel Aviv, BG 25)

friendly and sociable. She radiated femininity and warmth (in
contrast with Ben-Gurion, who found personal relations difficult). Somewhat of a busybody, she was also unreservedly frank
and spoke her mind regardless of convention. She had a discerning eye and could read people instantly, an ability Ben-
Gurion lacked. When they met, Paula was already a relative
veteran in New York and spoke English fluently. One day in
summer 1916 she offered to help him in his work at the library.
It was the start of a relationship that blossomed into love and
marriage. Their courtship lasted about a year. On 5 December 1917 they went before the city clerk at City Hall and, in the

presence of American officials only, were married in a brief civil ceremony. That day Ben-Gurion was fifteen minutes late for a meeting at the Poalei Zion offices, and when he arrived he apologized, explaining that he had just gotten married. Those present were stunned, since none knew of the relationship between him and Paula.

Ben-Gurion was thirty-one and ready for a relationship. Not handsome, short and thin, and without a profession or regular income, he was hardly an attractive prospect. But Paula was impressed. "As soon as he opened his mouth—I felt he was a great man," she later asserted.[1] She made him her life's work. For her, looking after him and assuring his well-being were preeminent tasks. She accustomed him to bathing regularly, brushing his teeth, and changing his underwear, standard practices of American hygiene but not widespread among Eastern European immigrants. She cooked according to the most advanced dietary theories of the day and zealously protected his health in general. But she did not share his spiritual world. She was not a Zionist; according to Ben-Gurion, she admired the anarchist Emma Goldman. She did not speak Hebrew. He knew he was marrying a woman who did not share the ideals that inspired him, did not read books, and did not share his other interests. Before they married he told her that she would have to leave America and immigrate to Palestine, a backward country without electricity and the other comforts of American civilization. He even warned her that if the Jewish Legion materialized, he would enlist. She accepted all of his conditions.

A few days before the wedding, two decisive events occurred. In England, Lord Balfour sent a letter to Lord Rothschild informing him that "His Majesty's government views with favour the establishment in Palestine of a national home for the Jewish people . . . it being clearly understood that nothing shall be done which may prejudice the civil and religious rights of existing non-Jewish communities in Palestine, or the rights and political status enjoyed by Jews in any other country." The second event was the Bolshevik (October) Revolution in Russia. These two events shaped Ben-Gurion's world for years to come.

Shortly after arriving in America, Ben-Gurion had met a fascinating, extraordinarily charismatic man. Pinchas Rutenberg was an assimilated Russian revolutionary who had made a name for himself in the Russian Social Revolutionary (SR) movement. He was attracted to Zionism while studying in Italy. When Ben-Gurion met him in New York in 1915, he was working to set up the Jewish Legion, in order to enable Jews to fight in the war. He told Ben-Gurion that the three Entente Powers endorsed the establishment of a Jewish "kingdom" (as he put it) in Palestine. Germany too was prepared to accept it, he claimed, but added that the Germans would be defeated in the war. These two assertions were remarkably prescient, since at that time Weizmann had not yet managed to sell the notion of a Jewish political entity in Palestine to the British, while the Palestinian exiles were not expecting a victory by the Entente Powers and still assumed their fate was tied to the Ottoman Empire.

In March 1917 the February Revolution in Russia toppled the tsar's oppressive regime. That April the United States entered the war on the side of the Entente Powers. The British, advancing toward Palestine from Egypt, announced the formation of Jewish battalions to serve on that front. Meanwhile the Turks bore down harder on the Jews—for example, deporting residents of Tel Aviv and Jaffa as the front moved closer. In the face of these momentous events, which seemed to be changing the course of history, Ben-Gurion and Ben-Zvi quickly realized their mistake and switched their allegiance to support the Entente side as enthusiastically as they had previously opposed it. Rutenberg and Ben-Gurion went to see Justice Brandeis and asked him to persuade President Woodrow Wilson to form a

Jewish Legion in the U.S. Army. But since the United States had declared war only on Germany, not on Turkey, this did not happen. The only choice left to would-be volunteers was to serve in the legion of the British army.

But Ben-Gurion's shift in orientation went beyond switching sides. In his discussions with Rutenberg in 1915 he had argued that a country is achieved not around a peace conference table, but through labor. Only massive Jewish immigration that made the land bloom would give the Jews the right to it. "The Land of Israel will be ours," he declared, "when the majority of its workers and guards are ours." Giving priority to practical work in Palestine over diplomatic achievements was in the spirit of the Second Aliya's opposition to the declarative Zionism of the Zionist Congresses, which since Herzl's death had been the refuge of idlers. "A country is not attained at congresses. A country is not given as a gift—a people's homeland is created and built by the power of its people," he contended.[2]

Now he changed his reasoning. At the peace conference following the war, the Zionists must demand not the rights to immigration and settlement, as he had previously insisted, but Palestine for the Jewish people. This shift from an evolutionary approach to a shortcut would recur in the future. Ben-Gurion had an ability to sense the greatness of a moment, the historic opportunity it presented, and this ability was first manifested in his volte-face toward a political orientation. Yet at the same time, just as it seemed that Herzl's dream of a charter was about to come true, he did not lose his sense of reality and insisted that only through mass immigration could this political promise be realized. "Over the next twenty years we must create a Jewish majority in Palestine. That is the essence of the new historical situation," he wrote.[3]

The simultaneous occurrence of the Balfour Declaration and the Bolshevik Revolution made the Socialist-Zionists ponder: what comes first, Zionism or socialism? Like many socialists, Zerubavel and Heshin chose to go to Russia, where the true revolution was taking place. Russia was also their homeland, and they now had the chance to return to it after several years of exile. Ben-Gurion himself had been cut off from his family in Plonsk for three years and did not know what had become of them. But in April 1918 he enlisted in the Jewish Legion—in the 39th Battalion of the Royal Fusiliers, which was being organized in Canada for deployment to England and thence to Palestine. When he got home and told Paula what he had done, she burst into bitter weeping. The first five months of their marriage had been a honeymoon filled with love and passion. The tenderness she lavished on him reminded him of his mother, whom he continued to adore. Paula's devotion melted the wall of loneliness that had surrounded him since he left Plonsk. He had warned her that she might be separated from him before they were married. But now she discovered she was pregnant and would have their baby while he was on a distant front.

Her tears hurt him very much, and he demonstrated his concern for her and their unborn child by writing a will and taking out a life insurance policy before leaving. She complained that if he truly loved her he would not go, to which he replied, "It is only because you do not yet know me well enough that such an idea would occur to you." He declared his love for her effusively: "You are for me my beloved and wife, mother and sister, and mother of my child. All that is tender and delicate in my heart is fused into my love for you." Nevertheless, "there is something else great and sacred, which in my eyes is greater and more sacred than anything in the world," and so "you must believe that I have done what I was duty bound to do."[4]

His letters to Paula from the army were in the same vein: acceptance of unending blame for leaving and causing her unimaginable hardship; expressions of love capable of melting a woman's heart; and justification of her sacrifice in the name of the Zionist ideal that was bigger than both of them and would eventually bring them divine happiness. "I shall give you the happiness that uninhibited love is capable of giving. I know you are suffering because of me, and I believe that I and my life's ideal will make it up to you," he wrote, signing, "Yours forever."[5] Just as his father had to pay for his studies in Istanbul for the sake of his ideal, Paula, too, must understand that he and his ideal were twins and be prepared to shoulder a similar burden. Since their love made them one flesh and one heart, he believed "that not only I volunteered for the Legion, but both of us."[6] Not joining up would have sentenced them both to a life without meaning: "Had I stayed with you now I would have been unworthy of you bearing my child."[7]

He liked serving in the British army. Military life, with its clear rules, rights, and obligations, agreed with his love of precision and order. The constant activity of a new recruit suited his bursting energy. Although he looked like a boy in his uniform, he wore it well and it set off his resolute chin. The new recruits were former Hechalutz volunteers and other young men who were attracted to the notion of a Jewish kingdom in Palestine. They were Ben-Gurion's natural audience, and he had more influence among them than did Ben-Zvi, who outranked him in the party hierarchy. Demonstrating organizational ability, adaptation to the military structure, diligence and perseverance, Ben-Gurion became the intermediary between the volunteers and the British officers. Although he preferred doing this informally, he was soon compelled to accept promotion to corporal. His popularity among the volunteers warmed his heart: "The whole camp knew I was coming and awaited my arrival impatiently," he proudly wrote Paula.[8]

This was the only military service in his life, and it was a formative experience. For him the British army always remained a superb regular army, worthy of being a role model. By their nature, the volunteers were a select group, and not all the English instructors kept up with their ability to learn quickly. Ben-Gurion concluded that the Jewish volunteers could learn their new profession in half the normal time and still become excellent soldiers. The discovery that Jews could make superb soldiers was an important lesson for him.

The voyage from Canada to Britain and then to Egypt was uneventful. In Egypt, Ben-Gurion suffered a severe bout of dysentery and was hospitalized in Cairo, where he received a cable from Paula informing him of the birth of their daughter on 11 September 1918. In his will he had requested that a son be named Yariv (one of King David's generals, and the name his daughter gave his first grandson) and a girl be called Geula (redemption). It seemed at the time that the redemption of the world in general and the Jewish people in particular was imminent, and names like Geula and Yigal (from the same Hebrew root) were popular in the milieu of Hebrew culture. In a letter, Paula wrote jokingly that the child was pretty, even though she looked like her father. Ben-Gurion responded: "Send me a photograph of you and the baby, and write whether our daughter is somewhat clever like her father, and as graceful as her mother"—following the standard gender division of the time between wisdom and beauty.[9]

Ben-Gurion's time in Cairo turned out to be notable in Yishuv history, for while he was in the hospital he read an anthology titled "Ba'avoda" (At Work), edited by Berl Katznelson. This booklet led to the most important alliance in his life—with Katznelson—and triggered a revolutionary process of unifying the workers in Palestine that propelled him into the front rank of the movement's leadership.

The three years Ben-Gurion was away from Palestine, which was completely cut off because of the war, were a period of internal coalescence of the remnants of the Second Aliya. New ideas of settling the country cooperatively, through independent workers' communities that took responsibility for building an economy and society and even nurturing Hebrew culture, replaced belief in the power of the Jewish proletariat to conquer all the labor professions. The independent farmer tilling his soil in different types of settlements supplanted the worker who had nothing to lose but his chains. Nationally owned land and national capital, placed at the workers' disposal by the Zionist Organization, would provide the worker-settler with the necessary means of production. The wandering and loneliness of the Second Aliya would cease, for the worker would be able to raise a family. In this manner a Jewish Palestine would be built without capitalism, without hired labor, without Arab workers, and without exploitation, resulting in an egalitarian Zionist society that fulfilled the workers' highest ideals. These ideas floated around in Palestine and coalesced into a program accepted by the agricultural workers' associations—the leading forces of the Second Aliya. These were years of decline for the political parties, which had been unable to cope with the war crisis. The leaders of Poalei Zion and Hapoel Hatzair went into exile or left the country. But the heads of the agricultural workers' associations, who as a group were dubbed the "Nonpartisan" party and led by Katznelson, remained in Palestine.

Berl Katznelson's path was the complete opposite of Ben-Gurion's. Whereas Ben-Gurion's road to Zionism and Palestine was clear to him from his youth and he was never tempted to follow other lights, Katznelson, who had been born in Bobruisk in White Russia and was the same age as Ben-Gurion, wandered from party to party, passing through all the tendencies in Jewish political circles. He wavered between Yiddishism and Hebraism, between territorialism and Zionism, and flirted with communist and anarchist ideas. Arriving in Palestine in 1909, in the second wave of the Second Aliya, he was like a completely desperate man reaching the last shore.

While the closed-up, introverted Ben-Gurion made few friends, Katznelson was gregarious, seeking to plumb the depths of every person he met. During this period Ben-Gurion rarely read literature; Katznelson read both Hebrew and foreign-language works and promoted writers. He was close friends with two Second Aliya icons: the elderly A. D. Gordon, the symbol of Hebrew labor, and Yosef Haim Brenner, the writer who exposed hypocrisy among Jews and the Zionist project generally. Katznelson's experiences in Russia had left him sick and tired of political parties. What interested him was the workers' culture and quality of life. For him, creating real, substantive benefits for the workers of Palestine was far more important than any political theory. Therefore, while Ben-Gurion focused on his struggles within Poalei Zion and went to Istanbul, Katznelson focused mostly on the workers' association. He set up a mobile lending library for workers, a room where they could sit at ease and read a newspaper; the Kupat Holim sickness fund; and, during the war years, Hamashbir, a cooperative that offered reasonably priced supplies. Within a short time he became the leading voice of the few Second Aliya "refugees" who remained in the country.

Ben-Gurion and Katznelson had met several times during the Second Aliya period, but no spark ignited between them. Ben-Gurion was studying in Istanbul, and his Turkish student clothing was not in tune with the proletarian austereness of Katznelson and his comrades. Once they walked together for several hours without Ben-Gurion opening his mouth. Now, however, they encountered each other again at the legion camp in al-Halamiya, Egypt, at the emotional meeting between the battalion from Canada and the one from Palestine.

Although the American battalion was fired up with hopes of a heroic war that would achieve a homeland for the Jewish people, the volunteers' Zionist commitment was not very deep, and after their discharge most returned to the United States. In contrast, the best of the idealists who stayed in Palestine during the war joined the Palestine battalion. There was much debate in Palestine over whether to enlist. On one hand, people heard the wings of history beating, and how could they stand idly by while Australian and British soldiers conquered the country for them? On the other, there was the argument that a country is conquered not with blood, but only by hard labor, and they must not abandon the few positions held by the workers. Poalei Zion supported enlistment enthusiastically as a continuation of its activist ideas from the Hashomer days. Most members of Hapoel Hatzair, with their feet planted firmly in the practical world, opposed enlisting. The Nonpartisans deliberated and in the end split into two camps.

Katznelson also deliberated, but eventually decided to enlist, not because he hoped to conquer the country due to his own efforts, but because like all anarchists he believed in the power of the great revolutionary deed that shatters conventions, sweeps along the hesitant and the weak, and creates the psychological basis for a new and better world. The depth of emotion and the intensity of the discussions that attended the formation of the Palestine battalion were foreign to the American battalion, but not to Ben-Gurion. As he lay in the hospital in Cairo after the historic encounter at al-Halamiya, reading a speech Katznelson had delivered to the agricultural workers' conference earlier in 1918, he suddenly realized that he agreed with every word. Katznelson's great vision saw the Jewish worker as the basis of Jewish society in Palestine ("You are the rock on which the Temple of the future will be built"). He expressed great hopes "for the forthcoming days" and described his concept of settlement as a working Jewish community that lived by the sweat of its brow without exploiting the labor of others. All these aspirations depended on the recognition that in order to achieve them the workers had to unite, for unity was the source of power. In moving prose, Katznelson expressed what Ben-Gurion, in his pragmatic dryness, believed and wanted to say. Given this "revelation," as Ben-Gurion called it, he did not hesitate to take the initiative. He had found the ally he had prayed for, and it was time to unite the workers of Palestine. He proposed an idea for a unified socialist Zionist movement of workers, and Katznelson agreed to work with him, though—being an eternal skeptic—with some hesitation.

Ben-Gurion came up with a plan that was revolutionary. He wanted not only to unite the agricultural workers as Katznelson envisaged, but to eliminate the political parties and establish an institution that would combine their political functions with the practical functions of workers' unions. This was the twilight hour: the destabilization of Jewish life in Eastern Europe due to the revolution and civil war in Russia and the pogroms against the Jews, together with the transition to British rule in Palestine, all indicated that it was time to change the scope of action in Palestine and to create new sources of power. Unification of the workers was designed to lay the foundations for absorbing the expected waves of immigration. If these immigrants found a unified political and social structure, they would be absorbed into it and not bring into Palestine the ideological battles and hairsplitting that characterized Jewish political parties in the Diaspora.

What was more, Ben-Gurion was sick and tired of Poalei Zion, in both Palestine and the Diaspora. The party had not freed itself from the Marxist model and previously had aspired to be accepted by both the Bund on the left and Zionism on the right. Now, the waves of the Bolshevik Revolution swept large parts of it toward the left. In order to strengthen the nondogmatic forces in Palestine, Ben-Gurion worked to unite with elements who were not constantly looking over their shoulders to see what people were saying about them in Moscow or Warsaw. Of the two partners, Ben-Gurion had the job of engineering the political suicide and elimination of Poalei Zion in Palestine. Persuading the Nonpartisans to unite was not difficult. Katznelson, who was also close to members of Hapoel

Hatzair, took on the task of persuading them to end their activities and join the new organization.

Their efforts to get rid of the two parties and form the Zionist-Socialist Union of Jewish Workers in Palestine—Akhdut Ha'avoda—were only partly successful. After hours of argument, and with Ben-Zvi's help, Ben-Gurion managed to forge a massive majority in his party. "I had not seen such stormy meetings as these in my life," he proudly reported to his wife; "it is a pity you did not see it, you would have been proud not only of your daughter, but a little of your husband too."[10]

The members of Palestine Poalei Zion were aware that the magnetic effect of the Russian Revolution had pulled many members toward the left and wanted to strengthen the party's allegiance to Zionism. The leadership had been weakened by the leftward tilt of some, the departure for Russia of others, and the lack of public stature among still others. These factors made it possible for the party to accept the union proposal. Hapoel Hatzair, on the other hand, did not want union. Even though its ideology was essentially no different from what Ben-Gurion and Katznelson advocated, the members contended that their party had its own message, and that they were a different type of people. In fact they loathed Poalei Zion's political and military activism, preferring to preserve past achievements and follow a slow, evolutionary path without revolutionary leaps. Although they too saw the workers as the ones who would realize the Zionist enterprise, they refused to accept socialist terminology and concepts, even in Katznelson's watered-down version. There was also a rumor that a large movement called Tse'irei Zion (the Young of Zion) had been founded in Eastern Europe that considered itself their sister-movement. Its members intended to immigrate to Palestine. In that case, why should they unite? Thus Katznelson's efforts to bring Hapoel Hatzair under the wedding canopy with Poalei Zion and the Nonpartisans failed. Full union had to wait eleven years.

The union was to be founded "on the basis of the unity in life . . . not on the basis of beliefs and dogmas."[11] It was to be a broad-based party, so dogmatic definitions were to be avoided. Katznelson wisely described the aspiration to world reform as a moral one, with the goal of establishing a just Jewish society in Palestine based on national capital, nationally owned land, and the immigration of pioneers who would create a broad working class, "a community of free and equal workers, living by the sweat of their brows," who would form the basis of a nation.[12] One of Akhdut Ha'avoda's missions was to impart cultural treasures to all, and this included inculcating the Hebrew language. In order to persuade the members of Poalei Zion to join, Ben-Gurion and Katznelson agreed that Akhdut Ha'avoda would be a part of the World Federation of Poalei Zion. They also agreed to its joining the Socialist International.

Addressing a workers' rally, mid-1920s, Tel Aviv (The Lavon Institute for Labor Movement Research)

The resolutions on the founding of Akhdut Ha'avoda contained a clause on "our national claim" that demanded civil and national rights for the Jewish people in the Diaspora and "international guarantees for the establishment of a free Jewish state in Palestine, which until such time as a Jewish majority was created in Palestine, would be under the aegis of a representative of the League of Nations."[13] The Mandatory government would be the League of Nations' representative in the transition period until the Jewish majority came into existence. This formula postulated that a Jewish state would be established at the end of the road, but indicated willingness to accept less than that in the meantime. Indeed, the hostile attitude of the British military administration in Palestine toward the Balfour Declaration, as well as the Arabs' agitation in response to the declaration and the rise of Arab nationalism, among other factors, mandated caution. Ben-Gurion later quoted this clause to prove that even then his intention was to create a Jewish state.

Ben-Gurion's alliance with Berl Katznelson was one of the most important associations he formed in his life. His lasting friendships tended to stretch backward in time, to Plonsk: Shlomo Zemach, Rachel Beit-Halakhmi, Shlomo Lavie, a pioneer from the Second Aliya who for Ben-Gurion symbolized dedication to principle. Except for Ben-Zvi, for whom he maintained warm feelings, it is doubtful that he had a deep connection with anyone outside this small circle. He developed contacts with people in the political system, forging and breaking alliances as the need arose. Katznelson was one of the only people Ben-Gurion was connected with both politically and emotionally. Katznelson understood Ben-Gurion's importance for the movement and had a very high opinion of him. In later years he repeatedly called him "history's gift to the Jewish people." But Ben-Gurion loved Katznelson. The emotional commitment of this introverted, closed man to this friend was exceptional in his life. "The only friend I ever had," he called him. Although they often disagreed, the disagreements never led to a real split. When they did disagree, it was most often Ben-Gurion who deferred to Katznelson. And when they agreed, they were a formidable coalition.

4

◆◇◆

Labor Leader

ON THE THRESHOLD of the 1920s, the Zionists believed that with the Balfour Declaration and the British conquest of Palestine, the political struggle for international recognition of the Jews' right to establish an independent entity in Palestine was over. It did not take them long to realize that this was a mistaken notion. The missions to be tackled next involved strengthening the Jewish foothold in Palestine, and their success would decide the fate of the Zionist experiment. The focus must be on development and immigrant absorption, with everything else subordinate to those initiatives. In the coming decade, Ben-Gurion's conviction that these were the central aims of this period led to his efforts to build a force that could accomplish these goals, the newly formed trade union organization known as the Histadrut (General Federation of Jewish Workers in Palestine).

In November 1919, Paula and Geula finally reached Pales-

62

Ben-Gurion's family, late 1920s. From left to right: Ben-Gurion, baby daughter Renana, wife Paula, daughter Geula, father Avigdor Green, and son Amos. (The Lavon Institute for Labor Research)

tine after a six-week journey from New York. Paula insisted on traveling first class so the baby would be comfortable, and her husband had to shoulder the resulting debts. After the founding of Akhdut Ha'avoda, Ben-Gurion was sent to London to set up an office of the World Federation of Poalei Zion (which Akhdut Ha'avoda had joined), which was supposed to develop a relationship with the Labour party in Britain, and his family went with him. In the meantime contact between Plonsk and the outside world had been restored. Old Avigdor and his family were impoverished. Before the war Ben-Gurion had invited them to immigrate to Palestine, and now Avigdor sought to take him up on this invitation. But Ben-Gurion was dismayed by the financial burden that absorbing them would impose on him. Paula was pregnant again, and their son Amos was born in London. With heartless frankness Ben-Gurion explained to his father that he would be unable to help him find work in

Palestine, for as a dedicated opponent of the accepted practice of favoritism, he could not overlook his principles for his father's sake.

Instead of bringing the Green family to Palestine, the Ben-Gurion family went to Plonsk for a visit. Ben-Gurion soon left for conferences and other meetings, leaving his wife and two small children in Plonsk for over a year. Relations between Paula and her husband's family were difficult. She was very critical of her in-laws' house; she complained about the low standard of hygiene, demanding that the contaminated water of Plonsk be boiled and that the room she and the children were in be heated. Ben-Gurion was caught between his father and his wife. He maintained warm relations with his father, but thenceforth, to his regret, there was no love lost between Paula and his family. When Avigdor reached Palestine some years later, he lived with his daughter Zipporah, a registered nurse who managed on her own in Haifa. Ben-Gurion apparently helped him find office work in one of the Histadrut institutions, but Paula excluded her husband's siblings from their home. Throughout the many coming years the Ben-Gurions and the Greens celebrated the Passover Seder together only once. In 1925, Renana, their second daughter and third child, was born. Paula was busy keeping house and raising the children. Ben-Gurion was usually away from home for at least three months every year to attend conferences, meet with important people, and take breaks abroad to rest and recuperate from intense work. As the years went by, his letters to Paula became less personal and more like reports intended not only for her, but also for the party central committee. The warmth and love he had lavished on her in their early years together had dissipated.

In December 1920, while Ben-Gurion was in London, a new organization, the Histadrut, was founded in response to pressure from the pioneers, mostly the newcomers. The new immigrants of the Third Aliya had encountered two parties competing for their support—Hapoel Hatzair and Akhdut Ha'avoda. The newcomers set up two prominent organizations, Gedud Ha'avoda (the Joseph Trumpeldor Labor Battalion, hereinafter "the Gedud") and Hashomer Hatzair (Young Guard), which pressured the veterans of the Second Aliya to establish a single labor union, politically unaligned, that would focus on the everyday interests of immigrants: settling them in a place to live and finding work for them. Since the new immigrants outnumbered the Second Aliya veterans, the latter were forced to agree to their demands.

The World Federation office in London was not particularly successful, and Poalei Zion in America, which had bankrolled it, ceased its support. Ben-Gurion returned to Palestine in 1921 and energetically assumed the post of Histadrut secretary general. Until then the Histadrut had marked time; the form it should take was still unclear. Now he took on the task of molding it into a powerful tool for realizing Zionism.

During the 1920s Ben-Gurion's salary was set at the Histadrut "family grade": a basic monthly salary of ten Palestine pounds plus allowances for a wife, children, and support of parents. Thus his total salary was around twenty pounds a month, which was enough to live on. Most workers made do with seven pounds a month. But starting in the early 1920s, Ben-Gurion became the slave of an obsession: he bought expensive books, often at the sacrifice of his family's welfare. On every trip abroad he found supporters willing to locate and send him hundreds of books he asked for, on Judaism, history, Jewish history, political science, philosophy, and later, Buddhism. His library eventually housed 18,000 volumes and thousands of booklets. He was not interested in collecting first editions or rare books; he only cared about their content. Once, when someone brought him a first edition of an important book, he thanked him but said he already had it.

The library also required more space than most people had,

so in the early 1930s Ben-Gurion built an unusually large two-story house in the workers' neighborhood near the sea in Tel Aviv (on today's Ben-Gurion Boulevard). The mortgage and loan payments added a further financial burden. Since Ben-Gurion was usually abroad during the summer, Paula rented rooms to vacationing families while she and the children crowded into one room. In the early 1930s Ben-Gurion published two books, *We and Our Neighbors* and *From Class to Nation*, that sold well both in Palestine and overseas, providing some financial relief. But not until he started work in the Zionist Executive, where salaries were high, did the family's financial hardships end.

Ben-Gurion never actually received a formal appointment as secretary general of the Histadrut. He was part of a collegium of three who were supposed to share the various tasks, but his activity so outshone his colleagues' that nobody remembered that he did not have exclusive status. Although his colleagues acknowledged his capabilities, his extraordinary energy and resolve, he was never more than first among equals. He did not exude charisma like Tabenkin and Katznelson, for instance, whose authority people accepted out of love and respect. People admired Ben-Gurion but did not like him; nor did they accept his authority unquestioningly. Every move he made was subject to his colleagues' criticism, which they never hesitated to offer.

The early 1920s were the years of belief in the "shortcut." Just as the Soviet Union had bypassed capitalism, the phase that according to Marxist theory would precede the socialist revolution, and moved directly from the quasi-feudal regime of old Russia to communism, the Jewish workers believed they could do the same in Palestine. The capital coming into Palestine was mainly national, raised by the Zionist Organization and its institutions; land for settlement was nationally owned (by the Jewish National Fund); and the pioneers who streamed into Palestine in the Third Aliya were idealists seeking national

and social redemption. Soon after beginning work in the Histadrut, Ben-Gurion proposed the establishment of a general commune of all workers. The Histadrut would allot work to all,
receive all the wages, and allocate to each worker enough to
live on. In an article he suggested that the Histadrut assume
ownership of all the farms and urban cooperatives, including
all their produce. Meanwhile, until the general commune was
established, all the members of Akhdut Ha'avoda would be
conscripted into "a disciplined army of labor that organizes
and manages the work, produce, and supply of its members on
the abovementioned principles."[1] This radical concept, probably influenced by news of the War Communism introduced
in Russia during the civil war, was rejected by his leadership
colleagues. Katznelson said it was an interesting idea, but not
something that could be imposed on people. This was the first
occasion—but not the last—when Ben-Gurion revealed a hidden fervor (quite detached from reality), like lava smoldering in
his heart, that he cloaked with deliberate rationalism.

Even after this concept was shot down, Ben-Gurion retained an abiding ambition to impose a centralist regime managed by one headquarters within the Histadrut. He referred
disparagingly to the lack of discipline in the Histadrut as "an-
archy" and strove to bring the workers' councils, labor settlements, and various cooperatives under Histadrut authority.
Every time one of them approached an institution outside the
Histadrut on its own initiative, Ben-Gurion swiftly fired off a
severe reprimand for breaching Histadrut discipline. Unfortu-
nately, the Histadrut Conference did not accept his centralist
concept. In fact, during the 1920s the Histadrut was run as a
sort of confederation of institutions. The Agricultural Union
dealt with labor settlement, the Workers' Councils negotiated
with employers and allocated work to job seekers, Solel Boneh
was awarded construction contracts and employed its own work-
force, and the Culture Division and newspaper were also run

autonomously. Someone once described the Histadrut's managers as "Chinese generals." However, whenever one of them found himself in a bitter internal conflict—a strike that had spun out of control, or a struggle between two workers' groups—Ben-Gurion seized the opportunity to intervene and impose the authority he sought to achieve.

In 1923 the Histadrut was invited to send two representatives to an agricultural exhibition in Moscow and display its produce. Ben-Gurion was excited by the chance to see with his own eyes what was happening in that amazing country where the greatest social experiment in history was taking place. Like the left the world over, Labor Palestine was fired up by the Bolshevik Revolution, though it was also concerned by the unprecedentedly harsh pogroms that accompanied the civil war in Russia. As a result of the war and the revolution millions of Jews lost their livelihoods and were doomed to starvation. Furthermore, the communists were anti-Zionist. The Comintern, founded in 1919, branded Zionism reactionary, a tool of British imperialism, and viewed the Arabs of Palestine as the harbingers of revolution there. The revolution had swept a large portion of Poalei Zion to the left, and these people founded the Communist party in Palestine or joined Left Poalei Zion (founded by Poalei Zion members who did not join Akhdut Ha'avoda), which continued to waver between communist and Zionist loyalties. The competition between Zionism and communism for the hearts and minds of idealistic Jewish youths remained a part of the history of Zionism and even of the State of Israel. Meanwhile, Comrade Ben-Gurion was happy to receive the invitation from Russia, and together with Meir Rothberg sailed to Odessa and traveled through Ukraine ("I was shown the swath of pogroms and massacres from a few years ago. The entire route was soaked with Jewish blood") to Moscow.[2]

The Palestine pavilion at the exhibition was a great success. The agricultural exhibits received high praise, and Russian farmers asked for seeds of the wheat on display. Jews and non-Jews alike crowded the pavilion every day. A blue and white Zionist flag flew over the exhibition—much to the displeasure of the *Yevsektsia* (the Jewish section of the Communist party), which was hostile toward Zionism, and even of the local Poalei Zion, which feared government reprisals. Almost all of the officials Ben-Gurion met were Jews who were willing to help. He met with people from Hechalutz, which, because it presented itself as nonpolitical, had recently been given a permit to act as a legal body training Jews for agricultural work in Palestine. He also met people from ZS, the Zionist-Socialist party, which was hounded by the authorities but continued to exist. The meeting that left the deepest impression was with members of the Hashomer Hatzair (SSSR) youth movement. This explicitly Zionist socialist group (which had no connection to Hashomer Hatzair in Palestine) had to go underground, since the communist regime prohibited Zionist activity. Although the activists were persecuted, they continued functioning throughout Ukraine.

For his part, Ben-Gurion appeared to these youngsters brave and cool-headed. At a secret meeting between him and their leaders, news arrived that the Soviet secret police were about to break into the room. To avoid considerable embarrassment for Ben-Gurion if he were arrested too, they decided to smuggle him out immediately. As they discussed what to do, he sat calmly, showing neither nervousness nor fright. His oratorical and analytical abilities also impressed them. At one interminable debate, someone asserted that the revolution would shortly spill over into Central Europe. Ben-Gurion stood up and delivered an impromptu lecture on why he believed that the revolution had halted and would not spread to Europe.

An unforgettable experience for Ben-Gurion on this trip was a Habima Theatre production in Moscow of S. Ansky's *The Dybbuk*, translated into Hebrew by Bialik. As the play began,

Ben-Gurion was afraid he would be disappointed, but soon he was swept up in its "tremendous, compelling impression of the inner life of generations of Jews."[3] After the second act, with its shocking dance of the beggars, Ben-Gurion wrote, "I am stunned, agitated, beside myself . . ." He returned the next day to see the play again, met with the actors, and heard about their impoverished lives and yearning for the Land of Israel. The Hebrew writers of Kharkov gave him a legally printed Hebrew anthology of poems, *Tsiltselei-shema* (Psalm 150:5, "The high-sounding cymbals"). As was his wont he wrote the names of all the poets in his diary, noting that "the poems are à la Blok"— which demonstrates that he was au courant with Russian modernist poetry.[4]

Despite a busy schedule he still managed to order books to ship home and also tried unsuccessfully to have the peerless Baron Ginzberg collection of Hebrew manuscripts transferred from the Lenin State Library in Moscow to the National Library in Jerusalem. Ben-Gurion's concern for cultural matters is also evident in his smuggling of a collection of Yosef Haim Brenner's letters, held by Brenner's good friend Shimon Bichovsky, to Palestine. Brenner had been murdered in the 1921 riots in Jaffa.

After three months in Russia, Ben-Gurion left with mixed feelings. From that time on he sought to persuade Soviet Russia to change its attitude toward Zionism, in order to ensure the safety of the Zionist-Socialist movements struggling for existence there, prevent international communist incitement against the labor movement in Palestine, and perhaps facilitate the emigration of Jews who wanted to leave the Soviet paradise. During the 1920s groups of ZS and Hashomer Hatzair members reached Palestine from Russia. They later became the movement's leaders in Palestine. Ben-Gurion continued to support the Soviet Union, at least until 1928, when hopes of improving relations finally faded as the noose tightened around the Zionist movement's neck and Hechalutz was outlawed.

In Ben-Gurion's impressions of Russia, light and shadow intermingled. When a young Muscovite member of Hashomer Hatzair asked whether the members of Akhdut Ha'avoda were communists, he replied, "We think we are communists"—in other words, "We are not communists according to Marxist dogma, but by our own criteria"—but he was still very left-leaning. He was disappointed by the New Economic Policy (NEP) in Russia, which had led to a retreat from the egalitarianism of War Communism. In strong, almost poetic prose he described "a country of revolution and speculation, of communism and the NEP, of holy suffering and filthy corruption, devotion and bribery, idealism and avarice, change of values and the tyranny of generations, the religion of labor and gilded idols."[5]

It was Vladimir Ilyich Lenin who made the most profound impression on him. Just as in his youth he had seen Herzl as the epitome of Jewish leadership, as an adult Lenin symbolized for him the ideal qualities of the leader of a nation in crisis and at times of revolution. Reading Lenin's words at the Seventh Communist Party Congress in 1918, in a debate over whether to accept the terms of peace Germany dictated to Russia in the last year of World War I, he was struck by the leader's greatness: "The man possesses the genius of looking at life face to face, of thinking not in concepts and words, but in the fundamental facts of reality, and courage . . . and a keen-farseeing eye . . . that plucks from the depths of reality the ruling powers of the future." At the same time, "a set objective paves the road of this master of stratagems who deviates neither left nor right . . . from the road leading to the objective."[6] Later, out of reach of the Soviet regime, he described Lenin with admiration but also emphasized his opportunism and cruelty: "a man of iron will who will spare neither human life nor the blood of innocent babes for the sake of the revolution," the complete opportunist "who will not fear to deny today what he favored yesterday, and favor tomorrow what he denied today." Yet through all his twists and turns he never loses sight of "the objective of the great revolution, the fundamental revolution, that uproots the existing reality."[7]

Ben-Gurion was not the only admirer of Lenin in Palestine. In 1923, the "shortcut" that the people of the Second Aliya had dreamed of shattered on the rock of the economic crisis caused by the Zionist Organization's lack of resources, and Zionism seemed unachievable. In such circumstances Lenin's success in achieving the impossible encouraged many to persevere. Thus, on his way to Odessa, Ben-Gurion wrote in his diary: "How similar is the economic problem of rejuvenated Russia to our issues in Palestine. Clearly, there is one small difference— Russia has a state and a government and a Red Army and unlimited natural resources, whereas we are armed only with an ideal and goodwill."[8]

In 1924 Palestine saw another wave of immigration that became known as the Fourth Aliya. In the wake of new U.S. immigration laws, which closed the country to immigrants from Eastern Europe, and in response to a nationalist policy in Poland designed to bolster the Polish middle class at the expense of the Jewish minority, many Jews chose to immigrate to Palestine. Over the next two years the Yishuv grew by tens of thousands. These immigrants, families and middle-class people, had no interest in becoming pioneers; most settled in the cities. Tel Aviv, Jerusalem, and Haifa enjoyed a surge of construction. This aliya was scathingly criticized by Chaim Weizmann, president of the Zionist Organization, who deplored what he saw as the transfer of the petty-trader Jewish society of Warsaw— operators of soft-drink kiosks, land speculators, and all sorts of peddlers—to Palestine.

For the labor movement this development meant the end of their hopes for a socialist utopia; Palestine could not escape the capitalist system. The question now was how to maintain the morale of rank-and-file workers and their sense that they were the elite ("the rock on which the Temple of the future will be built") who were realizing Zionism, as opposed to the middle class, who were simply perpetuating a petty-bourgeois society. It was also necessary to ensure that Zionist Organization funding, now devoted almost exclusively to the agricultural settlements, was not diverted to assist the middle class, as demanded by the right, which included the General Zionists, the largest party in the Zionist Congress, representing the middle class, Hamizrachi, the party of religious Zionists, and the newly formed Revisionist movement headed by Vladimir Jabotinsky.

Ben-Gurion undertook to conduct a "class war" in Palestine. Since at the time the country hardly had a working class, an economy, or a level of industry that could fuel a Marxist-style class war, he made do with the attitude and the mood of class war. In 1925 he published an article titled "The National Mission of the Working Class," in which he explained that private capital's aspiration for profit drove its owners to hire Arab workers, who cost less than their Jewish counterparts. Thus, instead of strengthening the Jewish foothold in Palestine, private capital was impeding immigrant absorption, since the jobs it created were not open to new immigrants. In one of the characteristic dialectic expressions that became his trademark, Ben-Gurion wrote, "It is doubtful if the private capital invested so far in the Jewish economy employing Jewish workers is private insofar as it is capital, and if it is truly capital, to what extent it is private."[9] In other words, what seemed to be "private" capital was actually public—for instance, money invested by Baron Edmond de Rothschild and Jewish philanthropic associations— or it represented such small amounts of money that it did not justify the term "capital." Certainly there were idealistic capitalists who came to Palestine motivated by Zionism and hired Jewish workers, but they numbered only a handful and were in fact acting against their class interests. By contrast, "the working class is unique *in its objective adaptation* to the historic needs of the nation." Ben-Gurion therefore reaches a paradoxical conclusion: "The way to realize the unity of the nation is through a class war."[10] His militancy against employers in the coming years—especially the farmers of the moshavot who employed Arab workers—was aimed at maintaining the workers' faith in the movement and creating commitment to it.

In 1925 the Polish government amended its currency laws, leading to the bankruptcy of thousands of Jews who had begun building houses in Tel Aviv and suddenly found themselves unable to meet their financial commitments. With one third of Tel Aviv's labor force unemployed, and workers going hungry, Ben-Gurion appeared at a workers' assembly where he spoke about the realization of Zionism and the primacy of the worker in it. "Leader, give us bread!" shouted one of the workers. "I have no bread," Ben-Gurion replied. "I have a vision."

The economic crisis that followed the Fourth Aliya developed into a crisis of faith among Zionists in the possibility of realizing Zionism. The high hopes of large-scale immigration and the settlement of many thousands of people within a few years were proved false. The Jewish people did not place the necessary resources at the disposal of the Zionist enterprise. The rate of construction in Palestine was far slower than that predicted in the early days of the British Mandate. For a while it seemed that the Fourth Aliya would settle the country with the Jewish private capital it brought in. The failure of this aliya symbolized the failure of capitalism too. The response of the labor movement leaders was: We told you so, the country cannot be built "in the natural way" but only through productivization of the Jews, hard work, and changing the Jewish psyche.

Yet it was the workers more than any other group who were hit by the unemployment and hunger caused by this failure.

The Zionist Executive was the governing body of the Zionist Organization, elected by its biannual congress, which functioned as a parliament. In 1927 the first Zionist Executive with no workers' representatives on it was elected to slash the budget and prevent the Zionist Organization from going bankrupt. It set up a committee of experts that in 1928 submitted a damning report on labor settlement, asserting that the kibbutz mode of life was unsuited to normal human nature and that investment in the kibbutzim was not only too high but unnecessary. At this desperate moment—when twice as many people left the country as immigrated to it, and Solel Boneh, the large construction company that was the pride of the Histadrut, declared bankruptcy—the labor leadership found the mental fortitude to turn the tide. That is, Ben-Gurion and Katznelson concluded that they must take over the Zionist Organization. To do so they needed first to found a broad-based party by amalgamating Akhdut Ha'avoda and Hapoel Hatzair. In 1930, after protracted discussions, this union was formed, creating Mifleget Poalei Eretz Yisrael (Workers' Party of the Land of Israel), better known by the acronym Mapai. This party was the anvil on which Ben-Gurion forged his leadership.

In 1931 Ben-Gurion and Katznelson took the first step toward labor movement hegemony, though no one realized at the time what was happening. In the elections to the Seventeenth Zionist Congress, the workers got twenty-nine percent of the vote. The Revisionists, whose party was only six years old, won twenty-one percent. These two groups were on the rise, while the center-right General Zionists were in decline. Labor and the Revisionists represented the Jewish masses in Eastern Europe. The charismatic Jabotinsky, a gifted writer and translator and undisputed leader of the Revisionists, called for activism against the British government: making a broad public campaign of the Jewish people to force it to uphold the pro-Zionist promises it had made in the Balfour Declaration and in the Mandate.

This policy was opposed by Weizmann, who believed that the window of opportunity for the Zionist movement that had opened at the end of the world war had closed, and that the best tactic now to ensure that Britain would not renege on its commitments was moderation, cooperation, and appeal to the goodwill of supporters of Zionism in the government. He also thought that the British had no intention of establishing a military "iron wall" between Jews and Arabs, as Jabotinsky demanded, and would not subdue Arab opposition to Zionism. The workers supported Weizmann's evolutionism, partly because they were dependent on Zionist Organization budgets, but also because they did not believe that political changes favorable to Zionism could occur before solid Jewish economic and social foundations had been created in Palestine.

At the Seventeenth Congress it was clear that forming a Zionist Executive without a coalition between the General Zionists and Mizrachi and either the Revisionists or Labor was impossible. The General Zionists and Mizrachi inclined toward the Revisionists, but Jabotinsky placed conditions on joining the executive that his potential partners found hard to accept. Negotiations continued, but the two groups also conducted parallel negotiations with the labor delegates. Like Jabotinsky, these delegates were hesitant; an ideological movement that joins a coalition loses its integrity, since coalitions always involve concessions and compromises. In the end, under pressure from Katznelson and Ben-Gurion, Labor decided to join a coalition with the General Zionists and Mizrachi. When Jabotinsky agreed, after a sleepless night, to waive his conditions, he learned that the new Zionist Executive had already been set up. This was the closest he ever came to power.

Thus began the race for Labor hegemony, which was ultimately won and lasted until 1977. Achieving it involved a bitter struggle against the Revisionists. The years between 1931 and 1934 were a time of struggle between these two movements for control over Jewish public opinion in both Palestine and the Diaspora. In this struggle Ben-Gurion played a leading role. In the early 1930s members of the Revisionist youth movement, Betar, appeared in Palestine. They were penniless young people, no different from the left-leaning pioneers, except that they rejected socialist ideology and demanded the right to work without becoming members of the Histadrut. When the Histadrut employment exchange refused to accept them, they directly approached employers, who were happy to pay the Histadrut back for its militancy by employing non-organized labor. When the Histadrut declared a strike in such a workplace, the Betarists showed up for work. Jabotinsky fueled the flames with an article titled "Yes, Break It," in which he urged the Betarists to weaken the Histadrut's power by strikebreaking. From there the road to violent clashes between the strikers and the strikebreakers was short.

Meanwhile, developments in Europe included the rise of fascism in Italy, led by Mussolini; the appearance of proto-fascist regimes in Eastern Europe; and the meteoric rise of the Nazi party in Germany—all against the backdrop of the global economic crisis that began in 1929. The workers in Palestine identified with the European left, which had been thrown on the defensive, and saw the Revisionists as the Jewish branch of world fascism. Ben-Gurion shared these sentiments and did not hesitate to magnify the contrasts between the Revisionists and the labor movement. Between 1932 and 1934, politics in Palestine shifted from conference rooms to the street and turned violent. Ben-Gurion did not object to violence. His good friend Berl Katznelson resigned from the Mapai Central Committee and his positions in the Histadrut in protest of a concerted attack by workers on a Betar parade in Tel Aviv, but Ben-Gurion's stance was ambiguous. Instead of sharply criticizing the use of violence in politics, he called for the violence to be supervised by the leadership and under its control. In one stormy debate he shouted, "The Yishuv can be destroyed so long as the Histadrut survives!"

But even as relations between left and right in Palestine neared the boiling point, and mutual insults reached a climax (the Revisionist paper *Hazit Ha'am* [Popular Front] referred to the "Stalin–Ben-Gurion–Hitler Alliance," and Ben-Gurion referred to Jabotinsky as "Vladimir Hitler"), Ben-Gurion's mind was elsewhere. He was devoting all his energy to taking over the Zionist Organization. At the Mapai Council in 1932 he offered the slogan "From Class to Nation"; that is, the working class had to see itself as representing the entire Jewish people. He developed the concept that "in order to maintain the vital compatibility between the Zionist enterprise in Palestine and the world Zionist movement, the labor movement is called upon to become a decisive force in the Zionist Organization."[11] It was possible to interpret this transition "from class to nation" as relinquishment of the class concept—that is, as abandoning the class for the nation. And indeed, not all his colleagues were willing to accept the new formula, but he succeeded in bringing the majority along with him.

Ben-Gurion set himself the objective of achieving a labor movement majority at the next Zionist Congress, to be held in Prague in the fall of 1933. In a party discussion, the majority expressed doubts about whether this was possible. The Zionist middle class was leery of the young leftist party that had rapidly developed into a real force. When the Zionist Executive for 1931 was installed, highly respected newspapers both inside and outside Palestine expressed doubts about the ability of a workers' representative to serve on the executive body of the Zionist Organization in a role resembling that of a foreign minister. At the time, Mapai's most prominent representative was Chaim

Arlosoroff, a brilliant young German-educated intellectual and former member of Hapoel Hatzair. He took over the political department of the Jewish Agency Executive. (The Jewish Agency had been established in 1929 to broaden the scope of the Zionist movement by including very wealthy Jews. This did not work out, and the Jewish Agency Executive soon became practically identical with the Zionist Executive.) Arlosoroff had managed to surprise everyone by establishing good communications and relations of trust with the British high commissioner in Jerusalem, more successfully than any of his predecessors in the political department. Despite this success, when Ben-Gurion proposed taking over the Zionist movement in Eastern Europe, his colleagues in the leadership remained doubtful. But they did not stop him. Once Ben-Gurion had decided to execute a mission, it would have been easier to stop a raging bull.

Ben-Gurion approached his objective with the thoroughness of a party functionary who knows that the secret of electoral success lies in organization. In April 1933 he went to Poland, the primary stage for high drama in the upcoming elections for the Zionist Congress. In previous elections, 67,000 people in Palestine had paid the shekel (Zionist Organization dues), whereas in Poland there were some 250,000 members. The Revisionists were in the ascendancy there. Ben-Gurion put his finger on the Archimedean point of the elections. He ignored Mapai's enfeebled Polish sister parties, which lacked enthusiasm and were preoccupied with the finer points of ideological debates. Instead he approached the Hechalutz Central Committee and the youth movement delegates and enlisted them for the election campaign. These enthusiastic, dedicated, energetic young men and women ran the campaign for him. Each activist was assigned to sell shekels in a specific area and required to bring in an ever increasing number of shekel payers—not just movement members, but their families as well.

Week by week Ben-Gurion received progress reports on

shekel sales. In areas showing lack of progress, he urged, scolded, and encouraged movement members to greater efforts. Meanwhile he traveled to large and small towns throughout Poland, Galicia, and the Baltic states, delivering speeches morning and evening. Masses welcomed him at the railway stations, and he filled the halls to capacity. But he was not the only one filling halls. Jabotinsky, too, ran a dynamic, turbulent campaign. Polish Jewry had never been so Zionist or so polarized as it became in the 1933 elections.

These were stormy times. The Nazis had taken power in Germany. The Reichstag fire and the persecution of Jews occurred during the election campaign. The anti-Semitic movement in Poland was gathering momentum, and the Jews there sought refuge. As a result, the Zionist movement was able to double its strength in the elections. In the 1931 elections, less than a quarter million voters had cast ballots, but in 1933 more than half a million voted. When the count was concluded, Ben-Gurion could feel satisfied with his efforts. Although the labor movement did not gain fifty percent of the vote, it got forty-four percent, making it the swing party in the Zionist Organization.

On 16 June 1933, with the election campaign at its height, Chaim Arlosoroff was shot and killed on a beach in Tel Aviv. He had just returned from negotiations with the German government on a transfer agreement that would enable German Jews to take their capital out of the country and settle in Palestine. To the Revisionists, who were trying to organize a worldwide boycott of Germany, Arlosoroff's act was akin to treason, as their paper, *Hazit Ha'am*, said on the day before the murder. It is therefore not surprising that Betarists were suspected of the murder. A new wave of tension and violence erupted both in the Yishuv and in Poland, and again later during the trial of the three who were arrested. Two of them were cleared, and the third, Avraham Stavsky, was convicted, but his sentence was overturned on appeal. Stavsky afterward attended the Great Synagogue in Tel Aviv, where workers instigated a riot and prevented him from being called to the reading of the Torah— behavior that Ben-Gurion termed "a wise act." Despite his great triumph in the congress elections, he still retained the temperament of a militant labor leader, unbefitting a leader with national responsibility.

When the new Zionist Executive was set up after the elections, the workers were careful not to exploit the majority they held and took only four of the executive's ten seats. Ben-Gurion stepped into Arlosoroff's shoes and was appointed head of the Jewish Agency's political department. To achieve broad legitimacy among the Jewish public, the respected veteran Dr. Arthur Ruppin, a liberal Zionist and supporter of the labor movement since the Second Aliya days, was appointed chairman of the executive. In the meantime Ben-Gurion remained in his post as secretary of the Histadrut. For the next two years he wore two hats, but his heart was in his new position. Later, no one remembered that for his first two years on the executive he was not its chairman.

5

From Labor Leader to National Leader

SINCE THE DAYS of the Second Aliya, Ben-Gurion had been aware of Arab opposition to Jewish settlement—the "Arab problem"—as both a potential danger to the settlers' security and a political problem of relations between two peoples living in the same country. He also knew there were nationalist undercurrents in the Arab street, as seen in the Arab who had been pleased by Ben-Gurion's deportation in 1915, despite his regret as a friend. The Arabs were apprehensive about and hostile toward Jewish settlement, since they saw it as endangering their national interests. The worrying signs that had been evident during the Ottoman period took on new dimensions during British rule, for at the same time that the Balfour Declaration raised Jewish nationalist aspirations, Palestinian Arabs experienced a nationalist awakening as a result of the "rebellion in the desert" against the Ottoman regime by the Hashemite king Faisal, instigated by British officers.

The Poalei Zion leadership had earlier taken up a romantic notion that the Arab *fellahs*, peasants or agricultural laborers, in Palestine were descendants of the Jews and had espoused Christianity before becoming Muslim. Ben-Gurion discussed this subject in *The Land of Israel Past and Present*, the book he published while he was in the United States. He considered the large number of Arab villages in Palestine that had names dating from the biblical and Talmudic periods to be evidence of the fellahs' Jewish origins. However, he never pursued this idea further. Instead, he learned from his encounters with members of the Labour party in Britain and people on the Jewish left that the question of the Palestinian Arabs was an important international issue. If the Jewish workers' movement was to gain legitimacy in the eyes of the world, it would have to propose either a social or a political perspective on the Arab question.

Ben-Gurion as well as his comrades believed that at this stage of the Yishuv's development it would be unwise to engage with the Arab question. Any proposal put forward would have to take into account the existing balance of power, in which the Jews constituted only ten percent of the country's population. It was in the Zionists' interest to delay any discussion of the Arab question until there was a critical mass of Jews in the country. Yet how could they justify impeding the Arabs' right to self-determination to the international workers' movement? Ben-Gurion and his comrades' answer was that the Arab leadership, which consisted of *effendi* landowners and benighted clerics, was reactionary. It was impossible to communicate with them because their hostility toward the Jews was based on class motives: they feared the progress and modernization Jewish workers were creating in the country. Instead, the Jewish labor movement was to enhance the standing and progress of the Arab worker. "The Arab worker is an organic, integral part of the country, just like one of its mountains and valleys," Ben-Gurion declared. Therefore "the destiny of the Jewish worker is linked to the destiny of the Arab worker. Together we shall rise or fall."[1] This mission was in tune with the class orientation of the time, and because it was long term it did not require concessions in the present. Organizing the Arab workers thus became one of the tasks that the Histadrut under Ben-Gurion's leadership took upon itself in the 1920s.

In the end, this "joint organization" was not a resounding success. The Arab workers were far from possessing class consciousness; they identified above all with their co-religionists and their people. Each outburst of Arab violence against Jews (in 1920, 1921, and 1929) led to greater separation between the two communities. National solidarity was stronger than that of class.

During this period Ben-Gurion's idea of a long-term perspective regarding the "Arab question" involved the development of two autonomous communities, Jewish and Arab. Jewish settlement in Palestine was moving toward the creation of territorial contiguity. Jews tended to settle in separate rural or urban settlements, and Ben-Gurion hoped that this spontaneous process would lead to the creation of contiguous Jewish areas, as opposed to the mixed-population cities. He contended that the combination of autonomy and land was the basis for developing Jewish sovereignty. In 1924 he stated, "With the increase in national urban and rural settlements, with the expansion of their area . . . our territorial autonomy will be formed, grow, and be strengthened, and the Jewish state will be built."[2]

In the following years, a period of relative quiet and stability, Ben-Gurion held several discussions with members of Brit Shalom (Peace Alliance), a liberal group of intelligentsia centered at the Hebrew University in Jerusalem and among Zionist Organization officials. The Brit Shalom people proposed the establishment of a bi-national regime in Palestine. Jews and Arabs were two peoples with equal rights in the country. Each would be autonomous in its own territory and would be represented on a legislative council in a way that would draw the sting from the majority minority question. To alleviate the Arabs' concerns about Jewish immigration, they proposed not using the phrase "a Jewish majority" but rather saying "many Jews."

Ben-Gurion rejected these ideas. In his view any proposal containing concessions regarding the Jewish people's potential to constitute a majority was inappropriate. He recognized the Arabs' rights to complete national and political equality, but rejected their claim to exclusive possession of the country. He also rejected the bi-national concept, asserting that for the Jews Palestine had a different value than it had for the Arabs. The Arabs had numerous countries; the Jews had only one. One side in this conflict consisted of a fragment of the Arab nation, while the other side included the entire Jewish people, dispersed over the world. In the end, all these discussions amounted to exercises in imagination among the Jews themselves, since no Arabs were prepared to accept the Brit Shalom proposals. A few years later, Arthur Ruppin, the Brit Shalom chairman, summed up the attempts at talks with them: *"What we can get* [from the Arabs] *we do not need, and what we need, we are unable to get."*[3]

This realistic, considered, mature conclusion did not suit Ben-Gurion. As long as he had not repeatedly tried negotiating himself, and seen firsthand that there was no chance that the Arabs would agree to any kind of Jewish sovereignty in Palestine, he would not stop trying. This confidence that he would succeed in persuading where others, less resolute than he, had failed was a manifestation both of his self-assurance and of his constant need for action and deeds—that is, for a Lenin-like effort to achieve a historic breakthrough.

These attempts during the 1920s to find political formulas that would not impair the Jewish people's right to Palestine while also granting self-government to the Arabs, as well as the somewhat naive attempts made to organize the Arab workers, were aimed at settling the internal contradiction of the Zionist-

Socialist movement: recognizing the right of nations to self-determination while opposing granting these rights to the Palestinian Arabs. One way to resolve it was to claim that an Arab national movement did not exist and that the Arabs' animosity toward the Jews was incited by the effendis, or feudal landowners. But in 1929, rioting by Arabs against Jews erupted on a previously unknown scale. By the time the British authorities managed to subdue the rioters, 133 Jews had been killed, as well as a similar number of Arabs, most by the security forces.

The riots were a turning point in Ben-Gurion's thinking about the Arab issue. Whereas in 1924 he had declared there was no such thing as an Arab national movement, he now asserted that "the debate on whether or not there is an Arab national movement is just empty words. The main thing for us is that the movement is mobilizing masses." And in the vein of brutal Leninist realism that observed unpleasant reality without blinking, he went on: "We do not see a revival movement in it, and its moral value is dubious. However, in the political sense it is a national movement."⁴ Not all of his colleagues agreed, but from then on he stopped talking about organizing the Arab workers and about effendis and fellahs.

The early 1930s were his apprenticeship years in Zionist policy. The utopianism of the early 1920s was over, and the world had become sober and worrying. As the Nazis rose to power in Germany, their virulent anti-Semitism began to spread throughout Europe. The world entered a period of tensions, with the Western democracies on the defensive. In Palestine, the riots of 1929 were followed by a political crisis. The Passfield White Paper, issued by British colonial secretary Lord Passfield in 1930, expressed anti-Zionist positions. It asserted that the Mandate was not directed solely at the Jews but rather represented a "dual undertaking" to both Jews and Arabs, and that it applied only to Jews living in Palestine, not the Jewish people as a whole. It stated further that Jewish settlement in

Palestine was expropriating land from the fellahs. Beatrice Webb, Baroness Passfield, the colonial secretary's wife, declared that there was "no room to swing a cat" in Palestine. Based on these assumptions the White Paper concluded that from then on, immigration would be conditional not only on the Jewish economy's absorption capacity, but also on Arab unemployment. Land sales to Jews by Arabs would be severely restricted. And to give the Arabs political hope, a legislative council would be established in Palestine that would represent the existing majority—that is, the Arab majority.

The Passfield White Paper created a storm in the British parliament, in the League of Nations Permanent Mandates Commission, and among the Jewish people. Weizmann resigned from the Zionist Executive in protest, and there were anti-British demonstrations throughout the world. Following an intensive political struggle, Ramsay MacDonald, the British prime minister, sent Weizmann a letter that supposedly did not annul the White Paper, but did retract its harsh anti-Zionist statements. The MacDonald Letter stated that the undertaking in the Mandate was not confined solely to the Jewish population of Palestine, but applied to the entire Jewish people and that the obligation to encourage Jewish settlement in and immigration to Palestine still stood. Thus the Zionist project was given a reprieve that lasted until 1939. In these years the Zionist enterprise in Palestine reached critical mass, enabling it to prevent the Arabs from establishing a majority state.

During this crisis Mapai was founded, and the labor movement became increasingly involved in political activity. Mapai held a comprehensive debate on the Arab question: was it time to take up this problem and propose an overall political plan? Ben-Gurion laid before his party a well-formulated proposal: "Hypotheses for a State Regime in Palestine." In his vision, the development of the national home, the improvement of Jewish-Arab relations in Palestine, and the reduction of the Mandatory government's powers and their subsequent transfer to the country's inhabitants would be interdependent processes. He spoke of three stages: the present founding period, which would continue for several more years; the strengthening period, in which the Jews would constitute forty to fifty percent of the population; and the concluding period, when the Jews would constitute at least fifty percent of the population. He assumed that the Arabs' attitude toward the Zionist enterprise would improve as they came to accept the fact that they could not uproot it and that in the third stage they would accept the establishment of the national home. As the stages progressed, Mandatory authority would be reduced and self-government institutions would be established based on territorial autonomy. At the conclusion of the process, separate national cantons would be established and combined into a federal state run by the House of the Peoples, in which there would be Jewish-Arab parity, and the House of the Inhabitants, in which the cantons would be proportionally represented. This plan foresaw a protracted process during which the national home would continue to develop.

In the end Mapai accepted a plan on parity proposed by Katznelson. The legislative council would represent the two peoples equally, regardless of the ratio between them. This plan was weighted on the side of the Jews, who at the time constituted only fifteen percent of the population. Still, from the Zionist perspective it contained an important concession in that it relinquished the Jewish people's exclusive right to the country and recognized that the Arabs had an equal right. During these exhausting discussions, Ben-Gurion's mind was on more practical matters. He checked and compared the number of Arab and Jewish men between the ages of twenty and forty in the census figures that reached his desk, and wrote down his calculations as to how many more pioneers were still needed to reach military parity between the two communities.

At the time Labour was in power in London. In the summer of 1930, Ben-Gurion had attended the British Commonwealth Labour Conference and was amazed by the rise to greatness of Ramsay MacDonald, the son of a poor family who now governed the greatest of empires. Ben-Gurion believed in labor fraternity. He felt he could talk man to man with Prime Minister MacDonald and his son Malcolm, trade union leader Ernest Bevin, and other leading Labourites and make them understand the Zionist position. He thought that Weizmann, who had frequented the corridors of power in Britain since the world war and was in close contact with Conservative politicians, looked down on the Labour people and as a consequence had missed opportunities. "Our safest and truest external political ally is the British Labour Party," he wrote in his diary.[5] His meetings with Labour party leaders gave him new hope for a change of direction. He was therefore very hurt when, after all his cordial talks, the lethal White Paper was published.

At the Mapai Council, held at the end of October 1930, he expressed disappointment and helpless anger, as well as the revolutionary zeal still burning inside him. This smoldering lava spewed out in one of his volcanic eruptions: "If the creative force revealed within us is to be arrested by this malicious empire, then our explosive power will be revealed and we shall destroy that bloody empire." Shaking his fist threateningly, he continued, "Beware, British Empire!"[6] This explosion was not well received by his leadership colleagues, to whom it sounded hysterical, bordering on ludicrous. They reverted to the course of patient efforts to create a shift in British policy, while continuing to build the country. The notion of blowing up the British Empire entered Mapai's historical memory as an example of the irrationality in Ben-Gurion that erupted at times of crisis. In the early 1930s there were enough leaders in Mapai to bridle him and induce him to back realistic positions.

At the Seventeenth Zionist Congress in Basel (summer of

1931), Ben-Gurion received another lesson in political intricacy. Weizmann, the admired president of the Zionist Organization, attended the congress after his reconciliation with Britain following the MacDonald Letter. But the delegates' anger at Britain was great. More than any other, Weizmann was identified with Zionist-British collaboration. His moderate policy provoked criticism from many delegates who felt that the times demanded more assertive leadership. The opposition was headed by Jabotinsky and the Revisionists, but the American Zionists and the Hamizrachi religious party also supported a change in the Zionist line. In an interview he gave to the Jewish news agency, Weizmann made the mistake of saying that the Jews did not need a majority in Palestine, and that this claim was construed as a desire to drive the Arabs out. From that moment it was clear that he would not be reelected to the presidency.

As part of his efforts to gain support, Weizmann sent Ben-Gurion to meet secretly with MacDonald at Chequers, the prime minister's country residence. Giving Ben-Gurion this mission was a compliment that made him feel he had penetrated the heart of political activity. On this trip he was exposed to the perquisites of power: a limousine awaited him at the airport to take him to Chequers; when he needed a transit visa in France, it was taken care of within minutes. He never forgot the experience of this relatively intimate meeting with the British prime minister. He had come a long way from Plonsk.

A new era began, as the hostile high commissioner in Palestine was replaced by Arthur Wauchope, whom Ben-Gurion later described as "the best of commissioners," and Arlosoroff became head of the Jewish Agency political department in Jerusalem. Ben-Gurion chose not to join the Zionist Executive elected at the congress. An interesting relationship evolved between him and Arlosoroff. Although Weizmann was the leading personality Arlosoroff consulted, alone among all his movement comrades he chose Ben-Gurion to share his thoughts, reflections, and the negotiations he conducted.

On 30 June 1932, less than a year after taking up his post, Arlosoroff wrote a long letter to Weizmann that was a masterpiece of statesmanship. He estimated that the Zionist movement had only a short period of time at its disposal. Within five to ten years Europe would be engulfed in war, and the Yishuv would likely find itself facing either an Arab-British alliance or an Arab revolt and be cut off from the Jewish world, its source of people and resources. The slow evolutionary process was not advancing the Yishuv to the next critical stage of its development, and certainly would not do so in the short time available. Arlosoroff detailed four options. The first three were to continue in the present mode and hope for the best; to despair of the Zionist path and choose a different track; and to establish a Jewish canton in Palestine that would serve as a strategic basis for future progress. The fourth option involved a transitional period during which a revolutionary Jewish minority government would change the face of the country through mass immigration and settlement—an option probably reminiscent for his reader of the Bolshevik coup d'état. He concluded with a declaration of faith more on the model of Ben-Gurion than in his own moderate style as a former member of Hapoel Hatzair: "All I feel, and with overwhelming force, is that I should never accept the defeat of Zionism before an attempt was made which would be equal to the grim seriousness of our struggle for national life, and to the sacredness of the trust which the Jewish people had laid in our hands."[7]

In his own hand Arlosoroff wrote on a secret copy of this letter: "Ben-Gurion. Just for you. . . . C.A." Ben-Gurion's response is unknown, but it is certain that the two discussed more than once the critical question of the time remaining for the realization of Zionism. Both men shared the sense of impatience

and urgency that underlay the balanced tone of this letter—
hence their secret collaboration.

Arlosoroff's gloomy forecast regarding the development of
the national home turned out to be erroneous. In 1932 another
wave of immigration, the Fifth Aliya, began and continued for
four years. Wauchope allowed a larger scope of immigration
than his predecessors, with the aim of bringing the Jews to
forty percent of the country's population. Though the whole
world was immersed in the economic crisis, prosperity reigned
in Palestine. The Nazis' rise to power in Germany pushed
wealthy Jews to emigrate to Palestine, and the agreement signed
by Arlosoroff on the eve of his murder in June 1933 helped
transfer their assets there. Most of the new immigrants were
from Poland, but the immigration from Germany included
numerous intellectuals and academics who changed the face of
the Yishuv and helped modernize it. In the meantime the country's fate was put on hold, and the evolutionary process was
given another chance.

Over the next two years Ben-Gurion was engaged mainly
in struggles with the Revisionists, both in the Yishuv and in
Poland, to achieve dominance in the Zionist movement. But
after the Eighteenth Congress in Prague in 1933 he joined the
Zionist Executive in Jerusalem to fill Arlosoroff's shoes. Moshe
Shertok (later Sharett), Arlosoroff's assistant in the political department, was promoted to membership in the Zionist Executive and remained there to help Ben-Gurion. Shertok, a member of the first graduating class at the Herzliya Gymnasium in
Tel Aviv, had studied at the London School of Economics. An
extremely talented linguist, he was fluent in English, a language
Ben-Gurion had learned in the United States during the war
but never felt comfortable writing in. Shertok also spoke fluent
Arabic and mediated between Ben-Gurion and his Arab interlocutors. During these two years Ben-Gurion continued as secretary of the Histadrut, but saw himself as responsible for the

Yishuv's foreign affairs. He held talks with the high commissioner and was very impressed by his courtesy, goodwill, and understanding of Zionist positions. At the same time Ben-Gurion sought to hold talks with Arab leaders to test the possibility of reaching a comprehensive agreement between the Jewish national movement and its Arab counterpart.

In the 1920s the directors of the political department had tended to develop connections with Arab leaders prone to bribery in exchange for adopting non-hostile positions on Zionism. Ben-Gurion sought out honest leaders who could not be bought with either money or positions. Thus he contacted Musa Alami, a legal adviser to the Mandatory government who was close to the mufti of Jerusalem, Haj Amin al-Husseini, considered not only the foremost Arab leader but also a nationalist and Jew-hater. Ben-Gurion opened his talk with Alami in the accepted Zionist manner by describing the development and economic growth the Jews had brought to Palestine. Alami responded that he would prefer the country to remain backward for another hundred years until the Arabs were capable of developing it themselves. "I felt that as a patriotic Arab he had the right to say that," Ben-Gurion wrote.[6]

Ben-Gurion then changed tack and sought to explore the possibility of reaching a comprehensive agreement between the two national movements. The Zionists wanted a Jewish state in Palestine, including Transjordan; in exchange they would be willing to support the establishment of a sizable Arab federation in the Middle East. This federation would include Palestine, with its Arabs constituting a minority within it, while the Jews would be a minority in the federation. In addition the Arabs would be part of the larger Arab nation. Aware of the Palestinian Arabs' fears of Jewish domination, Ben-Gurion sought to create an equilibrium whereby the Arab federation would compensate for the loss of the Arab majority in Palestine while ensuring the Arabs' status in the country. This was an updated

Ben-Gurion with the mufti of Jerusalem, Haj Amin
al-Husseini (at left), 1930s (Collection of Ben-Gurion
House in Tel Aviv)

version of previous attempts by the Zionist leadership to negotiate with the heads of the Pan-Arab movement (the Weizmann-
Faisal Agreement of 1919, for example) instead of with the Palestinian Arabs, on the correct assumption that such an agreement
would be easier to achieve than one with the locals. Ben-Gurion
was happy to meet with Syrian and Lebanese leaders in Europe
under a romantic cloak of secrecy—secrecy that his interlocutors did not preserve. The talks revolved around possible Jewish
assistance in establishing an Arab federation, but the Arabs neither wanted nor were able to make a commitment on behalf of
their Palestinian brethren.

Ben-Gurion's meetings with Musa Alami were pleasant and sincere, but they led nowhere. Ben-Gurion believed it was possible to find common ground, since it seemed to him that his interlocutor was impressed by his frankness. However he seems to have been prey to unrealistic optimism due to his lack of experience in such talks. He tried to meet with the mufti himself, but failed. As time passed the Arabs' basic positions—which had been outlined by the experienced Arthur Ruppin back in 1931—became clear. They were prepared to agree to the Jews being a permanent minority in Palestine, but nothing more. Ben-Gurion, however, was not prepared to relinquish the idea of a Jewish majority and Jewish sovereignty. Parity in the legislative and executive bodies of the Mandatory government was the limit of the concessions he could make. But the Arabs had no good reason to accept this. Even in 1936, after the large Fifth Aliya, they still constituted two thirds of the population. Ben-Gurion's persistence in his talks with Arab leaders—which fell into a fixed pattern that all parties anticipated in advance—was an expression both of his difficulty in accepting failure and of his recognition of the importance of this issue.

His attempts to negotiate with the Arab leadership were part of his perception of his role as head of the Jewish Agency's political department. He also held innumerable talks with the high commissioner, repeatedly plying him with Zionist arguments and occasionally persuading him to increase the immigration quota slightly in view of the impressive increase in the absorption of workers into the Jewish economy. Most likely his long speeches exhausted the high commissioner, but Wauchope was a patient man and welcomed the Yishuv's new, energetic leader.

Ben-Gurion acted vigorously to transfer the center of Zionist activity from London to Jerusalem by annulling procedures that gave priority to London and shifting the movement's propaganda and public relations efforts to Jerusalem. Weizmann, who at the time had no official position in the Zionist Organization, was the most important conduit to the government in London, where the Conservatives had regained power, and also to the Zionist movement notables there. Ben-Gurion tried to persuade both the British and the Jews that immigration—which was increasing year by year—was not keeping pace with the increased absorption and economic capacity of the growing Jewish economy. If fifty thousand people per year were allowed to immigrate over several years, he argued over and over, all of Zionism's problems would be solved and the Arabs would bow to the inevitable. The British were unconvinced.

His new position changed his worldview. He was no longer the militant labor leader seeking to impose a working-class outlook on the Jews of Palestine, but a leader responsible for the destiny of the entire Jewish people at this time of crisis. This change underlay a dramatic turnabout that to his contemporaries seemed incredible. In October 1934, Pinchas Rutenberg arranged a meeting between Ben-Gurion and Jabotinsky in Rutenberg's London hotel room. To their surprise these two great rivals, so different in character, education, and focus, found a common language. In this and several subsequent meetings, they spent many hours together, revealed to each other their visions, their hearts' desires and hopes, and in the end realized that with respect to Zionism there was no great distinction between them. Both wanted a Jewish state in Palestine. In the end they signed two agreements and formulated a third.

But their differences also came to light. When they sought to mark the great achievement of meeting and coming to terms with a particularly impressive act, Ben-Gurion proposed a large-scale settlement plan, whereas Jabotinsky suggested a petition from the Jewish people to the nations of the world. The difference between the advocate of practical Zionism, for whom laying the foundations for Jewish power in Palestine was the main objective, and the political Zionist, who believed in the magical effect of words on world public opinion, had never been starker. But on the personal level there was a breakthrough. Ben-Gurion wrote to Jabotinsky: "From now on nothing that happens will change the fact that we met, and for many hours forgot everything that stood behind us—and motivated by a great anxiety for the movement and the success of its [Zionist] enterprise, with mutual trust and respect driving us to a joint effort."[9] Jabotinsky replied in a similar vein: "There is a great deal more than sentimentality here if I am moved to the depth of my being on hearing, after so many years—and what years!—words like 'comrade and friend' from your lips. I had long since forgotten that language, perhaps I myself was the cause of it being forgotten between us." And regarding the agreement, he added: "A week ago I would have been surprised by anyone who believed it possible, but now I too believe it."[10]

The first agreement they signed was simply aimed at stopping violence in the Yishuv; the second dealt with labor relations, to prevent clashes between Betarists and Histadrut members over workplaces, strikes, and so forth. The third agreement, on Zionist issues, was formulated but not signed. They both knew they faced a tough internal battle over the agreements. In fact the hatred and mutual defamation in recent years had reached such a level that people on both sides had difficulty digesting this about-face. Jabotinsky could have imposed his will on his movement—even as one young man (whose name was Menachem Begin) reminded him reprovingly that Ben-Gurion had dubbed him "Vladimir Hitler." Ben-Gurion's situation was different. He led a broad-based movement that did not accept a leader's dictates. Even Katznelson's steadfast support was not enough. The entire leadership from the days of the Second Aliya, except for Tabenkin, supported the agreements. But the people from the later aliyot, leaders of city workers' councils who clashed every day with the Betarists, opposed them. The struggle against the class enemy was the foundation of their identity, and they were not ready for this conciliatory move, which had come unexpectedly, without previous preparation of public opinion.

In addition to the urban rank and file, two important kibbutz movements joined the opposition—Hakibbutz Hameuhad, led by Tabenkin, and Hashomer Hatzair, led by Meir Ya'ari and Ya'akov Hazan. Hakibbutz Hameuhad was Mapai's pioneering avant-garde, the organization that controlled the Hechalutz movement in the Diaspora that had made possible the victory in the Zionist Congress elections of 1933. Now Tabenkin, one of the founders of Akhdut Ha'avoda, came out against the agreements Ben-Gurion had signed with Jabotinsky. Threatening to split Mapai, the opposition forced the leadership to bring the agreements to the Mapai special council and then the party conference for ratification. Both bodies had a majority that favored the agreements, but to avoid a split Ben-Gurion and his comrades were compelled to have them ratified by a Histadrut referendum—a thing never done before and never repeated. In a mutiny by both rank-and-file and mid-level leaders against the top leadership, a large majority of the Histadrut membership rejected the agreements. This was the first hint of increasing tension in Mapai between Tabenkin on one hand and Katznelson and Ben-Gurion on the other. Whereas the latter two now saw themselves as responsible for the fate of Zionism and as moving "from class to nation," Tabenkin and his comrades remained entrenched in their labor-constructivist worldview.

Despite this resounding defeat, Ben-Gurion did not threaten to resign. "It was clear that a grave mistake had been made, but I accepted the decision without mental anguish. I knew I must bow to majority opinion and do everything in my power to ensure that the mistake made by the majority would not harm the movement," he explained to his children in a letter after the Lucerne Zionist Congress in September 1935.[11] His colleagues recognized his talents and his vigor in the Zionist struggle, but they did not see him as an outstanding, irreplaceable leader. The agreements were filed and forgotten, but they still affected life in the Yishuv. There were no more violent clashes between workers and Betarists, and the latter stopped breaking strikes. The struggle between the two movements pulled back from the street and into politics. The failure to ratify the agreements led Jabotinsky to despair of the Zionist Organization. His movement seceded from it, and he founded the New Zionist Organization.

The Zionist Congress in 1935 completed Ben-Gurion's apprenticeship in national leadership. He learned that in order to achieve his objectives he had to compromise and not bang his head against a brick wall. Such compromise became the very essence of Mapai leadership. A symbol of it was his decision to address the congress in Yiddish, despite his deep love of Hebrew. Most of the delegates did not know Hebrew, and since he wanted to make them understand the immense problems and broad scope of Zionism, he chose to speak Yiddish, even though this cost him a great effort both ideologically and physically. "When I finished even my jacket was soaked with sweat," he wrote afterward.[12]

Ben-Gurion now made a number of decisions that prove he understood the weight of national responsibility resting on his shoulders. Gone was the labor leader prepared to destroy the Yishuv if the Histadrut fell, who saw violence as a useful tool in fighting a political rival. His first decision was to restore Weizmann to the presidency of the Zionist Organization. Weizmann, the aristocrat of the Zionist movement, a leader without a party behind him who by the force of his personal charm had captivated and won the trust of British politicians, was the statesman with the greatest influence in representing the movement to the outside world. He had shortcomings: he was hasty, did not consult with anyone, and did not know how to take criticism. But Ben-Gurion accepted him with all his faults, knowing that he, above all others, was the man to represent the Zionist cause on the world stage.

Second, Ben-Gurion formed a broad coalition representing all the parties at the congress. The most important one was Hamizrachi, which represented the religious sector, and he wooed it until it agreed to join—even though this meant having to agree in turn that the kibbutzim would observe kashrut and the Sabbath. This was the beginning of a "historical alliance" between the labor movement and religious Zionism that held firm until 1977. When his son Amos sent him a note asking why he had not spoken about class war at the congress, Ben-Gurion explained that unlike labor movements in existing states, the Zionist-Socialist movement had to establish a state, an economy, a society, and a culture, and it was impossible to do so without the cooperation of all the nation's forces. For the same reason he also agreed to assume the chairmanship of the Zionist Executive, even though he initially acted hesitant. Only after many hours of persuasion from Tabenkin did he accept the post. Ben-Gurion hoped that he was thereby guaranteeing the cooperation of Hakibbutz Hameuhad, which was close to his heart. "My presence on the Executive increases the responsibility of the workers in Zionist affairs," he explained to his son, exemplifying the shift of focus in his life from his role in the Histadrut to that in the executive.[13]

He left the congress exhausted and drained after a month of intense activity. Together with Paula he settled into a modest chalet in a beautiful, remote Swiss village in the snow-covered mountains, and rested from his labors. In recent years his relations with his wife had seen ups and downs, and this was one of his efforts at reconciliation. It is doubtful that she enjoyed the scenery, the natural beauty, and the clear mountain air as much as he did; she did not join him on his walks around the area. He used this respite to write long letters to Amos and Geula, which

Ben-Gurion speaking at the Zionist Congress, apparently at
Lucerne, 1935 (The Lavon Institute for Labor Research)

were actually intended as a historical record and perhaps also
for the party central committee. In them he elucidated his policy and tactics at the congress and in the Zionist arena generally. He was very much aware of himself and his new standing
in the Zionist movement. But in the international arena, he was
still considered a minor leader.

6

◆─◆─◆

Days of Hope, Days of Despair

IN APRIL 1936, the Arab Revolt erupted in Palestine. After
several days of rioting and the murder of Jewish passersby,
Palestinian Arab leaders took charge and announced a general
strike that would continue until the Mandatory authorities met
three demands: cessation of Jewish immigration, cessation of
land sales to Jews, and the handover of government to the Arab
majority. With the outbreak of the revolt, the Zionist Executive went on high alert. The most important question was how
to prevent the British government from acceding to the Arab
demands. The leadership declared a policy of "restraint." Based
on experience, the Jews sought to prevent the rioting from
being presented as two-sided, as the authorities had done on
previous occasions. Accordingly they would not respond to the
Arab terrorism with terrorism of their own—it was the Mandatory government's job to protect them. At the same time the
Zionist leadership demanded that the government recruit Jews

as supernumerary policemen, that it not stop immigration, and that it permit the construction of a jetty in Tel Aviv, since Jaffa Port was strikebound and it was impossible to unload goods or disembark immigrants there. For Ben-Gurion, ensuring continued immigration was the core issue of Zionist policy at the time, in Palestine and London alike.

After several years in which the focus of Zionist activity had been in Palestine, the center of activity now reverted to London. The leading personality in the small team housed at 77 Great Russell Street, the Zionist Executive office in London, was Chaim Weizmann. Charming as always, with his extraordinary rhetorical talent and exceptional grasp of the ins and outs of the British political system, Weizmann was the one who presented the Zionist case to the British governmental authorities. He would go on his own to talks at the Colonial Office or unofficial talks with the pro-Zionist lobby. Ben Gurion, as chairman of the Jewish Agency Executive, went to London to support Zionist activity. He and Katznelson, who was in the office part of the time, formed a sort of Palestine guard ensuring that Weizmann made no mistakes. But they were not told what he said in his tête-à-têtes with the British, with Arab leaders such as the Iraqi prime minister Nuri Sa'id, or with people like Harry St. John Philby, a Briton who had converted to Islam and was a confidant of Ibn Saud, the king of Saudi Arabia. Weizmann kept his British government contacts to himself and hardly ever confided in Ben-Gurion. The Great Russell Street staff were devoted to Weizmann, although they did not always agree with him. Two people in the office who had independent opinions were Blanche Dugdale, Lord Balfour's niece, known as "Baffy," and Lewis Namier, a Jew of Polish extraction who was an eminent professor of history at the University of Manchester. They were important members of the office, with excellent contacts in the British oligarchy, and they had Weizmann's trust. They recognized his unreliability and his tendency to make irresponsible statements and leak things he shouldn't. In his memoirs, Namier wrote. "Much as I loved and admired Weizmann, I suffered severely from his indiscretions, and Baffy and I would sometimes withhold from him even important things if the danger of their being repeated exceeded the possible loss from their being withheld."[1]

What the British partners in the London office accepted with forbearance, Ben-Gurion found intolerable. At a meeting with Nuri Sa'id, Weizmann, in a slip of the tongue, suggested that the Zionists might be willing to stop immigration for a while in order to facilitate negotiations with the Arabs. Reports of this conversation whipped up a storm in the Zionist camp. In such cases Ben-Gurion was not the easiest or most forgiving partner. He would erupt in rage—often approaching the level of irrationality of "Beware, British Empire!"—and cause chaos in the office. It became increasingly clear to him that Weizmann remained Weizmann, and that he came as a kind of package deal—if you wanted his virtues, you had to bear his shortcomings.

Ben-Gurion needed to obtain not only the trust of the people in the office, but their esteem. Even though he and Namier had similar views, however, his outbursts of rage were not conducive to winning over Namier or anyone else. He was never part of the inner circle that Baffy used to invite to dinner at her home, though she sometimes invited him to join the after-dinner conversation. He did win both admiration and affection from the Oxford-educated Doris May, a young Englishwoman who worked as a secretary at the office. She treated Weizmann with appropriate respect and distance, but she developed a friendliness with Ben-Gurion that deviated from stereotypical British aloofness. It is difficult to imagine Ben-Gurion developing the degree of emotional intimacy and closeness with an educated young Englishwoman that their correspondence reveals.

Their point of contact was a mutual love of classical Greek literature, especially Plato. They exchanged views on writers and books, and she was in charge of sending his book orders from Blackwell's bookshop in London to Tel Aviv. May and Ben-Gurion remained friends for years, even when their political opinions and approach to the Zionist struggle with Britain diverged. "I told you once, I think, that I could foresee that we should one day find ourselves on opposite sides of a fence," she wrote him at the end of a letter in which she disagreed with him, "and that when it happened it would make no difference to my friendship for you, because whatever happened I should believe in your utter honesty of purpose."[2] Ben-Gurion's friendship with her was some compensation for the frustrations caused by Weizmann and his colleagues, not to mention the representatives of the British government.

It was only after some six months—and the intervention of the Arab kings of Transjordan, Iraq, Saudi Arabia, and Yemen— that the Arab strike and the terror ended, making it possible for the British government's Palestine Royal Commission, headed by Lord Peel, to come to Palestine, hear the claims of both sides, and suggest a new policy. Ben-Gurion appeared before the commission, but only in a minor role. Except for one aphorism— "The Mandate is not our Bible, the Bible is our mandate"—his statement did not make an impression. By contrast, Weizmann addressed the commission with brilliant oratory about six million superfluous Jews in Europe and claimed that Palestine would be able to absorb several million over thirty years. In February 1937, Weizmann visited Nahalal, in northern Palestine, with Professor Reginald Coupland, the commission's driving force. During their conversation Coupland raised the idea of partition—not cantonization, which is a form of autonomy— but partition into two independent states. Weizmann was ecstatic. So was Ben-Gurion, but he knew that if the Jews were too enthusiastic there would be overwhelming Arab opposition to the idea. Therefore the Jews should play the part of the reluctant bride who must be persuaded until she says yes.

That same month Ben-Gurion drew up a partition plan of his own and presented it for preliminary discussion before the Mapai Central Committee. Knowing his audience, he began with the possibility of a negative change in British policy in the wake of the Arab Revolt. For him the worst-case scenario was for the government to change its policy on immigration, and instead of determining the number of immigrants by the country's "absorption capacity," as had been the policy to this point, it would decide arbitrarily how many Jews could enter based on the reactions of the Arabs. Such a politically motivated cap on immigration would force the Yishuv to be an eternal minority. Ending immigration during this period of crisis would make Zionism irrelevant for the Jewish people, as they fought for their life and sought refuge, and the Yishuv would sink into decline. As an alternative he proposed his own plan, with a detailed map. This was the first discussion of a partition plan among Jewish institutions. When Golda Meyerson asked what would happen when there were three million Jews in the small state he had sketched, Ben-Gurion replied: "What will happen after three million Jews come to this Jewish state we shall see afterward. The future generations will take care of themselves; we must concern ourselves with this generation."[3]

Despite his enthusiasm over the vision of imminent Jewish sovereignty, he accepted the reservations of his colleagues, especially Katznelson, who thought the partition to be proposed by the Peel Commission would probably be far less advantageous than Ben-Gurion's. Nevertheless, he asserted that when the possibility of a Jewish state, even a tiny one, was on one side of the balance, and on the other the de facto annulment of the pro-Zionist clauses in the Mandate instrument—that is, a moratorium on the national home—he preferred the first. But deep in his heart he did not see partition as the lesser of two evils: for him the vision of a Jewish state that suddenly seemed achievable was a dream come true.

On the eve of the Peel Commission report's publication, the members of the Jewish Agency Executive in Jerusalem learned its main points when a Jewish worker at the Palestine telegraph office leaked a telegram the colonial secretary sent to Wauchope, which contained an abstract of the report. Moshe Shertok hastened to Cairo, where he could call his colleagues in London without fear of British wiretapping, and gave them the details of the partition proposal, which went beyond Jewish expectations. Ben-Gurion, on fire, leaked the proposal to the Palcor news agency, and soon telephones started ringing all over the world. Weizmann was enraged, but Ben-Gurion innocently explained that he wanted to prepare public opinion in the Yishuv before the report was published and had purposely not informed Weizmann so that his hands would be clean. Ben-Gurion's colleagues in the executive did not accept this excuse, and Baffy Dugdale was given the task of reprimanding him about acting on his own initiative. He apologized, but it remained true that just as Weizmann often did not consult his colleagues, Ben-Gurion also acted solo when he wished to. This particular incident demonstrates his ability to manipulate both the press and his audience, proving that he had learned a trick or two from his London colleagues.

In the history of the Zionist movement, the debate over partition was one of those moments of truth when realism clashed with myth, the possible with the desirable. The opponents of partition included those for whom the mystical connection with the Land of Israel tipped the scales: Hamizrachi, the Revisionists, and also some circles in the labor movement. "How can you divide a mother's body?" asked one member of a socialist youth movement. Others doubted that the British would ever actually try to implement partition. The debate was informed by the Jews' distrust of the Mandatory power; opponents claimed that even if the British ratified the proposal, there was no chance that it would materialize. The same reasons that led Britain to curtail immigration and try to appease the Arabs would also prevent the implementation of partition. Still others thought the Yishuv was not yet ready to stand on its own two feet. Katznelson likened partition at that stage to the premature birth of a stillborn child. There were also opponents who raised a whole series of practical reservations about one or another of the proposal's clauses, arguing that without massive amendments it would be impossible to accept.

In contrast, the proposal's supporters saw a Jewish state within their grasp: the Zionist dream was about to be fulfilled. Not only the leaders were excited by this prospect. In Poland, the oppressed Jewish masses with no hope of a future were set afire by this sudden prospect of rescue. Their enthusiasm was unrestrained; delegates from Poland at the Twentieth Zionist Congress, held in Basel in August 1937, brought with them lists of ministers for the future state.

Ben-Gurion believed in seizing historic, once-in-a-lifetime opportunities. This was one of Lenin's characteristics that captivated him. In a Jewish Agency Executive discussion that took place before the arrival of the Peel Commission, he expressed the feeling that "in history, too, there are chances. There are chains of circumstances, and a man or a movement must possess the ability to seize an opportunity and hold on to it."[4] To him the partition proposal was one of those historic opportunities in which the heavens open and what was impossible suddenly becomes possible. He lived with a sense that the times were fateful: "I am totally impassioned in that I feel we are on the eve of events liable to change the course of our history, events that have occurred only twice or three times in our three-thousand-year history," he wrote to his party comrades.[5]

His exhilaration left him unable to sleep for weeks. Therefore when he met the American Socialist-Zionist leader Chaim Greenberg, who opposed partition, in the hallway at the Zionist Congress, he shouted at him, "You should be executed!" But he could still offer a cogent argument. In a long, reasoned letter to his son Amos he tried to explain his motives, not in emotional terms ("political questions are not a matter for emotion"), but in a rational and considered way, with the aim of convincing him and others that the Jews had no choice but to accept partition, since the alternative was reduced immigration and the deterioration of the Yishuv.[6] He spoke not of the advantages of the Jewish state, but of the dangers inherent in an anti-Zionist British interpretation of the Mandate now that the Palestine question was being comprehensively reassessed after the Arab Revolt. Still, every now and then sparks from his inner turmoil flew off, revealing the scenarios his imagination played out. In trying to persuade his party comrades who doubted the Jews' ability to withstand Arab resistance on their own, he described a state that organized mass immigration, created an economy, and set up an army. "We will bring all the pioneers undergoing training, give them khaki uniforms, and invite foreign officers who will train them to be soldiers. And in one month we shall have good soldiers." He went on to explain, "a Jewish boy needs only one month of instruction to become a good soldier."[7]

Ben-Gurion knew he must tread a fine line. So long as the Jewish state was not a fact, the Zionist movement must not lose the Mandate instrument recognizing the Jews' status in Palestine. The question was how to hold on to the Mandate while supporting partition. The answer was that partition must be a British plan, and overenthusiastic support from the Jews might ruin it. For this reason he saw an advantage in his opponents' caution. They all, especially his comrades in Mapai, dictated a draft resolution to the Zionist Congress that empowered the executive to negotiate partition with the Mandatory government,

but bound it to bring the final proposal before a special congress to be convened for that purpose.

Weizmann's speech in favor of partition was considered the
best one delivered at the congress. He was at pains to warmly
praise Moshe Shertok, but said not a word about Ben-Gurion.
If Ben-Gurion was affronted, he did not say so. When Paula,
who had come to the congress, complained about Weizmann's
attitude toward him, he replied: "I am not interested in how he
treats me. I am not dependent on him and I have no need of his
favor. I view him as an important instrument in our enterprise,
and the enterprise, only the enterprise, interests me."[8] It is hard
to believe that Weizmann's contemptuous attitude did not vex
Ben-Gurion. But in the struggle over partition they were allies
who needed each other against large sections of the Zionist Organization. He therefore made an effort to reconcile with Weizmann and wrote him a letter acknowledging his primacy: "You
are now King of Israel," the emissary of Jewish history on whom
"the historic Providence of our people has imposed the rebirth
of the Kingdom of Israel."[9]

At the end of 1937 the members of the Zionist Executive
perceived the first signs that the British government, which
had ratified the partition plan, was about to renege on it. Ben-
Gurion, electrified by his vision of the Jewish state, was unwilling to believe these ominous signs. In contrast with the usual
division in the Great Russell Street office—in which he was the
pessimist and the others the optimists—the roles were now re-
versed. While Baffy and Weizmann warned that the government was about to go back on its commitment, Ben-Gurion
still believed that partition would happen and rejected their
pessimism. "Even if there are people in the cabinet who seek to
kill off Zionist policy out of fear of the Arabs and Muslims, or
of Hitler and Mussolini—I do not believe that British public
opinion will allow such a betrayal."[10] This belief in public opin-

ion and its ability to influence the government was more like Jabotinsky than like Ben-Gurion the realist.

The aggressive policies of Italy and Germany created fears of war in Britain, and Palestine was not high on the public's agenda. Appeasing the Arab monarchs had a higher priority for the government than assurances to the Jews. The Woodhead Commission, which the government set up ostensibly to resolve the problems of implementing partition, in fact gave the partition plan a decent burial. But until the Woodhead report was published, Ben-Gurion refused to accept the actual situation and demanded continued pressure on the government for partition. Nothing Weizmann and his colleagues said—not even Katznelson's realistic reasoning—had an effect on him. He continued to see partition as the only option for preventing sanctions against the Yishuv. Even though he recognized the danger of a world war after the Munich crisis in the autumn of 1938 and understood that war would prevent any revolutionary change such as partition from being carried out, he still clung to the idea of the state as a realistic possibility.

On 18 September 1938, Weizmann, Ben-Gurion, and Colonial Secretary Malcolm MacDonald held a long talk. It was the height of the Munich crisis, with the Czechs' supposed ally Britain demanding that they submit to Hitler. MacDonald informed Weizmann and Ben-Gurion that he was currently studying correspondence written during World War I between Sir Henry McMahon, the British high commissioner in Egypt, and the Hashemite Arab ruler of Arabia, Hussein bin Ali, and had learned that the Arabs had suffered an injustice and that contradictory assurances on Palestine had been given to Jews and Arabs. Considering that over the preceding twenty years the British government had continuously rejected the Arabs' claims, and that McMahon himself denied that he had accepted them, MacDonald's assertion that he had just "discovered" these documents seemed to be laying the ideological and legal ground-work for reneging on the assurances given to the Jews in the Mandate instrument, particularly with regard to immigration. Weizmann and Ben-Gurion reported to Baffy Dugdale on their talk, and she wrote in her diary, "They are going to sell the Jews too—give up partition, for fear of the Arabs and the Germans and the Italians. . . . We were all stunned. Ben-Gurion's first reaction—and mine—was that the Jews will fight, physically, rather than go back to the Mandate as it will be."[11]

In the following days Weizmann's inclination was to break off contact with MacDonald and stop the talks with him, while Ben-Gurion demanded that they continue, that the last word had not yet been uttered, that perhaps there was still hope. But the outlook became gloomier by the day. In the meantime the Czech crisis was resolved by the Czechs' surrender, Britain having abandoned its tiny ally. Jan Masaryk, foreign minister of the dying Czech Republic, made an analogy between the fate of the Czechs and that of the Jews using a poignant metaphor. With bitter sarcasm he suggested to Weizmann that they buy a three-story house in London. The first floor would be for Haile Selassie, emperor of Ethiopia, who had been expelled from his country by the Italians; the second would house Masaryk, representing the Czechs; and the third floor would be for Weizmann—all three victims of British duplicity.

The same Ben-Gurion who until a few weeks earlier had asserted his belief in British public opinion now contended that in the era of power politics no one listened to claims for justice and fulfillment of promises. Even Jewish protests in Poland or New York would make no impression on the British government now. The Yishuv had only one thing at its disposal—its own force, which must be prepared for this struggle to prevent it from being handed over to the Arabs. The Jews must purchase land, bring in people, and buy arms either legally or illegally. Ben-Gurion revealed his musings in this direction to

Lewis Ruskin, a wealthy young American Jew who was prepared to purchase arms for the Haganah, the Jewish militia in Palestine, and apparently suggested that the Jews attempt to take Palestine by force. Indeed, like his leadership colleagues, Ben-Gurion felt that Ruskin's proposals were premature, but at the same time Ruskin got the impression that Ben-Gurion had devoted a great deal of thought to this subject, for he was prepared with answers to Ruskin's questions about strategy and the military balance of power between Jews and Arabs in Palestine.

Ben-Gurion was incapable of accepting a situation of helplessness. Although the Woodhead report had effectively delivered the coup de grâce to the partition plan, a government decision had not yet been made. The Jews and the Arabs were invited to talks at St. James's Palace, ostensibly to find a solution to the Palestine question that both could agree on. In the meantime, Ben-Gurion went to New York and tried to mobilize American Jewry against the imminent sanctions. The Jews of America, however, were leery of any action that might identify them as fighting for a particular Jewish interest. Attempts to enlist President Franklin D. Roosevelt to the Zionist cause also failed. This trip to America is memorable only because it marked the first time Ben-Gurion addressed an audience in English.

Up to this point Ben-Gurion had zealously ensured that the Jewish Agency Executive's actions remained legal, opposing attempts to bring "illegal" immigrants to Palestine—attempts in which his good friend Katznelson was involved. Now, however, he began speaking about bringing masses of refugees to Palestine in order to create leverage for eliminating the political cap on immigration. Not much came of these grandiose plans. Meanwhile, despite their instinct to boycott the government-initiated St. James's conference talks, the members of the executive decided that they had to participate. Although, as Namier put it, "Malcolm MacDonald is prepared to promise everything in the future, admit to everything in the past, and not give anything in the present," Jewish and British public opinion would not understand a boycott of the talks.[12] And thus came about a fantastic spectacle that lasted for more than a month. In the magnificent setting of St. James's Palace, wearing tailcoats, the Yishuv and Zionist movement delegates sat at a round table with members of the British Colonial Office. The Arab delegates refused to sit at the table with the Jews and were seated at a separate round table. In this manner the two sides supposedly negotiated, with the Jews making powerful arguments to no avail, while MacDonald ably presented the Arab side to them.

On 15 March 1939, the day Hitler entered Prague, both delegations were given the clauses of a new White Paper. The tragic spectacle of the conference was over, and the delegates sailed back to Palestine. Aboard ship Ben-Gurion recuperated from the tremendous tension he had been under, played chess with Ruskin, and read books on sociology.

MacDonald's White Paper was published in May. It limited immigration to seventy-five thousand over five years, after which immigration would be conditional upon agreement from the Arabs. Land purchase by Jews was also restricted. After ten years Palestine was to be granted independence, meaning that an Arab-majority state would be established, if the Jews agreed. The White Paper signaled the end of the affair between the Zionist movement and Britain.

Between March and September 1939, Ben-Gurion was in a frenzy. He worked unceasingly to mobilize the Yishuv for a real physical struggle against the White Paper. He proposed mass immigration with armed defense of the immigrants as they came ashore, settlement without government approval, and significant reinforcement of Haganah units. He was prepared for armed clashes with British government forces. These activist notions were intended as an antidote to the Jews' sense of complete helplessness, which heightened as the specter of a world war drew ever closer. However, every time he made such a proposal to the Zionist Executive or the Mapai Central Committee—even to the Haganah National Command—his colleagues headed him off, rejecting his proposals out of hand. They saw no point in making relations with the government worse at a time when the Yishuv was dependent on the British and the prospect of war was in the air. Ben-Gurion's "fighting Zionism" was another of the man's volcanic eruptions his colleagues managed to block.

The Mandate authorities brutally quelled the Arab Revolt, and the White Paper pacified the Arabs politically. The Yishuv reacted with demonstrations, protests, and an acceleration of illegal immigration. But in response, the authorities took the gloves off. They incarcerated the Jews who sought refuge in Palestine from the approaching war, shot at illegal ships, and put down demonstrations with firearms. In mid-August 1939 the Twenty-first Zionist Congress convened in Geneva. It opened with the White Paper as the main item on the agenda and closed with the realization that war was imminent. While it was in session the Molotov-Ribbentrop Pact, a non-aggression agreement between Soviet Russia and Nazi Germany, was announced. Aware that war was about to break out, the delegates hurried home to their families. The parting was dramatic: no one knew what fate would bring and when, if ever, they would meet again. In tears, Weizmann parted from his friends: "My heart is full to overflowing. . . . It is impossible that some things may not come about, things without which the world cannot be pictured. The surviving remnant will continue to work, to fight, to live, until better times than these arrive, and for those times I wish you all: Au revoir in peace!"[13]

The Jewish people had no doubt about which side it was on. The White Paper was dwarfed by the need to fight Hitler. "We must assist the English in their war as if there were no White Paper, and resist the White Paper as if there were no war," Ben-Gurion declared in another of his dual formulas that became famous.[14] It made a wonderful catchy slogan, but its validity in reality was doubtful. In a situation of world war, the priorities of nations—and the Jews—change. When titans are in conflict, what good can come of pleas to the world's conscience by a small, helpless people that suddenly finds itself in existential danger?

In March 1940, when the Palestine Lands Transfer Regulations were published, limiting land sales to Jews, Ben-Gurion wanted to deploy the Haganah in violent demonstrations against them. But once again he found himself in the minority in the Zionist Executive. The notion of using force against the British when the country was swarming with British troops seemed implausible. Fears of iron-fisted British reprisals, confiscation of Haganah weapons, and putting all of Zionism's achievements at risk put a brake on any extreme action. Ben-Gurion was so frustrated that he resigned as chairman of the Jewish Agency Executive. But he remained active, and when Weizmann offered him a way out of resigning by inviting him to join him in London, he accepted, and his resignation was forgotten.

Ben-Gurion reached London on 1 May 1940 after sailing to Italy, which was not yet at war, and from there traveling by rail to Paris, where he was delayed for a few days waiting for a seat on a plane. He used the time to wander the bookshops, and sent home packages of volumes on military subjects, history, and philosophy. It was the period of the Phony War, and Western Europe was still calm. London was welcoming; he made common cause with Weizmann on the need to enlist American Jewry to the Zionist endeavor. But the false quiet was shattered by a thunderbolt when the Germans invaded the Low Countries. Neville Chamberlain's government of appeasement fell and was replaced by an activist national unity government, headed by Winston Churchill, that included the Labour party. Ben-Gurion was stunned by the speed at which events unfolded and moved by the response of the British people: "I am amazed by the level-headedness and inner confidence of this wonderful nation," he reported to Paula. "Nothing shakes its belief and confidence in its ultimate victory."[15] The evacuation of the British Expeditionary Force from Dunkirk seemed to him nothing short of miraculous. He considered Churchill's speech after the evacuation, with his admission of failure and simultaneous declaration that victory would eventually come, a political act of prime importance that expressed the resolve of the British people and their determination to keep fighting. He grieved over the defeat of France: "The last bastion of freedom of the spirit and human dignity has fallen in continental Europe—and now only two countries remain from which the hope of rescue and deliverance can be expected—England and America," he wrote Paula.[16]

From day to day his esteem increased, as the British people and their leaders continued fighting despite defeats: "Their will is the only thing presently standing between Hitler and world domination."[17] What most roused his admiration was Churchill's decision to bomb the French fleet at Oran: "Not only was the Nazi plot to seize French warships foiled, but it sent out a clear signal to the world that England is resolved to fight to the bitter end."[18] The Battle of Britain in August 1940, and Churchill's speech afterward, taught Ben-Gurion how critical a people's moral fiber, resolve, and love of freedom were in such a struggle. "I would like the Yishuv and the Jewish people to learn this lesson from Britain."[19] Though he was full of admiration for Churchill's leadership in Britain's darkest hours, he contended that history was made not by leaders but by the masses. However, at fateful times, when the scales of history waver between life and death, destruction and redemption, victory and defeat, "a courageous, cautious, farseeing, enterprising leader, or the absence of one, means the difference between ruin and salvation." Even so, Churchill's resolve still needed the bravery of the British people. "All Churchill's heroism would not have served him if he had to face Hitler—with the majority of the members of the Zionist Executive," he wrote ironically, settling scores with the colleagues who rejected his "fighting Zionism."[20]

During the London blitz—when he refused to go down into the air-raid shelter either by day or at night, and continued working or sleeping as usual—for the first time since being captivated by Lenin, Ben-Gurion adopted a new leadership model: the democratic leader. He maintained that Churchill had risen to power by virtue of British democracy, which even in wartime allowed parliamentary activity to continue and public opinion to be expressed. Despite the talk from both left and right on the weakness of democracy, the war proved that it could cope with a great crisis. All of the examples of its inadequacy when faced with dictatorships were evidence not of the weakness of democracy, but of a failure of government. A resolute and wise leader backed by a brave people ready for war was the combination that ensured victory. In 1948 he would attempt to emulate Churchill's model.

The Zionist question faded into insignificance before the dramatic events of those months. The instinct of people like Weizmann, whose formative experience was in World War I, was to attempt to replicate the relations that had led to the Balfour Declaration in the completely different reality of 1940, where the Jews' bargaining power was nonexistent. The war against Hitler was the war of the Jewish people together with the rest of the civilized world. By contrast the Arab states and the Arabs of Palestine were in the comfortable situation of being wooed by both sides in the conflict. The Palestinian leader, Haj Amin al-Husseini, found sanctuary in Berlin, from where he assisted the German propaganda machine in the Middle East. Maintaining the Arab states' loyalty to the Allies was of prime importance; thus the British quelled a pro-Nazi revolt in Iraq. Therefore, the Zionists' expectation that the pro-Zionist Churchill's rise to power would lead to the suspension of the White Paper policies turned out to be mistaken.

But in the meantime they tended to put their faith in the apparently positive development represented by the new government in London, and repeatedly offered the help of the Jewish people in general, and the Yishuv in particular, in the war effort. Weizmann attempted to recreate the scientific success he had achieved in the World War I effort by working on strategic materials for the Allies. The Zionists offered the Yishuv's production capability and its organizational and creative talent. The jewel in the crown was their request to establish a military unit under British command—another item from the previous world war that was replicated in the latest one. The Jews hoped that a unit under the blue-and-white flag would accord them the rights of a fighting party. It was also a good opportunity to train young people from Palestine in a modern army and give them military experience.

Precisely for these reasons, the Colonial Office did everything in its power to thwart this possibility. It and the Foreign Office viewed the Balfour Declaration and the entire Zionist enterprise as a historic mistake and were determined not to allow the Jews to establish an independent entity in Palestine. Therefore any expression of Jewish nationalism linked to Palestine must be opposed—particularly any measure that could nurture Zionist hopes that Palestine might become a refuge for millions of Jews after the war. It would be stupid to give the Jews arms and teach them how to fight, for those weapons could be turned against the British in the future. The British tactics of evasion, delay, and deceit in this matter could fill an entire textbook on governmental duplicity. Churchill attempted to intervene, but every time someone else spiked his guns: there was insufficient matériel, there was no need for additional troops, Palestinian battalions should be established with equal numbers of Jews and Arabs, not units under a Jewish flag. It was not until 1944 that a Jewish Brigade was created; it fought in northern Italy, but its main activity was after the war, aiding Holocaust survivors and helping rehabilitate the Jewish people. In the meantime thousands of young people enlisted in the British army. Some twenty-seven thousand Jews from Palestine served in the war, feeling duty bound to fight Hitler, even though not under a Jewish flag. One volunteer was Amos Ben-Gurion, who was commissioned in August 1941.

In the fall of 1940 Ben-Gurion felt that he had nothing more to do in London, since the Palestine issues had become marginal. He decided to test the Jewish political waters in the United States and reached New York in early October. No one awaited him at the port. Completely incognito he disembarked, and an immigration officer detained him for several days since he was unable to provide good reasons for such a voyage in wartime. The ambiguity of his "dual formula"—assisting Britain in the war while struggling against it in regard to Palestine—plagued him in the United States. The question was how to mobilize American Jewry on behalf of Zionism without encouraging anti-British tendencies. He found a public with strong Jewish identification and definite Zionist instincts, but confused and disorganized, with a leadership embroiled in petty quarrels over honors and positions.

Ben-Gurion demanded that American Zionists formulate a plan of action. The plan he proposed included supporting the establishment of a Jewish army and fighting the White Paper, but the focus was on its third point: assuming that the British won the war, it would end with a terrible Jewish disaster—five million displaced Jews, for whom the only solution would be bringing them to Palestine. This transfer could only be accomplished by the Jews themselves, and to do it they needed a state. "It is vital that Palestine become a Jewish state, not as a final objective, but as a means of transferring millions of Jews there after the war as fast as possible."[21] Not authorized to present such a plan, Ben-Gurion scrupulously stated that it was his personal plan. From then on, however, he strove unceasingly to make it the accepted Zionist one.

No one, including Ben-Gurion himself, imagined that this trip to the United States represented the first stage of his transformation from leader of the Yishuv to leader of the Zionist movement—the one who expressed the collective will not just of that movement but also (given the circumstances of the Holocaust) of the Jewish people as a whole. Yet though he had already adopted the frame of mind of a national leader, at this time he was not seen as such outside Palestine. His prestige was far lower than Weizmann's, both in the United States and elsewhere.

Ben-Gurion was certain that American Jewry had to assume the role of leadership of the Jewish people. Whether it was indeed ready to take up this fateful role is not clear, but history had placed this mantle on its shoulders, and history cannot be argued with. Ben-Gurion learned very quickly that the U.S. State Department was under British influence and hostile toward Zionism, so the Jews could not look for salvation from it or from Roosevelt. Although Roosevelt had advanced Jews more than any other president, he believed that Palestine was too small to solve the Jewish problem, and another country had to be found for the Jews. Fighting Roosevelt was out of the question, since he was a friend of the Jews even though he did not believe in Zionism. Therefore, "the way to win over the American administration is to win over the people, win public opinion," Ben-Gurion opined. In one of the flashes of crystal-clear thinking that he displayed several times in the coming years, he declared that the Zionists must reach out to the press, members of Congress, churches, labor leaders, and intellectuals, "and once they are with us—the administration will be with us. . . . The way to Roosevelt is through the American people."[22]

Thus within a few months Ben-Gurion, the anonymous traveler who had been detained on Ellis Island, achieved insights that no one had reached before. He defined the war's objective: turning Palestine into a Jewish commonwealth in order to bring in millions of Jewish refugees. He also defined the strategy: organizing masses of Jews so they could mobilize American public opinion to support the creation of the Jewish state. This would mean a complete departure from Weizmann's method of influencing policymakers through personal behind-the-scenes talks, and changing course to a grassroots mobilizing of Jewish and American public opinion. The only problem was how to accomplish it.

Ben-Gurion remained in America for three months, then needed an entire month to get back to Palestine from New York. He stayed several months, but there was no action there, so in August 1941 he returned to London, where the corridors of power were closed to the Zionists. The world was at war and the Palestine question was not at the top of the government's agenda. Ben-Gurion's need for constant activity came up against the frustrating reality that no real action was possible. In November 1941 he again sailed for New York and remained in the United States for more than ten months. In April 1942 Weizmann, too, reached New York as a guest of the American administration, for consultations on chemistry research. In stark contrast with Ben-Gurion's anonymous arrival, he was given a royal welcome by Jews and non-Jews alike.

The United States had not yet entered the war, but within a few weeks the Japanese attack on Pearl Harbor changed everything. Ben-Gurion viewed this event as creating a revolution in the outlook of the United States that mandated a similar drastic change in the Zionist camp. His main focus during his first few months was to establish lines of communication between Zionists and non-Zionists. The horrors of the war, the sense of the fatefulness of the hour, the danger of a German invasion hovering over Palestine, all made it possible to create harmonious relations between the Jewish-American financial elite, which was organized in the American Jewish Committee (AJC), and the Zionists, whose wartime organization was the Joint Emergency Committee (later, Council). Ben-Gurion believed he could bring the members of the AJC to agree on a joint statement with the Zionists that would include recognition of the claim to establish an independent Jewish entity in Palestine after the war. These efforts gained the support of most AJC members, but the minority, led by Justice Joseph Proskauer, rejected them and threatened to resign. The negotiations, conducted over many months, foundered on this rock. In the end, Ben-Gurion's efforts at unity failed, and the two main non-Zionist bodies in America—the Jewish Labor Committee, led by the unions, and the AJC—did not join the Zionists. Nonetheless, he enjoyed a heartening moment when, on 10 May 1942, the American Zionists convened a conference at New York's Biltmore Hotel and proclaimed the Jewish people's war objectives.

There is controversy among historians as to whether Ben-Gurion or Weizmann should be credited with the Biltmore Program, as it became known, which was passed unanimously by the American Zionists. As we have seen, during his previous trip to the United States, Ben-Gurion spoke of bringing millions of displaced Jews to Palestine after the war and of creating an independent Jewish commonwealth there that would carry out this process. In January 1942, Weizmann published an article in *Foreign Affairs* propounding the same ideas. In talks held after arriving in the United States in 1941, Ben-Gurion reiterated these ideas. So the Biltmore Program, which called for opening Palestine to immigration, Jewish control of the country, and establishment of a Jewish commonwealth there, did not present any new ideas. Its importance lay first in its declaration of these aims as the war objectives of the Jewish people, which should determine the arrangements to be made at the end of the war, and second in its being a joint statement by all American Zionist organizations.

Apparently Weizmann attributed less importance to the Biltmore Program than Ben-Gurion; to him it was just another Zionist declaration like many others made at the conclusions of Zionist conferences. He saw it not as a binding program, but as a vague document open to various interpretations: perhaps an independent state, perhaps a part of the British Empire, or part of another supranational organization that would be incorporated into the new order in the Middle East. With regard to immigration, Weizmann thought in pre–world war terms. For him mass immigration meant at most perhaps one hundred thousand people a year.

By contrast Ben-Gurion, as Weizmann remarked ironically, saw the Biltmore Program as a new version of Herzl's original Basel Program. He emphasized the independent Jewish state as a war objective, and stated that his goal was the immigration of two million Jews within three years; once the scope of the annihilation of European Jewry became known, he spoke about one million within two to three years. The gradual approach that the Zionist movement had taken before the war faded into insignificance in the face of the terrible hardships of the Jewish people (evident even before news of the Holocaust came out) and the vast population movements expected as a consequence of the war: millions of refugees and the resettlement of millions of Germans, Poles, and various minorities. Amid this vast migration of people the Jews would need to ingather their own millions. The combatants' ability to move millions of troops hinted at tremendous logistical and economic possibilities that suddenly acquired practical meaning. For Ben-Gurion, American involvement in the rehabilitation of Europe after the war seemed inevitable: "Hoover's relief activities in the last war are child's play compared to what this country will have to under-take in the feeding of Europe after this war."[23]

Ben-Gurion's revolutionary concept seemed to challenge twenty-five years of Weizmann's cautious gradualism. Like other eminent leaders, Weizmann identified with his own enterprise and was not open to changing his modus operandi in response to the world's radically changing situation. He quite naturally tended to minimize the importance of the Biltmore Program, even though he took part in formulating it, whereas Ben-Gurion turned it into a banner, a symbol of the revolutionary turnabout in Zionist action.

Weizmann and Ben-Gurion did not disagree as to the final goal: both wanted a Jewish state. They argued over Zionism's political orientation, its course of action, and their own roles in relation to each other. Weizmann, a master of one-on-one meetings, represented the Zionist Organization to the British and American governments. The doors of Lord Halifax, the British ambassador to Washington, of senior American ad-ministration officials, and even of the Oval Office were open to him. He held talks with the elite and rarely addressed the Jew-ish masses in America. Ben-Gurion's meetings were mainly limited to Jews—he met with very few non-Jews—and he saw organizing the Jews into an ethnic pressure group that could exert its political and electoral power as the lever to change the administration's negative attitude toward Zionism. Weizmann opposed aiming propaganda at the masses as a risky tool that might arouse opposition to the government and thereby dam-age relations not only with the American administration but also with the British government. The very idea of exerting Ameri-can pressure on the British over the Palestine question seemed rash to him; he was, after all, a loyal British subject and did not want to do anything to damage Britain's vital interests in Amer-ica. Ben-Gurion contended that Weizmann was unable to say "no" to the British. This was unfair, but it was true that Weizmann was far more sensitive toward British interests than Ben-Gurion. His identification with Britain was probably strengthened after his pilot son was killed on active service in the Royal Air Force.

What attitude to take toward Britain was one of the main bones of contention between them. Since the outbreak of the war, and in fact since the publication of the White Paper, Ben-Gurion had been ready for a change in the Zionist movement's orientation. He saw the United States as the prime candidate to replace Britain as Zionism's principal ally. Initially, he spoke cautiously of nurturing the relationships with both Western powers, but as the course of the war unfolded, and the more the British rejected the Zionists' overtures, Ben-Gurion's orientation toward the United States became stronger. As early as February 1942, in a letter to his favorite daughter, Renana, he wrote that after the war ended, Europe would be in need of American aid, "and thus America's power will be great, and its opinion more decisive, maybe, than any other country. This is why I believe that our future also depends much more on this city [Washington] than on London."[24] In the aftermath of the war he foresaw the breakup of the British Empire and the rise of two new superpowers, America and Russia. Weizmann reported on this prediction to Baffy Dugdale with shock and derision: "He attaches a decisive importance to America, in contradistinction to Great Britain, repeating the slogans which one hears occasionally here that the British Empire is doomed, that the greatest force which will emerge out of the war is America, and therefore we have to rely primarily on what can be done here."[25] In Weizmann's view the British Empire was fundamental to world order, and even if the war did lead to changes on the worldwide political scene, Britain would still play the leading role in determining the future of Palestine. America was important, but Britain even more so.

These differences in attitude should not have caused a schism between the two men, since while the war continued no decision on the Palestine question would be made anyway. Palestine was under threat of a German invasion from the south by Erwin Rommel's forces, which had pushed into Egypt, and from the north by a German invasion from the Caucasus following the rapid advance of Wehrmacht forces through the Ukrainian steppes. The country's defense was in the hands of the British army. All Britain's sins paled into insignificance amid concern for the fate of the Yishuv. But there were also personality conflicts between Ben-Gurion and Weizmann. It is hard to imagine two men so different yet so similar in their personal ambition and authoritarian inclinations. Weizmann derided Ben-Gurion and did his best to humiliate him. Ben-Gurion claimed with justification that Weizmann had a "court" and excluded him from negotiations in London and Washington. As always, Weizmann preferred to attend important meetings on his own and report on them at his discretion. After reaching the United States he did not meet with Ben-Gurion for policy-setting talks, but acted on his own initiative and revealed that he had met with so-and-so only after the event. Ben-Gurion demanded recognition of the fact that the president of the Zionist Organization was part of the Zionist Executive of which he, Ben-Gurion, was the chairman—in other words, that Weizmann was part of a collective leadership and must set policy not according to his impulses but through preplanning and in consultation with him. But Weizmann was a master of the art of improvisation with no interest in precise planning. He was also unwilling to accept the humiliation of being supervised by Ben-Gurion.

The tension between the two came to a head after the Biltmore Conference. Ben-Gurion boycotted meetings that Weizmann had proposed; there was an exchange of letters filled with scathing accusations; and in the end relations between them

Chaim Weizmann and Ben-Gurion, early 1940s (Collection of Ben-Gurion House in Tel Aviv)

were severed. At the end of June 1942, Ben-Gurion initiated a meeting at the home of Rabbi Stephen Wise, president of the American Jewish Congress and chairman of the Joint Emergency Committee, that was attended by American Zionist leaders. It was a difficult experience for the attendees, who witnessed an exchange of defamatory remarks between the two men. Nor did Ben-Gurion get what he wanted. Weizmann refused to include him in the political negotiations, and the Americans were not prepared to force him to do so. Despite its diminished brightness, Weizmann's aura was still powerful enough to repel Ben-Gurion's assault.

Relative to the amount of energy he expended, Ben-Gurion's activity in America was low-level. He continued to negotiate with the non-Zionists and supported a new star that had appeared in the American Zionist firmament, Rabbi Abba Hillel Silver from Cleveland, who impressed him with his drive. Engulfed by loneliness, he found no one he could talk with uninhibitedly. He confided some of his concerns, which he hid from his daughter, to Doris May: "I do not know how and when final victory will come, but come it will, as sure as the day. But what is going to happen to us until then? It is sometimes very very hard, almost unbearable to be alone with these gnawing doubts and apprehensions—and I am so terribly lonesome here!"[26] He found some consolation reading Plato's *Republic*, which he described as "a modern book." He also found relief from his loneliness in the alluring form of Miriam Cohen, a thirty-four-year-old Jewish woman who worked as a secretary for the Emergency Committee. Educated and well-mannered, she caught his eye, and he managed to have her assigned to him as his secretary while he was in Washington. After considerable wooing, he captivated her. The love letters he sent her from Beaver Lake House, a resort in Ulster County, New York, where he spent a few days vacationing on her advice, were full of descriptions of nature, Socrates, and his colleagues. Above all, they testify to this impersonal man's hidden romantic soul.

The letters led to the intimacy he sought in their relationship. According to Shabtai Teveth, they spent several days vacationing together, and he devoted the day before his return to Palestine to her. It was a serious, profound relationship. She learned some Hebrew and even a little Greek. He signed his letters to her "D," while she addressed him as "David" and signed her letters "Miriam," in Hebrew. Over the next two years their correspondence was warm and loving. She was also important to him as a source of information about what was happening in American Zionism. He intended to return to New York soon, and the hope of reuniting kept their relationship alive. More than to any other person, he opened his heart to her. Thus, for example, he allowed himself to tell her about an encounter that shocked him, with a young woman from Hechalutz in Sosnowiec who had come to Palestine from Poland with a group of fifteen other survivors. He went to Haifa to meet her, and for three hours listened to her story: "I heard a story of horrors and misery, which no Dante or Poe could have ever invented, and you are completely helpless, and you cannot even go mad—and the sun shines in all her glory and you must go on with your ordinary work, for that is the only thing one can do."[27] He did not allow himself to reveal these emotions of shock and helplessness to anyone else. In January 1944 he wrote to her that he was miserable, adding that in existing circumstances there was no justification for being happy or aspiring to personal happiness: "What really happened (and is not yet finished) is worse than anything we imagined so far. Hitler will be destroyed—but he in the meanwhile has wiped out almost half of our people." But he convinced himself—and her—not to be preoccupied with this: "We must, must still look forward and save what may remain, at least let us save our self-respect."[28]

He never spoke or wrote such expressions of despair and pain publicly. It seems that Ben-Gurion's relationship with Miriam Cohen revealed his innermost personality, which he took great pains to conceal beneath his tough, impersonal persona. In April 1944 she replied with no less profound emotion: "I am here for whenever you need me—wherever it is, for whatever I can do."[29] But it is hard to nurture love with correspondence alone. In 1945 Miriam married Eddie Taub. After that their correspondence became more infrequent, yet it maintained its intimate tone and continued until Ben-Gurion's death.

On 18 September 1942, Ben-Gurion at last obtained a seat on a plane (no small feat at the time) and left for Palestine. His journey took him through India and South Africa, and from there, on exhausting flights in military aircraft with no air-conditioning or seats, to Cairo. The journey exposed him to British colonial racism. "When you pass through India, Africa, and so on, you feel that you belong to the white race and are ashamed of it," he noted. England the homeland is a wonderful nation, "but outside England, England sees itself as a *Herren-*

volk."[30] He reached Cairo after ten days, and on 2 October 1942 arrived in Palestine, where he immediately embarked on feverish activity. As usual, he reported at great length to the Zionist Executive on his meetings and activity in America, and within a few days the executive in Jerusalem adopted the Biltmore Program as binding Zionist resolutions. On 10 November 1942, the Zionist Executive approved the program, which from then on was known as the "Jerusalem-Biltmore Program."

The first burning issue on the agenda requiring a decision was party unity. The dissident Faction B, led by Hakibbutz Hameuhad's Yitzhak Tabenkin, controlled a third of Mapai, and since it was well organized and always voted en bloc it made life in the party unbearable. Berl Katznelson had demanded that party factions be abolished, but was unable to make this happen. Now, with Ben-Gurion back, Mapai held its conference in Kfar Vitkin, where in effect the party split. Faction B, whose membership included a large proportion of the activists who supported Ben-Gurion politically, left Mapai. Ben-Gurion and Katznelson found themselves in a party that was disciplined, but did not take the assertive political line that Ben-Gurion wanted.

Meanwhile, tumultuous events occurred on the world stage. During the conference, the decisive battle between Bernard Montgomery's Eighth Army and Rommel's Afrika Korps took place at El-Alamein. The British victory there enabled the Jews in Palestine to heave a sigh of relief; the danger of a Nazi invasion was over. A month later, news of the destruction of European Jewry was confirmed by Washington. More significantly, an exchange of Palestinian and German civilians brought to Palestine a group of survivors who testified about what had taken place in the Nazi-occupied countries. The shock was dreadful; it traveled throughout the Jewish people in Palestine and the United States. Accusatory voices were heard in Palestine asking why no warning had been given, why there had been no rescue operations. In public Ben-Gurion did not reveal the feelings that roiled within him. He opposed picking at these open wounds and demanded that whatever could be done to rescue the survivors should be done, but without what he called "this sadistic campaign" of mutual accusations.[31]

The impasse with Weizmann remained unresolved. During 1943 Ben-Gurion tried repeatedly—threatening to resign, and then actually resigning—to get Mapai's support for his demands regarding Weizmann. The most extreme of these was that the president resign. But what Ben-Gurion really wanted was for Weizmann to accept joint leadership and stop behaving like an American president. His movement rejected his position and demanded that he cooperate with Weizmann. Weizmann asked Moshe Shertok to join him in the United States, and when Shertok did so, Ben-Gurion broke off relations with him for a while. In the summer of 1943 some fragmentary news filtered through about talks that Weizmann was holding in London. Citing health reasons, Weizmann rejected repeated demands from Palestine that he come for consultations. He had no intention of conducting the battle with Ben-Gurion on his adversary's own turf at a time when he had no real achievement to point to. Ben-Gurion refused to go to London, and in any case Weizmann announced that he would not cooperate with him.

In fall 1943 Ben-Gurion resigned as chairman of the Jewish Agency Executive, triggering a crisis. He refused to withdraw his resignation, and all his party colleagues' attempts at conciliation and compromise did not move him. Even a severe reprimand from Katznelson, who had previously reined in Ben-Gurion during his volcanic outbursts, was useless. A compromise was finally reached in the form of a Zionist Executive delegation to London that induced Weizmann to send Ben-Gurion a telegram inviting him to London and promising to share responsibility with him. The drama between them was still unfinished;

this was only the second act. But for now cooperation seemed assured. In any event, the frozen sea of British policy on Palestine had not yet thawed, and neither Weizmann nor Ben-Gurion could change that reality.

In August 1944, Berl Katznelson died suddenly. For Ben-Gurion his death was a blow that was hard to recover from. A month later he wrote to Miriam Cohen: "Nothing that happened to me personally affects me so deeply," and further, "I feel as if half of myself is gone, dead."[32] To his dying day, the only photograph he had on his desk was of Katznelson.

In 1944, hopes rose in Great Russell Street. The Jewish Brigade was formed, and Churchill initiated a cabinet committee on Palestine. It submitted findings to the prime minister containing a recommendation that Palestine be partitioned. Then matters became complicated by the assassination of Lord Moyne, resident minister of state in Cairo, by members of Lehi (the Stern Gang), as well as Foreign Secretary Anthony Eden's bitter opposition to the partition plan. As a result the British cabinet postponed its decision on partition. Churchill informed Weizmann that a decision on Palestine would only be made at a peace conference after the war—that is, at an unspecified date, not immediately after the war ended, as the Zionists had believed. This was a harsh blow for Weizmann. That summer Hungarian Jewry was annihilated, even as the Great Powers led by Britain thwarted attempts to rescue them.

In March 1945 Ben-Gurion left Palestine for London, not to return until November. During those six months, major changes occurred on the world political map. President Roosevelt died and was replaced by Harry S. Truman, a midwesterner who had no connections with Jews and owed them nothing. In May the war in Europe ended. Shortly thereafter Churchill, the architect of victory, was voted out of office in a general election. His government was replaced by the Labour party, whose platform included a pro-Zionist plank on Palestine that demanded abrogation of the White Paper and even spoke of a transfer of the Arabs of Palestine. By now, however, the Zionists were experienced in the ways of British politics, and knew that Labour's position while in opposition would mean little once it came to power.

Roosevelt's death stunned Ben-Gurion. "I know [that] this is a great loss for America and the world—but I fear that this tragedy has hit us more than anyone else," he wrote.[33] The entire relationship created between Roosevelt's confidants and the American Zionist leadership was now put into question. In February 1945, on his way back from the Yalta conference, after a meeting with Ibn Saud, Roosevelt had remarked that he had learned more from it than from all the memoranda on Palestine—a bad sign for the Zionists. Still, Ben-Gurion was more concerned by the new, complete unknown in the American equation. But he also knew that now American public opinion— and Jewish public opinion as part of it—would carry more weight, because the new president needed support. He recorded these thoughts during an enforced rest in his London hotel, after miraculously escaping death in a road accident a few days after arriving in the city. He suffered only a mild concussion, but was ordered to rest for several weeks. From his hotel room window he watched the joyous crowds celebrating the end of the war in Europe, and wrote in his diary, "The day of victory. Sad, very sad," adding a verse from the Bible that highlighted the contrast between the general jubilation and the mourning of the Jews: "Rejoice not, O Israel, unto exultation, like the peoples."[34]

7

On the Verge of Statehood

NEITHER THE END of World War II nor the rise of Labour to power in Britain brought about the change in the fortunes of Zionism that the Zionists expected. The White Paper was not annulled, and the Palestine question was not revisited in the British corridors of power. From a Zionist point of view, time was of the essence: as long as the sea of international policy, which had thawed during the war, remained unfrozen, there was a chance of revolutionary changes. If too much time passed, it would freeze over again.

Ben-Gurion was gripped by a sense of urgency, of an opportunity that must be seized. If a Jewish state were not established immediately, the Jews of Palestine were liable to wind up as a pitiful minority in an Arab state. Yet even as the Zionists sought a quick decision, the British government resorted to foot-dragging. If it delayed long enough, the world would perhaps forget the catastrophe that had befallen the Jews in the

Holocaust, whose horrors had been brought into every home by the war correspondents accompanying General Dwight D. Eisenhower's conquering army in Germany. The pictures from Dachau, Buchenwald, and Bergen-Belsen were imprinted on the public consciousness and created sympathy in the West for the Jews, as well as an understanding of the need of this unfortunate, homeless people for a state of its own in Palestine.

In the summer of 1945, in response to complaints that the army had treated Jewish refugees brutally, President Truman sent his personal envoy, Earl G. Harrison, to tour the refugee camps (or as they were then called, displaced persons [DP] camps) in the American- and British-occupied zones in Germany. Harrison submitted a damning report on conditions in the camps, and more particularly the condition of the Jews there. He described Jewish DPs who were unable to return to the "bloodlands" in Eastern Europe, where the killing of Jews continued even after their liberation by Soviet troops. Harrison recommended separating Jews and non-Jews in the camps, since many of the latter had collaborated with the Nazis; allowing them greater freedom of movement; and improving the food rations.

From the Zionist perspective, the main point of the report was its statement that the vast majority of the DPs wanted to emigrate to Palestine; Harrison quoted a figure of one hundred thousand. Truman issued orders to Eisenhower to ameliorate the DPs' conditions, allow the flow of Jewish refugees from Eastern Europe to enter the American-occupied zone, and grant them sanctuary in the camps. At the same time he requested that Clement Atlee, the British prime minister, grant immigration certificates to a hundred thousand Jews. From then on, the DPs were a central item on the international agenda. Atlee replied to Truman that any deviation from the White Paper was liable to lead to rioting that would require the use of force. He demanded that if this happened the Americans should contribute forces to quell an Arab uprising. It was an evasive response that avoided the problem.

The Jewish people had never been as stricken and helpless as they were now. But Ben-Gurion had learned to generate power from weakness. In mapping out the resources at his disposal, he defined three power sources: the Yishuv in Palestine, which would prepare itself for a violent struggle against British rule; American Jewry, which would exert pressure on President Truman; and the Holocaust survivors in the DP camps, who would turn an apparently marginal international policy problem into a central issue.

Since the publication of the White Paper in 1939, Ben-Gurion had harbored rage, a sense of insult, and a desire to pay Britain back with interest. While the war was still raging, he repressed these feelings, but now, after the Allies' victory, the time had come to cast the Yishuv's entire military potential into the struggle. To achieve maximum impact he was prepared to put aside his deep-seated hostility toward the secessionist organizations: the Etzel (the Hebrew acronym of Irgun Tsva'i Leumi, or National Military Organization, known in English as the Irgun) and Lehi (Lohamei Herut Yisrael, or Fighters for the Freedom of Israel, labeled the Stern Gang by the British).

The Etzel had been formed in the 1930s by young people who left the Haganah, the Yishuv's Histadrut-led militia, which soon came under the authority of the Zionist Executive. Some returned to the Haganah during the Arab Revolt, but the Betar members refused to do so and soon challenged the policy of "restraint" adopted by the Yishuv leadership by engaging in terrorist actions against Arabs. With the outbreak of World War II, the Etzel ceased these actions and collaborated with the British, but an extremist branch from within its ranks, led by Abraham Stern (Yair), seceded and formed Lehi, which was ready to negotiate even with the Nazis in order to rid Palestine of the British. Menachem Begin, former commissioner of Betar in Poland, arrived in Palestine in 1942 and was appointed commander of the Etzel. In 1944 he declared a revolt against the British, even though the war had not yet ended.

The terror activities of the Etzel and Lehi, which climaxed with the assassination of Lord Moyne in Cairo by two Lehi members, led the British to demand that the Jewish Agency Executive cooperate with the government to suppress the secessionist organizations. Since at the time the establishment of the Jewish Brigade and the rumor that a cabinet committee had proposed partition led the Zionist leadership to expect a positive shift in British policy, Ben-Gurion and his colleagues felt that stopping the secessionists' activities was justified. Moreover, Ben-Gurion considered the Etzel's rejection of the authority of the elected Yishuv and Zionist Organization leadership a grave attack on the nascent national authority. During the summer of 1944, which became known as the "saison," or "hunting season," hundreds of fighters were handed over to the British. Some were exiled to Kenya, while others were detained. Begin's order to his fighters not to fight back against other Jews, despite this controversial action by the leadership, became part of the Etzel myth, proof of its sense of national responsibility. On the other hand, although the "saison" was not Ben-Gurion's finest hour, he never expressed remorse for it.

Nevertheless the bitterness between the sides was apparently not deep, since it did not prevent them from cooperating after the war. In October 1945, Ben-Gurion instructed Moshe Sneh, head of the Haganah National Command (the organization's civilian authority), to reach an agreement with the secessionists on establishing "the Hebrew Resistance Movement" for the struggle against the British. This was a dramatic turnaround in Ben-Gurion's policy; until then he had opposed any agreement with the secessionist organizations that would grant them legitimacy as institutions with the same status as the Haganah. Just as he demanded that the members of the New Zionist

Organization return without conditions to the Zionist Organization after Jabotinsky's death in 1940, he also demanded that the Etzel members unconditionally join the Haganah as individuals. He now deviated from that policy and consented to an agreement that granted the two secessionist organizations de facto recognition.

At the same time he ordered Sneh to commence sabotage operations against the Mandatory government. He also called for stepping up illegal immigration and for readiness for clashes with the British forces, even if this meant using firearms. In Paris, where the government supported the Zionist cause, he set up an operations center that coordinated, organized, and trained personnel involved in illegal immigration. From then until 29 November 1947, Ben-Gurion acted with two parallel identities. On one hand he was chairman of the Jewish Agency Executive, which negotiated with the British government in London and the high commissioner in Palestine. On the other, he headed an underground organization based in the operations center in Paris that conducted actions that were both illegal and hostile toward the British government. He devoted incessant efforts to recruiting young Jews from the DP camps for what was known as Aliya Gimmel ("fighting aliya") and to finding the money required for training them, for purchasing vessels that could face up to the Royal Navy, and for buying arms. His agents were spread all over Europe in an efficient network whose members worked for him in the coming years. Reuven Shiloah, Ehud Avriel, and Teddy Kollek were all part of this logistical system. Their contacts and the methods of action they developed yielded great benefits in the War of Independence.

Ben-Gurion was compelled to spend much of his time outside Palestine. In 1945 he was out of the country for 249 days, and in 1946 for 310. Despite these absences he was recognized as the undisputed leader of the Yishuv as it readied itself for struggle. An insight into the change in his status is provided by

Baffy Dugdale, no admirer of his: "Had no lunch but a couple of sandwiches in the office with Ben-Gurion, who all day was his very nicest and most reasonable self, and made one understand, what sometimes seems inexplicable, why he has so much influence as a leader."[1]

The second locus of power—the DP camps—came into play in the struggle for immigration. In fall 1944 Ben-Gurion attempted to travel to Romania, whose surviving Jewish community was the largest in Europe. But he was thwarted by the British and the Soviets and had to make do with visiting Bulgaria, which had already been liberated and was under communist control. The enthusiastic welcome he received from the Jews of Bulgaria convinced him that quite possibly most of the Jews who had escaped the Nazis would join the Zionist struggle. The Harrison Report and Truman's response to it made clear to Ben-Gurion—if he needed further clarification—that the main thrust of Zionist activity at this time would be to guide Eastern European Jews (mainly from Poland) to the shores of the Mediterranean and thence to Palestine. The Jewish Brigade troops stationed in Germany, Austria, and Italy played a vital role in making contact with the survivors. But the "brikha" (escape), the movement of Jews to Mediterranean ports, came at the initiative of the survivors themselves, under the guidance of the ghetto fighters and partisans.

Ben-Gurion tried to visit Poland but was prevented from doing so. Instead, in October 1945 he visited the DP camps in Germany. It was the first visit to the camps by any Jewish leader. Ben-Gurion was the only Zionist leader to visit the camps several times. The first direct encounter between the survivors and the man who signified hopes of a new life for them occurred at the camp in Zeilsheim. He arrived in the car of Rabbi Judah Nadich, chief Jewish chaplain of the American army in Europe. When several survivors recognized the striking head with its mane of white hair, they began chanting "Ben-Gurion,

Ben-Gurion" and crowded around the car. Nadich assured them that Ben-Gurion was going to address them, and they streamed into the camp auditorium. In Nadich's description, "As Ben-Gurion stood on the platform before them, the people broke forth into cheers and song, and finally into weeping. At last he began to speak, his voice choked up, his eyes filled. He had to stop as he broke down for a moment. In the sudden quiet one could hear the muffled sobbing from all sides of the auditorium. Very few eyes were dry. For the incredible was true: the impossible had happened. Ben-Gurion was in their midst and they had lived despite Hitler . . . they had lived despite them all to this day when they could welcome Ben-Gurion!"[2]

He addressed them in Yiddish, opening with the words, "Dear Brothers and Sisters." They connected to him as if he were family, sending regards to relatives in Palestine whose names they gave him, and he wrote them all down and made sure their messages reached their destination.

The survivors and the Zionist leader had interests in common. Both saw Palestine as the survivors' only hope, since no other country was prepared to take them in and rehabilitate them. As the survivors fought to rebuild their lives, they were also fighting to open the gates of Palestine. Illegal immigration became Zionism's watchword, and the illegal immigrant its loyal soldier. Guerrilla actions and sabotage were not considered acceptable by the entire Yishuv, and certainly not by all Jewish people. But the struggle of the small immigrant ships against the Royal Navy, the desperate struggle of men and women with infants (very few children and elderly people had been saved) against arrest, and their later transfer to British-controlled detention camps in Cyprus fired the imagination of all Jews. World public opinion identified with the refugees, with Jewish public opinion at the forefront. The press constantly reported on illegal immigration: it was a matchless human story. Ben-Gurion gambled on the fact that the British were not the

Nazis and would not use Nazi methods against helpless people. It was an audacious struggle for world sympathy, and the ultimate triumph was his.

The DP problem was also the banner under which American Jewry could unite. If during the war Ben-Gurion had been unable to urge the American Jewish leadership to concerted action, the news of the Holocaust brought this young Jewish community out of its isolation. The world's indifference to the plight of the Jews during the war had proved to them the need to create a pressure group to fight for the Jewish people's interests. At the moment, these interests and the Zionist one coincided, since there was no chance that America would open its doors to the Jewish refugees. The non-Zionist Jewish Joint Distribution Committee (JDC) undertook to provide assistance to the DP camps, while simultaneously covertly funding illegal immigration. Although there was no official union of Zionists and non-Zionists, in fact American Jewish capital was placed at the disposal of the Zionist struggle.

The Zionists of America were now headed by an impressive champion in the shape of Abba Hillel Silver, a Reform rabbi from Cleveland, who did not shy away from confrontations with the president and turned the Jewish vote into an unparalleled pressure group. The president was inundated with letters and requests from citizens who demanded action on behalf of the DPs. American Jewry had never been as united and active as it was between 1945 and 1948. Ben-Gurion's insight in the early days of the war—that the road to the American president was via American public opinion—was proven correct.

President Truman's request that Britain grant one hundred thousand immigration certificates left British foreign secretary Ernest Bevin in a bind. Britain's dependence on Arab oil made him unwilling to change the White Paper policy. The Arabs would construe granting the certificates as an abrogation of the

White Paper, and the wrath of the Arab League states would descend on Britain. On the other hand, Britain was in dire economic straits. Only America could provide it with the loans and grants necessary for rebuilding. Fobbing off the American president was therefore out of the question. As a compromise, the Anglo-American Committee to examine the DP problem was formed.

Foreign Office and Colonial Office policy, adopted by Bevin, sought to separate the Palestine problem and that of the Jewish refugees. During the war the British had explained to the world that little Palestine was not a solution to the problem of five million Jewish refugees. Now, after the Holocaust, it appeared that the numbers were far smaller, but the British continued to argue that there was no connection between the two issues. They asserted that claims that the Jews wanted to get to Palestine, that they had fled Eastern Europe in order to avoid returning to their blood-soaked countries, were pure Zionist propaganda. The Jews must be rehabilitated in the countries of Europe; Bevin's motto was "repatriation."

Here ensued a covert contest between Ben-Gurion and Bevin. One sought to strengthen the connection between the refugees and Palestine, while the other wanted to break it. In January 1946, after word came that the Anglo-American Committee would tour the camps in Germany, Ben-Gurion went there for a second time to ensure that the DPs' leaders briefed their audiences properly. Thus on its visit the committee learned that the vast majority of DPs wanted to emigrate to Palestine. Even those who did not intend to immigrate made sure to identify themselves publicly with the national interest. The committee's unanimous conclusions included quite a few clauses that the Zionists disliked, but one clause compensated for all the others: the committee demanded the immediate issuing of one hundred thousand immigration certificates. Ben-Gurion asked the American Jewish activists to urge the president to focus on demanding these certificates, and he agreed. The other clauses were quickly forgotten.

Meanwhile there was turmoil in Palestine. Since November 1945 the Hebrew Resistance Movement had been sabotaging British installations used to thwart illegal immigration, the rail network, and the bridges connecting Palestine with its neighbors—operations designed to demonstrate that Britain could not continue ruling the country against the Jews' will. On Saturday, 29 June 1946, the British retaliated with Operation Agatha, known in Zionist history as "Black Saturday." They imposed a countrywide curfew; arrested young people suspected of membership in the Haganah and Palmach (the elite corps of the Haganah), members of the Zionist Executive, and Histadrut leaders; raided the Jewish Agency offices in Jerusalem, seizing documents in a search for evidence connecting the Zionist Executive with Jewish terror activities. The British conducted aggressive searches for arms—shooting kibbutz members who resisted—found a large arms cache, and confiscated it. Ben-Gurion escaped arrest because he was in Paris, at the Royal Monceau hotel. There he met the leader of a national movement from a distant country, Ho Chi Minh, who suggested that he form a government-in-exile. Ben-Gurion, however, preferred to form one that would gain international recognition.

In July 1946 the Etzel blew up Jerusalem's King David Hotel, a center of British administration, killing some one hundred British, Arabs, and Jews. The scale of the casualties shocked the Yishuv. Weizmann, who was in Rehovoth, ordered Sneh to stop violent actions against the British immediately, while threatening to resign as president of the Zionist Organization. Sneh obeyed, and from then on the Haganah ceased its sabotage operations and focused solely on protecting illegal immigration.

Matters reached a crisis in summer 1946, when the British

came up with a new plan formulated jointly by Deputy Prime Minister Herbert Morrison and U.S. Ambassador Henry F. Grady. They proposed establishing autonomous areas in Palestine for the two peoples under British trusteeship—leaving British rule in place. In the meantime they delayed responding to Truman's request while not allowing any immigration, hoping that the DPs would despair of reaching Palestine and return to their home countries.

In August, at a dramatic meeting of the Zionist Actions Committee in Paris, Nachum Goldmann, who headed the Zionist office in Washington, was authorized to inform the U.S. president and the State Department that the Zionists might agree to partition as an alternative to the Morrison-Grady Plan. This was a seminal moment in the movement's history: for the first time, the Zionist movement proposed its own solution to the Palestine question. As a result, Truman rejected the Morrison-Grady Plan and on October 4, the eve of Yom Kippur, expressed his support for the establishment of a Jewish state in part of Palestine (his "Yom Kippur statement"). On Goldmann's sixtieth birthday in 1954, Ben-Gurion congratulated him for two great achievements: "To the extent that one man succeeded in 'selling' . . . the idea of the Jewish state to the decision-makers in the American administration, that man is you."[3] (The second achievement was the reparations agreement with Germany.)

The moment of decision came at the Twenty-second Zionist Congress in Basel in December. The Zionist Executive had been split between supporters of Weizmann's moderate line of ending operations against the British and the activists led by Ben-Gurion, who demanded that they continue, but all agreed on not renewing violent actions before the congress. That October Ben-Gurion had visited the DP camps in Germany for the third time. One survivor asked, "When will we get to Palestine?" He burst into tears and replied that although he had no immigration certificates, he had no doubt that they would reach the country soon—he was bringing them hope. The visit demonstrated the survivors' increasing pressure for a speedy solution, since their endurance was almost spent.

In the end the Twenty-second Zionist Congress, the first to be held after the Holocaust, focused on one question: yes or no to Weizmann. At the end of October, Ben-Gurion had written Weizmann an amicable letter that began by congratulating him on his recovery from a second eye operation. He then tried to persuade Weizmann to refuse to discuss the Morrison-Grady Plan with the British and instead present them with a simple alternative: either uphold the terms of the Mandate instrument or support the creation of a Jewish state. He knew that Weizmann, whose power lay in negotiating with the British, would be unwilling to take this line. Thus Ben-Gurion's statement in the letter that for him Weizmann remained "the chosen one of Jewish history who, more than any other, symbolizes Jewish suffering and genius" amounted to a farewell to the man he had known in his greatness, but who now posed an obstacle to the expected political breakthrough.[4]

The balance of power at the congress reflected the dramatic changes in the Jewish people following the Holocaust. The American General Zionists, headed by the activist Silver, were the largest faction at the congress. Following its internal split, Mapai was the second largest. The Mapai faction supported Weizmann for reelection as president and even favored conducting negotiations in London, so Ben-Gurion found himself in a situation in which an absolute majority of the Yishuv and of his movement supported his activist line, but his own party's delegates to the congress represented the opposite position.

Ben-Gurion's conduct at the congress and his relations with Silver—compounded both of admiration and of deep suspicion of the latter's predominance—have provided material for numerous historians who have difficulty determining what actually happened there. The congress ended without electing an executive, which was eventually formed by the Zionist Actions Committee with delegates from Mapai, the General Zionists, and Hamizrachi. No president was elected. Silver became the leader of the Zionist Executive in the United States, and Ben-Gurion remained chairman of the executive in Jerusalem.

As in the past, Weizmann's inclination to improvise was his undoing. As he delivered a speech at the opening of the congress, the audience saw an old, broken man with failing eyesight; the speech, whose content he had agreed on with his executive colleagues, was bland. But as the congress progressed the old warhorse recovered. He seemed to have shed twenty years and was again primed for battle. His second speech, delivered in salty Yiddish, had not been agreed on with anyone. He used his favorite metaphor of a mother with two sons. One son needed frost to make a living, and the other needed heat, so she prayed for "warm frost." This was an attack on Ben-Gurion, who wanted both to fight the British and to negotiate with them. Weizmann recalled that when he was told about the British abuses in the Yishuv on Black Saturday, he replied, "What did you expect, that you blow up trains and the British will give you honey cakes?" and linked his political destiny with pro-British restraint. He also opposed Ben-Gurion's policy of getting the United States to exert pressure on Britain for a Jewish state. Although the delegates gave him a standing ovation, he had lost any chance of reelection by expressing understanding for British anti-Yishuv military actions; even to the moderates among the delegates, this was unacceptable. This was the end of the struggle between two great leaders. Even though Ben-Gurion greatly esteemed Weizmann, and even though he made sure Weizmann was elected Israel's first president, he did not invite him to sign the Declaration of Independence. The reason he gave was that only members of the People's Council (the provisional parliament) could sign it, but in fact this was a feeble and ungenerous evasion. Ben-Gurion acted purely from spite, for no one would have minded if Weizmann had been given the privilege of signing.

At the post-congress meeting of the Zionist Actions Committee, Ben-Gurion announced that he was assuming the defense portfolio of the Zionist Executive. Up to that point he had not been directly involved in defense activity, although no operations were undertaken without his approval. This change of status was designed to grant political significance to what he had told the Haganah people at a joint meeting of activists from the Haganah, the Palmach, and the Mossad for Illegal Immigration (which organized the ships bringing illegal immigrants) after the congress: the moment of decision was approaching. The Haganah people wanted to renew violent operations and were angered by the decision not to. Ben-Gurion explained that a Jewish state would soon be established, which would lead to war not only with the Palestinian Arabs, but with the Arab states. Therefore no actions must be taken that would provide the British with grounds for destroying the Yishuv's defense force. Furthermore, preparation must be made for what was to come. They did not really believe him, assuming that he had simply invented an excuse for not renewing operations.

Although many spoke of "a Jewish state now," only a few believed that it would be established in the next few years. It was more of a slogan than a political forecast. Ben-Gurion's assessment that the establishment of the state was imminent, and that it would bring in its wake a bloody war against the Arab states' regular forces, was one of his astonishing intuitions. During his first visit to the United States at the end of the war in Europe, he had revealed his thoughts on this subject on an extraordinary occasion. At his request, Henry Montor, future chairman of the United Jewish Appeal, gave him a list of seventeen wealthy Jews who were prepared to enlist in the Zionist cause. He called each one personally and invited him to a meeting at the New York home of Rudolf G. Sonneborn on Sunday, 1 July 1945. Although there were still transportation problems in America, since the war with Japan was not yet over, all of the invitees from all over the country arrived on time for the meeting, which opened in the morning and went on all day. Ben-Gurion presented his Zionist perspective and explained that a Jewish state would be established in Palestine after the war and would have to fight for its existence against the Arab armies. The Jews would withstand the onslaught, he said, but to do so they needed arms. In America, the sale of military surplus for scrap had begun, and equipment to create a military industry in Palestine could be purchased at very low cost. Ben-Gurion asked those present to set up a special fund for this procurement. Captivated by his vision, the Americans agreed.

Afterward Ben-Gurion referred to the establishment of "the Sonneborn Foundation," the special fund's codename, as one of the three great achievements of his life. The other two were his immigration to Palestine in 1906 and the establishment of the State of Israel. Many years later, when he was retired, he wrote to Sonneborn: "I will never forget—I think that our people will never forget—that meeting in your home on 1.7.1945 which enabled us to create our military industry."[5] The equipment was shipped to Palestine disassembled and camouflaged as spare parts and agricultural machinery, then reassembled. This machinery was the foundation of Israel Military Industries. At the 1946 Paris meeting of the Zionist Actions Committee, Ben-Gurion requested that three million dollars be allocated for military procurement, a vast sum at the time. The Zionist Executive approved the allocation, and Ben-Gurion sent Ehud Avriel and Yehuda Arazi to procure heavy weaponry that would be shipped to Palestine after the state was established.

Since the adoption of the Biltmore Program, the question of how the Arabs would respond had hovered in the air. There was no reference in the program to the Arab question, and that was one reason it came under attack. In opposition to the Bilt-more Program, Hashomer Hatzair put forward a plan for a bi-national state in Palestine. That was also the goal of Judah Magnes, chancellor of the Hebrew University in Jerusalem, a dyed-in-the-wool pacifist. The Aliya Hadasha (New Aliya) party, which consisted of immigrants from Germany, protested the establishment of a state without an agreement with the Arabs. In Mapai, too, voices in the spirit of Brit Shalom were heard. In public, Ben-Gurion dismissed the danger of the Arabs going to war against the Jewish state, contending that on the contrary, when the state was established they would come to an agreement with it. He also took this line in political memo-randa to the British and Americans. Off the record, however, he was well aware that the Arabs would not accept a Jewish state, and its birth would be attended by a bloody war. His in-sight that the Arab states would intervene in the Palestine con-flict was prescient, for they were still very far from a decision on this issue. Ben-Gurion based his forecast not on intelligence reports, but on his comprehension of the historical process.

Amid all these storms, another took place in the Ben-Gurion family. Amos Ben-Gurion, who was serving as an officer in the Jewish Brigade, fell ill and was hospitalized in Liverpool, where he was cared for by a lovely young student nurse. Love blossomed between Mary Callow, daughter of an Anglican fam-ily that had lived in the Isle of Man for generations, and the handsome young man from Tel Aviv. A short time later Amos told his parents that he loved Mary and intended to marry her. Nothing reflects the complex relationships in the Ben-Gurion family like the letter that Ben-Gurion fired off to Paula, in which he cautioned her not to exert pressure on Amos. "There is nothing to be gained and no point in being angry and re-proaching him," he wrote. "Nothing can be changed by force or shouting." He, the man of impulsive outbursts, understood more than anyone the power of this love over his son, who possessed the family trait of stubbornness. Ben-Gurion told Paula that he would try to explain to Amos how marrying a non-Jewish woman would complicate his life. "I am, of course, not sure that I will succeed, but if there is a chance then it lies only in dealing with it in a comradely, friendly way, without coercion."[6] But Amos and Mary's love was strong, and Amos did not succumb either to his mother's dictates (well described by Shabtai Teveth) or to his father's educational importunings. At the end of April 1946, Amos and Mary were married in a civil ceremony, without either set of parents present. The marriage was hasty because the bride was already pregnant.

Only afterward did Ben-Gurion meet his daughter-in-law for the first time, and it was love at first sight for both of them. Between his trips to London, Paris, and New York, he devoted much time to arranging Mary's immigration permit, her passport, and all her other needs. He bought the newlyweds everything they needed to set up house, making sure it was all sent from the United States and London—everything from nylon stockings (very scarce after the war) to bedding and items needed for the baby. The more he wrote in praise of Mary—"She leaves a good impression on everyone with her beauty, modesty, sense of humor, and good manners. She is independent, brave, and certainly no fool"—the angrier Paula became.[7] Left neglected in Palestine, bearing all the worries of the household, she was now supposed to welcome the gentile woman who had stolen her beloved son and even threatened to win a place in her husband's heart.

Ben-Gurion was sensitive to this young woman's difficulties landing in a foreign country, not speaking the language, and beyond that, carrying the taint of being a "non-kosher" convert. He had tried but failed to have her converted by an Orthodox rabbi, and she was converted quickly in London by a Reform rabbi—a conversion not recognized in Palestine. The young couple reached Palestine at the end of July 1946, and in

Three generations of the Ben-Gurion family, early 1950s. From right to left, standing, adjutant Nehemiah Argov, daughter Geula Ben-Eliezer, eldest grandson Yariv Ben-Eliezer, son Amos Ben-Gurion, Paula's sister Benia Munbaz; sitting, Paula, daughter Renana Ben-Gurion-Leshem, Ben-Gurion, daughter in-law Mary Ben-Gurion, granddaughter Galia (IDF Archive)

December their daughter Galia was born. But the conversion issue continued to trouble the family until 1970, when mother and daughter underwent Orthodox conversion, putting an end to this issue.

Throughout his life Ben-Gurion showed his love for Mary; the conversion issue did not bother him and he did not take it up again. Amos and Mary gave their children a Palestine secular-Jewish education. According to one of Ben-Gurion's letters, his attendance at the bar-mitzvah of Amos and Mary's son, at their request, was one of only two times that he had gone to synagogue since his immigration to Palestine. The other time, according to the letter, was on the eve of the establishment of the state. The Yishuv society reacted tolerantly to the marriage of its leader's son to a gentile woman. A popular anecdote focused not on the religious aspect of the marriage but on Ben-Gurion's political approach to everything: the story goes that Amos told his father, "I've met a nice girl and I'm going to marry her, but she's not one of us." To which Ben-Gurion replied, "No matter, there are nice girls in Hashomer Hatzair too." This was as far as his ability to imagine "not one of us" went.

The last meeting between the Zionist Executive, headed by Ben-Gurion, and Bevin and his senior officials took place in January 1947. It was the first time Ben-Gurion met Bevin, who had previously refused to see him, describing him as an extremist zealot, the Jewish doppelgänger of Haj Amin al-Husseini. Their talks made it clear that no solution acceptable to both Jews and Arabs could be found, and they ended in failure. In early February the British government announced that it was transferring the Palestine problem to the United Nations. It was the end of an era.

8

◆━◆◆◆━━

"We Hereby Declare . . ."

ONCE THE BRITISH DECIDED to hand over the Palestine question to the United Nations, Ben-Gurion began the countdown to the establishment of the state. Meanwhile, the U.N. set up the United Nations Special Committee on Palestine (UNSCOP) to examine the Palestine question and develop proposals to bring to the General Assembly. During the long months before the committee's submission of its recommendations and the historic General Assembly debate of 29 November 1947 that resulted in a vote for partition, the fate of the Zionist project hung in the balance. Afterward too, even though the British had announced that they would not cooperate with the United Nations in implementing partition and would evacuate Palestine on 15 May 1948, the political situation remained unsettled. But Ben-Gurion disregarded the uncertainties and busied himself preparing for both war and the state.

He devoted the first months of 1947 to examining the state

of the Haganah and its readiness for war. He found a militia with some thirty thousand members—most with no military training—and about ten thousand rifles. Despite the strength of their Zionist convictions, the majority of the Jews in Palestine were not eager to mobilize or devote their resources to the general good. The settlements purchased arms for themselves and were in no hurry to hand them over to the national leadership, and in any case they had only light weapons. The Palmach, numbering about three thousand, was the only regular force with any combat training, mainly in guerrilla tactics. The operational plans in place rested on the assumption that the British would remain in Palestine and the Haganah's role was to guarantee the inhabitants' safety from the Arabs until the army arrived. Everyone was still captive to the perception that the British were the enemy.

Ben-Gurion had to instigate a conceptual, organizational, and functional revolution. He had to inculcate in the Haganah command the concept that they were an army, not a militia, to redefine the enemy, and to build the organizational and command tools for dealing with the new reality. He was haunted by a feeling that time was short, and that the very existence of the Yishuv hung in the balance. He was irascible, impatient, and more given to outbursts than usual, but his sense of urgency and his incessant pressure on people eventually spurred them to action, even though they were not entirely convinced that his forecast was correct.

Procuring heavy weaponry was the first item on his agenda. He sent his aides to purchase tanks, artillery, aircraft, and ships to transport the equipment. Golda Meyerson volunteered to go to the United States in his place to raise funds to buy arms, and was very successful. The most important supplier was Czechoslovakia. But the British still controlled Palestine, and bringing in heavy weaponry was impossible. "Will the equipment reach *us*, and in time. That is the main question, and on it, perhaps, all else hinges," Ben-Gurion wrote to Meyerson and Shertok in New York. "We are preparing for D-Day. But all our preparations will be in vain if the equipment does not arrive."[1] He demanded constant updates from the procurement agents, trying to infect them with his own sense of urgency: "The equipment is a question of life [and death] that cannot be postponed, and there is nothing else of equal importance."[2]

It was difficult to convey to the Haganah commanders, who were used to a certain pace and scope of action, his belief that this time they would be fighting a different war, against regular forces, that mandated a different level of preparedness. To a Haganah that operated in units smaller than a platoon, armed with light weapons, he spoke of divisions, tanks, and aircraft— and the Haganah people whispered to one another, "The Old Man's gone mad." Seemingly overnight he forced them to change their thinking and organization; nor was he patient when they had difficulty adapting to this revolutionary reality. They did possess qualities that Ben-Gurion did not fully appreciate: the ability to improvise and to operate semi-underground without the rigid hierarchy of an army and under conditions of shortage. The Palmach's courage, resourcefulness, and willingness to sacrifice made up for its operational weaknesses and lack of experience.

But Ben-Gurion wanted a completely different structure: he had never forgotten his experience as a soldier in the Jewish Legion. Now, in the thousands of Jewish soldiers discharged from the British army, he saw the foundations of the nascent Jewish army, especially the command cadre. They knew what a regular army was, he contended. He considered any former British army officer preferable to the Haganah veterans and tried unsuccessfully to impose former British army officers on the Haganah command. They integrated well into the professional corps, and even constituted one third of the Haganah chain of command, but the Jewish Brigade was not reproduced in the way Ben-Gurion wanted. Some contend that this was the Jewish people's good fortune, since in the chaotic conditions of the inter-community war that broke out the day after 29 November and the war against the Arab armies that began the day after the declaration of the state, it was the Haganah and Palmach commands' flexibility and ability to adapt to changing conditions that saved the nascent state. But Ben-Gurion was right on another point: if the military equipment had not arrived in time, the Jewish state might not have survived.

Two key dates marked the road to the state: the U.N. decision on partition, and the Ben-Gurion declaration of independence. First came the U.N. General Assembly resolution of 29 November 1947, which by a two-thirds majority passed the UNSCOP proposal to partition Palestine and establish two states, one Jewish and one Arab. People at the time perceived this resolution as a miracle: the two great powers, the United States and the USSR, both supported it! With the Cold War rapidly hardening into a stalemate, it had seemed impossible that these powers would agree on Palestine. Yet Russia and the entire Soviet bloc voted in favor of partition. The USSR aspired to weaken Britain's standing in the Middle East, and to that end even a Jewish state was acceptable.

The night of 29 November 1947 entered the national memory as an unforgettable moment of exhilaration, a spontaneous outpouring of joy among massed circles of dancers. At the Dead Sea resort that night, Ben-Gurion was awakened and told that the General Assembly had voted in favor of a Jewish state. He did not celebrate; he knew full well how heavy the cost would be.

During the first months of the inter-community war, the Arabs held the upper hand. The roads were dangerous, Upper Galilee and various settlements were cut off, and Jerusalem— the heart of the Yishuv, where twenty percent of the Jewish population lived—depended on supply convoys that sometimes managed to reach the city, but often did not. In March 1948 three big convoys ended in disaster, triggering a crisis. The Jews seemed to be losing control. Ben-Gurion's proud declaration, when the British announced that they would evacuate Palestine on 15 May, that the Jews would assume the government was suddenly put into question: were they losing the battle?

This was when the United States began to pull back from the partition resolution; the American ambassador to the United Nations proposed a trusteeship in Palestine instead of independence. At this moment Ben-Gurion tipped the scales. He demanded that the Haganah command undertake an unprecedented large-scale operation, sending fifteen hundred fighters to break through to besieged Jerusalem. Operation Nachshon went down in history as the war's greatest turning point. Although the road to Jerusalem was again blocked a short time later, in the meantime huge supply convoys reached the city, enabling it to stand fast under the siege. The success of Operation Nachshon was due to the clandestine arrival of a weapons shipment; the Haganah managed to unload the light weapons and distribute them to the fighters. Following Nachshon an offensive began that was designed to take control of the territory assigned to the Jewish state by the partition plan. April saw the conquest of Tiberias, Safed, and most important, the port city of Haifa. This conquest told the world that the Jews now had the upper hand.

These were eventful months, filled with tension that heightened as 15 May approached. Despite all the pressure Ben-Gurion was under, he devoted much of his time and energy to the civil matters involved in establishing a state. He held exhausting negotiations with the National Committee, the Yishuv's representative body, the Yishuv's political parties, the ultra-Orthodox, and various other groups in order to form a provisional state council and a provisional government that would grant appropriate representation to the Jewish Yishuv and the Zionist Organization. The provisional government had thirteen members, including four Mapai ministers, one of whom was Ben-Gurion, who was both prime minister and defense minister. He thought it was important that Golda Meyerson be a member of the government, asserting not only that she should be included on her own merits, but that the first Jewish government should have a female member. "The participation of a woman in the government constitutes a banner—a banner of human liberty and equality."[3] However, his Mapai colleagues preferred someone else.

He asked the Hebrew Language Committee to provide Hebrew names for the entire governmental system, from the executive to the legislature and the foreign service, from the army to the police, and also for legal and parliamentary procedures. Everything was new, a first effort at running a state. Together with the vast procurement enterprise they undertook, he asked Meyerson and Shertok to recruit American Jewish volunteers for the Jewish army, like Colonel David ("Mickey") Marcus, a West Point graduate who had come to Palestine and gained Ben-Gurion's trust. "Send us ten Marcuses, some naval officers, pilots—and pray for the arrival of the equipment," he wrote them.[4] He also tried to recruit Jewish scientists: "The objective is scientists in the fields of physics, chemistry, technology, who can either increase the ability to kill many people, or the opposite—to heal people."[5] He also found time to take an interest in the list of Holocaust survivors from Plonsk who had reached Palestine, and to invite the writer Max Brod for a talk.

The tension intensified as 15 May approached. Jewish intelligence was extremely weak. Field intelligence was nonexistent. Everything was learned on the fly. The size of the forces that would attack the Jewish state, their war plans, and whether the Arab armies would coordinate their attacks were all unknown. Would Transjordan join the fighting? Many Jews lost their nerve. A war against Palestinian militias, and even the irregular Arab Liberation Army (which invaded Palestine during the inter-community war) was not the same as a war against the armies of Egypt, Syria, Iraq, and Transjordan. Golda Meyerson undertook a secret mission to King Abdullah of Transjordan, an enemy of the mufti who sought to annex the territories assigned to the Arab state in Palestine to his own kingdom; the Jews did not oppose his doing this. At the beginning of the year the king had promised to stay out of the war, but now, swept up into the Arab states' bellicose mood, he decided to take part and joined their joint command. Meyerson's mission failed.

In Washington, George C. Marshall, the much-decorated general and secretary of state, cautioned Moshe Shertok, who was about to return to Palestine, not to make the mistake of listening to generals intoxicated with victory. If you lose, we won't come to your aid, he warned, and suggested postponing the declaration by a few months. Conveying Marshall's warning to Ben-Gurion, Shertok added, "I think he's right." Ben-Gurion asked him to relay the warning to the provisional government, but without the last four words. At a dramatic meeting of the provisional government on 12 May 1948, Shertok made his report, Meyerson reported on her failed mission to Abdullah, and news came of the fall of the Etzion Bloc, four isolated Jewish settlements between Jerusalem and Hebron. On top of all this, Jerusalem was again cut off and under artillery fire from the Arab Legion (the Transjordanian army, which was under British command). The heads of the Haganah, Yigael Yadin and Israel Galili, were invited to the meeting and asked for their views on the chances of withstanding an Arab invasion. Yadin thought they were fifty-fifty. It was not a reassuring assessment. Using all the force of his personality and powers of persuasion, Ben-Gurion got the decision he wanted: with six votes in favor and four against, the state would be declared.

The subsequent discussions of the Declaration of Independence were something of an anticlimax. Should the borders of the state be declared according to the map proposed by the

Ben-Gurion declaring Israeli statehood, 14 May 1948 (Collection of Ben-Gurion House, Tel Aviv)

UNSCOP and approved by the General Assembly on 29 November? Ben-Gurion opposed this, arguing that even in the American Declaration of Independence there was no mention of borders. Deep in his heart he hoped for favorable adjustments to the 29 November map, which had assigned the Jews a territory he considered impossibly fragmented. Should the name of God be invoked or not? With everyone feeling the greatness of the hour, they found a compromise between religious and secular views, adopting the rather vague phrase "Placing our trust in the Rock of Israel." To simplify the declaration, Ben-Gurion cut out rhetoric and legal formulations, incurring the wrath of Moshe Shertok, who had drafted it.

At 4 p.m. on Friday, 14 May, the members of the Provisional

Council, the leaders of the Yishuv, dignitaries, and members of the press gathered in the Tel Aviv Museum on Rothschild Boulevard. Some council members from besieged Jerusalem did not make it to the ceremony. Ben-Gurion, wearing a dark suit and tie, with Paula in a black dress beside him, mounted the podium under the blue-and-white flag. The audience broke into a spontaneous rendering of Hatikvah. Then Ben-Gurion in his familiar metallic voice unwaveringly declaimed the Declaration of Independence: "We hereby declare the establishment of a Jewish state in Eretz-Israel, to be known as the State of Israel." Rabbi Judah Fishman-Maimon intoned the "Who has kept us in life and preserved us" blessing. A wave of joy erupted inside the hall and among the crowd outside. Everyone was crying and laughing, kissing, dancing and singing. Golda Meyerson and two members of the Mapai Central Committee bought a bouquet and brought it to Ben-Gurion's home, where he was sitting on the second floor with the general staff, checking the final plans to combat the imminent invasion. He came out to them, and when he saw that they wanted to congratulate him— as the one who more than any other had brought the state into being—he was embarrassed, almost shy, and words failed him. Unused to praise, he did not know how to respond. On that jubilant night he again felt, as he had on 29 November, like "a mourner among the joyful." Who more than he was aware of the magnitude of the risk he had taken? Only three years after the end of World War II and the Holocaust, he took a gamble on the very existence of the Yishuv. He did not share his feelings and fears with anyone, and even in his diary noted tersely, "At 4 p.m. Jewish independence was declared and the state was established. Its fate is in the hands of the defense forces."[6]

The month that followed was the hardest of the war, and there were moments when victory or defeat seemed to hang by a thread. All the borders were aflame. The Egyptian army advanced to within thirty-two kilometers of Tel Aviv. In the north, the Syrians advanced into the Jordan Valley, and it seemed that nothing could stop their tanks. In the center of the country the Arab Legion took the Latrun police station, blocking the road to Jerusalem. Jerusalem was being shelled, the Old City's Jewish Quarter fell, and the city fathers fired off messages to Ben-Gurion saying that the city itself was about to fall. Colonel Marcus explained to Ben-Gurion that the Arab Legion—considered the most highly trained of all the Arab armies, commanded as it was by British officers—had a choice. It could cut the Jewish state in two near Netanya, which would create a truly dire situation. Or it could try to take Jerusalem—which would save Israel, since its forces would have difficulty fighting in a built-up area.

The legion chose the second option. The pressure on Jerusalem was great, and part of the city's population panicked. Ben-Gurion was caught by the city fathers' fear and was afraid that Jerusalem was about to fall. Yadin tried vainly to convince him that there were sufficient forces in the city to prevent a catastrophe. Ben-Gurion could not keep still and made the high command's life a misery, demanding that they give preference to Jerusalem over everything else. The route to saving Jerusalem passed through the conquest of Latrun, and Latrun became Ben-Gurion's obsession. As, one after another, attempts to take Latrun failed, his lack of faith in the Haganah command became evident. Unwilling to listen to the military experts, he demanded that the newly formed and as yet unorganized Seventh Brigade be thrown into the battle. Shlomo Shamir, a former British army officer who commanded the brigade, reported to Ben-Gurion and received his orders. "Your wish is my command," he said, even though he knew it was a lost cause.

The controversy surrounding the six battles for Latrun, which made it part of the national mythology, reflected the different military traditions of the Haganah and the Palmach on one hand and the British army on the other. Ben-Gurion had put his trust in the disciplined and hierarchical regular-army traditions that the Jewish Brigade veterans brought with them. The Haganah commanders thought the attacks on Latrun were futile, since the new brigade was still too disorganized to win the battles. They also considered Ben-Gurion's involvement in operational decisions uncalled for. In retrospect Ben-Gurion argued that the battles for Latrun diverted Arab Legion forces from Jerusalem and saved the city. Yadin, however, considered the entire Latrun episode a needless mistake. We shall never know who was right. In the end, Latrun was not taken by the Israelis until the Six-Day War in 1967, but they did capture Arab villages to the south of the road, and from there an alternative route to Jerusalem was opened. When the truce was declared, the Jews had a road to Jerusalem that was not dependent on U.N. observers. The month of fighting ended with the halting of the Arab attack.

The truce began on 11 June and was set to last only four weeks. All the tensions that had been repressed during the fighting now surfaced: between Ben-Gurion and the Haganah command (which became the Israel Defense Forces command); between the young state and the Etzel (the Irgun); and between the left, which in January 1948 had founded Mapam, a Marxist party that worshiped the USSR, and Mapai. At the center of all these tensions was Ben-Gurion. Not only did he not defuse them, he seems to have deliberately tried to bring them to a boiling point in order to crush, once and for all, the numerous forces that he thought were challenging the state authority he had established. Clearly he identified totally with the state authority and treated his opponents as if they were plotting to harm the brand-new independent entity.

The first dramatic clash took place around the *Altalena* affair. The *Altalena* was a vessel carrying weapons, purchased by the Etzel, which reached the country during the truce. Begin, who had apparently heard of the ship's impending arrival only after it sailed, announced that fact to Galili, with whom he was negotiating terms for the Etzel to join the Israel Defense Forces (IDF). The agreement they signed stated that the Etzel forces in Jerusalem (which was not included in the Jewish state) would have a certain degree of autonomy, but apart from that the Etzel was to relinquish its separate arms sources, place its weapons at the disposal of the IDF, and instruct its battalions to join the IDF. When the ship arrived on 20 June, Galili told Begin to direct it to the Kfar Vitkin beach, on the assumption that no U.N. observers would be there. Although one of the terms of the truce was an arms embargo, Ben-Gurion had no intention of observing it, and the IDF rearmed as much as it could during the cease-fire. There was no sense in flaunting this in front of the U.N. observers, however.

When the ship stood off Kfar Vitkin, it became evident that the Etzel was not going to transfer the arms to the IDF but intended to store them in its own facilities, then prioritize their distribution to the Etzel battalions—or in other words, to maintain a certain autonomy within the IDF. To Ben-Gurion this was a challenge to the state's authority and an attempt to establish a power parallel to the IDF's. Clashes broke out on the beach, and both sides suffered their first casualties in fighting each other. That night the ship sailed for Tel Aviv, where it hit a reef opposite Palmach headquarters in full view of the world press. The Etzel troops left their military units and hurried to help the stricken vessel. Troops from the IDF's Kiryati Brigade, which was responsible for securing Tel Aviv and its environs, hesitated to use force against the Etzel. To Ben-Gurion this was a test of the state's authority vis-à-vis separatist organizations. The provisional government authorized him to take action, and he did not flinch: "This time any compromise is out of the question," he wrote to Galili. "Either they accept orders and obey them—or we open fire. I am opposed to any negotiations and agreement with them. The time of agreements is past and will not return." Here he added a statement that reflected his view of the difference between a state and a voluntary society: "If there is force—it must be used unhesitatingly." To this he added two handwritten words: "And immediately."[7] The Palmach, which passionately hated the separatists, was sent to put down what it perceived as the launch of a putsch. A curfew was imposed on Tel Aviv. The commanding officer at the Yonah army base north of where the ship was anchored was ordered to shell the vessel. The second round hit the ship and it caught fire. Fourteen were killed and close to twenty wounded among the Etzel and Palmach troops on the beach.

The trauma of Jews firing on Jews—of a vessel bringing arms to Israel being sunk by the IDF—was unforgettable. Thenceforth both left and right referred to it incessantly. Some praised Ben-Gurion's decision-making ability, while others viewed him as a political Satan who exploited a seemingly innocuous incident to settle old scores with the Etzel. Many years later, it seems that even in the minds of the Israeli right, the *Altalena* affair has become fixed as an extreme but vital expression of imposing the state's authority on those who still harbored hopes of preserving the old Yishuv mindset. Ben-Gurion never denied his sole responsibility for giving the order to use force against Jews. He seems to have viewed this decision as belonging to the category of Churchillian decisions made at critical moments. Perhaps he was thinking about the sinking of the French fleet at Oran, or even of another occasion when Churchill sacrificed civilian lives for the great cause. Years later, when the Camp David negotiations between Ehud Barak and Yasser Arafat collapsed, one of the Palestinians remarked: "We needed a Ben-Gurion, but we've got Arafat."

The *Altalena* incident was barely over when a new crisis blew up behind the scenes, leading Ben-Gurion to use his ultimate weapon—a threat to resign not only as minister of defense but also as prime minister—just a few days before the fighting was renewed. This time the face-off was between him and the IDF general staff. The first signs of an impending crisis regarding the country's defense structure had appeared on the eve of independence. In early May, Ben-Gurion announced that the post of head of the National Command would be discontinued; there would be no intermediary between the minister of defense and the chief of staff. Coming amid the preparations for invasion and the tumult of the war, this order was considered reckless. Galili, the head of the National Command and a Ben-Gurion appointee, had played the role of intermediary between Ben-Gurion and the general staff, moderating and interpreting orders that he gave emotionally, and that were not always possible to carry out. Discontinuing that position would affect the day-to-day functioning of the general staff, and the generals wrote Ben-Gurion a letter containing a veiled threat to resign if Galili was not reinstated. Ben-Gurion reinstated him, but without an official position. The message was: there is a single authority in matters of defense, and it is the minister. All the civil authorities, which were the result of compromises and agreements made in the Yishuv period, were thus annulled overnight by Ben-Gurion.

The crisis resurfaced immediately after the *Altalena* incident when Ben-Gurion attempted to impose his own choice of commanders on the military. This action reflected both his wish to promote former British army personnel and his lack of trust in former members of the Haganah and Palmach. Most controversial was his appointment of Mordechai Makleff, a young, recently appointed brigade commander, to command the central front, which would clearly be at the focus of the fighting after the truce ended. The general staff, headed by Yigael Yadin, wanted Palmach commander Yigal Allon, who was considered brilliant and experienced. Three generals, led by Yadin, tendered their resignations, and Galili sent Ben-Gurion a letter, with copies to all the members of the government, advising him of the seriousness of his act. Ben-Gurion thereupon announced to the government that there was a political rebellion among the general staff. The upshot was a commission of inquiry of five ministers, before which all the painful issues arising from the month of fighting were laid out, from Latrun to Ben-Gurion's intervention in operational matters. The commission, siding with the general staff, rejected Ben-Gurion's position. It also called for the establishment of a war cabinet that Ben-Gurion would have to consult with. Ben-Gurion now brought out his doomsday weapon, informing the government that if they wanted him to continue in office, they should shelve the commission's findings. No one even contemplated the possibility of letting Ben-Gurion resign. Yadin came up with a compromise: instead of commanding the front, Allon would command Operation Danny, which would be the main operation on the front. Ben-Gurion acquiesced, and Galili paid the price. He was relieved of his duties and quietly retired.

Underlying this episode was Ben-Gurion's suspicion of the political motives of the general staff and Galili. Mapam had been founded in January 1948; it included Hashomer Hatzair and the Akhdut Ha'avoda (labor unity) Movement, a party that had been established by Faction B, which had seceded from Mapai. It took the name of the original party formed in 1918 to assert its adherence to the basic values of the movement. Its dominant force was Hakibbutz Hameuhad. Mapam members were prominent among the Haganah and Palmach commanders. Hakibbutz Hameuhad was the Palmach's patron, and even if, as was claimed, promotion in the Palmach was determined on the basis of talent, not political affiliation, Ben-Gurion's suspicions were understandable. He now found himself under attack for preferring the nonpartisan Makleff over Allon, a member of Hakibbutz Hameuhad and Mapam. In those early days of the state, binding norms of separation between military service and political involvement had not yet been defined. Allon and Galili were among Mapam's leadership and well known for their party activity. The Palmach was known as "Yitzhak Tabenkin's private army." This elite military unit, which before becoming part of the IDF had borne the brunt of the early battles in the war, shedding its blood in every part of the country, had not been created by Ben-Gurion and owed him no loyalty. It had a different source of inspiration.

As we have seen, Ben-Gurion was never enthusiastic about the anarchistic, creative elements of the labor movement. He preferred clear, hierarchical, organized structures. The Palmach, with its total lack of formality, its opposition to ranks and blind discipline—not to mention its leftist political orientation—was the essence of everything he disliked. He did not wait until the war ended to settle his score with the Palmach. On the eve of Operation Yoav, one of the biggest, most difficult operations, he announced the disbanding of the Palmach command. This time he gave prior notice of his intention, and went to talk with the Palmach commanders, supposedly so they could explain to him why the Palmach needed its own command when the IDF had a general staff. In fact, though, once the IDF was established, the Palmach's separate command became obsolete. Even though it had symbolic and sentimental value for the country's young people, Ben-Gurion did not hesitate to dissolve its command, and shortly its brigades as well. Ben-Gurion was unforgiving; he bore grudges; and he did not forget that the Palmach was not his.

He also had a habit of choosing his moment when he caused a crisis. It was usually at a critical juncture, when responsible people found it hard to flout his authority for fear that he would threaten to resign. Galili used an evocative image to describe this power of Ben-Gurion's. In his nightmares, he said, he saw defeat, with thousands of people fleeing in panic. Yet there was one who stood facing the flow, arms extended, and he stopped the flight. That one was Ben-Gurion. This description, by a man whose very soul was permanently scarred by Ben-Gurion, expresses the force of Ben-Gurion's leadership. He was not blessed with charisma, nor was he one of those who, from the moment they enter political life, find their authority universally accepted. He was unfamiliar with the art of backslapping and idle chat, and as the years went by, increasingly cut himself off from people. Since Katznelson's death there had been no one he could consult with as an equal. He kept his anxieties and doubts locked in his heart, rarely sharing them with others. This self-imposed loneliness was the product either of his character or of a belief that it was appropriate behavior for a leader. Until and even during the War of Independence, even his party comrades did not accept his authority unquestioningly, and certainly his opponents on the right and left did not. But in the wake of the war and the establishment of the state, and given that he had so often been proved right, he slowly gained the standing, at least among the masses, of someone who is sui generis. It seems that he often recalled what he had written to Paula about Churchill: that "a courageous, cautious, farseeing, enterprising leader, or the lack thereof, means the difference between ruin and salvation."

During Operation Danny, which took place when the first truce ended, the tip of the iceberg of Jewish attitudes toward the Palestinian Arabs was revealed. Since the outbreak of hostilities the day after 29 November, there had been a steady flow of local Arabs from the Jewish-controlled areas, and of Jews from areas under Arab control. Contrary to expectations, Jews did not remain in Arab-controlled areas, and almost no Arabs remained in the Jewish areas. Before the first truce, the Arabs' flight was most often spontaneous, motivated by fear either of the fighting or of Jewish control. During Operation Danny, two Arab cities in the center of the country were conquered, and their residents did not have time to flee. A brief uprising by the residents of Lydda (Lod) exposed the danger inherent in leaving a large bloc containing a hostile population behind the advancing army, midway between Tel Aviv and Jerusalem. The commanders Allon and Yitzhak Rabin, who were considering a large-scale population evacuation, went to consult with Ben-Gurion. Ben-Gurion listened to them and did not react; he had an uncanny ability to keep silent when he needed to. It was only at the end of the discussion, as the commanders were about to leave for the battlefield, that, according to Rabin, Ben-Gurion waved his hand and said: "Expel them." This is as far as we know the only instance in which there is evidence of Ben-Gurion giving an order to evacuate Arabs. In other cases, such as Nazareth, he forbade expulsion. But there is no doubt that, like most of his ministers, he saw the Arabs' exodus as a great miracle, one of the most important in that year of miracles, since the presence of a hostile population constituting some forty percent of the new state's total populace did not augur well for the future.

As Ben-Gurion said repeatedly, he was prepared to accept the 29 November borders, including the Arabs within them. But if there was a war, then *à la guerre comme à la guerre;* he would no longer be committed to borders. What was more, those Arabs who left would not be allowed to return. And indeed, in July 1948 the government decided not to allow the Arab refugees to return. In the atmosphere of the time, when only a few years earlier there had been a forced movement of millions in Eastern Europe; when the expulsion of millions of Germans from territory they had lived in for a thousand years was justified with the excuse that the aggressor must pay the price of its aggression; when at exactly the same time in India there raged a brutal war over partition in which hundreds of thousands were killed and millions of refugees were exiled from their homes, the decision not to allow the return of the Arab refugees was accepted as self-evident, and gained broad public support.

Since the first truce, the IDF had had the initiative in the

Ben-Gurion with President Harry S. Truman (left) and Abba Eban, early 1950s (Collection of Ben-Gurion House, Tel Aviv)

war. Following Operation Danny, the focus of the fighting moved from the center of the country to the Negev. This area was cut off, and proposals were floated internationally to annex it to Egypt or Transjordan. Despite the second truce, signed after Operation Danny, the fighting continued all summer and winter; cease-fire agreements were not signed until 1949. During this period Ben-Gurion proved he could give not only attack orders, but also orders to withdraw. When he felt that the IDF was becoming embroiled in a conflict with Britain, and when the American president ordered him to withdraw during Operation Horev, as the IDF entered the Sinai Peninsula and reached the outskirts of El-Arish, he issued withdrawal orders. Having no delusions of grandeur as a result of these triumphs, Ben-Gurion imposed his will on the victorious IDF. He also demonstrated in those long months that he was willing to take calculated risks: for example, to go into an all-out battle with the Egyptian army, even when there were fears of intervention by the Arab Legion and Iraqi forces on the other fronts. He also did not flinch from provoking the United Nations by breaking the truce agreement. But the limit of his fearlessness was a clash with a Western power. Vainly, the right and Mapam accused him of defeatism. He did not flinch from confronting them but chose to maintain good relations with the United States, which he perceived as a potential ally of the new state, and also not to provoke the British lion, even though its fangs had been drawn. At the end of the war, when Yigal Allon, who represented the younger generation of commanders that had grown up in the war, demanded the conquest of the West Bank up to the Jordan River as the natural, defensible border of the state, Ben-Gurion refused. He recognized that the IDF was militarily strong enough to carry out the conquest, but he believed that the young state should not bite off more than it had already chewed. There was a limit to what the world was prepared to accept. Furthermore, the armistice borders—which later became known as the Green Line—were better than those he had dreamed of at the beginning of the war. In Ben-Gurion's opinion, in terms of territory Israel was satisfied. It was time to send the troops home and start work on building the new nation.

9

———◆◉◆———

Helmsman of the State

"THERE WAS NOTHING that the Jewish people yearned for
more over hundreds of years than a Jewish state," Ben-Gurion
wrote in 1951; "there was nothing the Jewish people was less
qualified for than a Jewish state." He thought that, by contrast
with its genius in the sphere of ethics and values, the Jewish
people was "flawed in its sense of statehood."[1] This question
never ceased to trouble him. "For hundreds of years the Jewish
people offered up a question-prayer: can a state be found for
the people? No one considered the horrifying question—can
a people be found for the state once it is established?"[2] These
words reflect the tremendous dilemmas Ben-Gurion con-
fronted and the concerns he faced. He saw himself responsible
not only for defense and foreign policy, but also for forming a
national identity for the hundreds of thousands of people who
came to Israel from different countries and cultures, not understanding each other's languages. He had to accomplish this

objective while also developing an economy—and swiftly, for the enemy promised a "second round," and there was no time to build a nation slowly and gradually, as had been done during the Mandate period. A new language of governance must be created appropriate to the "statism" he envisioned. Statism would be able to effectively use the new tools at the state's disposal to overcome the Jewish tendency toward schism and anarchism and harness for the state the energies that during the Yishuv period had been channeled into voluntarism.

To his party comrades, not to mention the opposition, it was "madness" to transfer power from labor movement institutions to the state. They could not understand why he wanted to abolish the "Labor stream" of secular socialist-oriented schools and the Histadrut employment bureau, fight the favoritism system, and so forth. They construed the transfer of authority to the state as a betrayal of the values of socialism, of the pioneering ethos, and of all the labor movement's glorious social creations.

The state's first four years were dramatic. The Jewish population doubled in size and had to be provided with food, housing, employment, and education. Ben-Gurion, who had always claimed that he did not understand economics, fired off cables to Israel's embassy in Washington: "The wheat and cereal situation is dire. By the end of February there will be no bread. By the end of January there will be no feed for the chicken farms."[3] The winter of 1951–1952 was particularly harsh, and the immigrant and transit camps suffered storms, flooding, and shortages. The waves of immigration that inundated the country were not planned. Some immigrants came from DP camps in Germany, others from the Cyprus detention camps, from Romania and Poland, which had not yet closed their gates, and from Bulgaria, which also allowed Jews to leave. But immigration from the European countries was quickly exhausted. Most of the immigrants came from the Mediterranean countries: Iraq, Yemen, Libya, and the Maghreb. They arrived impoverished, and the majority had never been exposed to Western culture.

The Yishuv had no experience dealing with immigration on such a scale and of such a nature. Voices were raised among decision-makers and in the press demanding that immigration be limited because of economic hardship and absorption difficulties, and also because of the Middle Eastern composition of this aliya, which the fathers of Zionism were quite unfamiliar with. Fear of "ruffians" drove the press—mainly the liberal press in the shape of *Ha'aretz* or *Haboker*—to warn against mass immigration as liable to change the country's cultural fabric by introducing "Levantine" culture ("Levantine" being the accepted disparaging term for non-European culture). "I am unable to be one-millionth of a party to this fear," Ben-Gurion declared in the Knesset.[4] He agreed briefly to grant better absorption conditions to Polish Jews, fearing that otherwise they would not immigrate, but immediately backtracked: "We cannot discriminate between one immigrant and another . . . anyone not wishing to come—should not come," he wrote to Yitzhak Gruenbaum, the patron of Polish Jewry.[5] It was true that when immigrants from Poland arrived in the late 1950s, Ben-Gurion agreed to give them better conditions, for the dubious reason that if they were not absorbed quickly, the gates of Poland might be closed. He also yielded to the people in charge of immigrant absorption and accepted a selection process that imposed restrictions on Moroccan immigrants in 1953. But overall there was no more spirited fighter against the elitist winds blowing among the intelligentsia and the press.

He lived with a sense of the loss of European Jewry and the need to establish the state through the ingathering of other Jewish communities. "The people that conceived, nurtured, and realized the great pioneering enterprise, the acme of which is labor agricultural settlement, that people has been annihilated and is no more. . . . This country needs, and from now on can

be built by, a different Jewish people, a people that did not acquire the Hebrew and humanist education given to European
Jewry, a people whose fate it was to live for hundreds of years
in downtrodden, backward, and poor countries."[6]

Ben-Gurion shared the feeling that European culture was
superior, and his attitude toward immigrants from elsewhere
tended to be patronizing. However, he was innocent of any trace
of racism. He ascribed the cultural differences to different living conditions: "From the standpoint of ability, there is no difference between a European and an African Jew, an Asian Jew
or an American Jew. Place them under the same conditions, the
same housing conditions, the same family life—they will be
the same Jews."[7] The problem was that the conditions were far
from equal. Ben-Gurion was sensitive to the ethnic gap being
opened and was concerned lest it create two separate peoples in
the country. He saw this as an existential danger but did not
know how to overcome it. He understood the scope of the task
and the type of changes required for the transition from Yishuv to
state, but never succeeded in finding creative new tools to implement the foremost enterprise of the generation—immigrant
absorption.

Ben-Gurion was prone to jump straight from conceptual-
izing an idea to putting it into effect, without the intermediate
stages of objectively examining its feasibility and the actual possibility of implementing it. In some respects this was a wonderful quality in a leader, for he set inspirational targets that often
led to accomplishing the impossible. A fine example of his skep-
tical reaction to experts who poured cold water on his visions
involved his idea of building a modern city in Beersheba. The
committee of experts he appointed to examine the idea concluded that it could not be done. When Ehud Avriel, director
general of the prime minister's office, asked him what they
should do next, he replied, "Appoint a new committee."

He used the same tactic with respect to the absorption of

mass immigration, but without much success. Demanding new efforts from a small, fatigued Yishuv that had been through terrible struggle and war, and now sought a little peace and quiet, he was bitterly disappointed when it did not respond. The distance between will and capability—the same gap that drove him out of his mind and led to his volcanic outbursts—also manifested in the distance between the statist ideology he promoted, which assumed that the state had unlimited powers, and his rapid realization that he needed the voluntarism of the old Yishuv. He demanded that the kibbutz movement absorb new immigrants and provide them with work in its kibbutzim. Until then the kibbutzim had not employed hired labor, which contradicted their ideology of equality since it was based on exploitation and created class distinctions. When Ben-Gurion called on them to open their doors to hired workers, the kibbutz movement duly gave him the cold shoulder. While it absorbed and educated young people from Youth Aliya, which included children and teenagers, it refused to change its social fabric by absorbing hired workers.

There was something simplistic and naive in Ben-Gurion's assumption that he could impose great social changes with a wave of his hand, by the power of his will, and his disappointment when it did not happen. In 1950 he declared in the Knesset that he was "ashamed" of the kibbutz movement. He was right in assuming that by alienating itself from mass immigration, the movement had sentenced itself to remain outside the mainstream of life in the state. But he also did not understand that it was impossible to artificially recreate the Yishuv's energy of volunteerism and replicate it in the state. Those who had carried that energy were now exhausted. They looked forward to tranquility, to reconstructing their lives, and they had neither the mental nor the physical strength to meet the demands of a leader who continued to forge ahead with new, revolutionary, and challenging missions.

Ben-Gurion testing Yemenite children's reading skills at a Ma'abara, or immigrant absorption camp, 1950. These transit camps were built in the early 1950s when the number of immigrants far exceeded the state's capability to provide them with permanent housing. The housing was usually built of temporary materials (tin shacks, tents, or wooden huts). It was miserable. (IDF Archive)

The great revolution of war and the creation of the state were followed by ordinary times of daily routines. But to Ben-Gurion this period was not ordinary, for it was the time of the true revolution of ingathering the exiles and creating a nation. He never stopped mobilizing participation in immigrant absorption and settlement throughout the country, now empty of its Arab inhabitants and with undefended borders. He envisioned the establishment of hundreds of *moshavim* (cooperative agricultural settlements) by new immigrants as the expression of the perpetual revolution he hoped to drive forward: moving Jews from petty trading to agricultural work and settlement on the borders. To him, productivizing the Jews was the most important process; he could not understand the trend in modern economics toward reducing the percentage of workers engaged in manual labor for the benefit of services and the technical professions. Even though he declared his acceptance of cooperation between the public and private sectors, he still equated private enterprise with avarice. To him, the essence of Israeli socialism was the central role played by the state in the economy and society. The state would ensure that class distinctions were reduced and the education system expanded for the benefit of disadvantaged populations. He bitterly opposed increasing the wage gap between manual laborers and the government-employed intelligentsia, and did not flinch from speaking out against the engineers, doctors, and high school teachers who demanded wage increases. For him it was the manual laborer who symbolized the productivization of the Jews. Even fifteen years later, after the Six-Day War, he still feared that the country would be flooded with cheap Arab labor that would lead the Jews to abandon physical labor, dooming the productivization process.

The early 1950s were the formative years of the Israeli nation. Although the plague of terrorist incursions made life very hard for the new settlers along the borders, from a security standpoint these were years of relative quiet. In 1952, the grave economic crisis led Ben-Gurion to reduce the size of the army to the minimum despite the opposition of Yadin, the chief of staff, who subsequently resigned.

Israel's Arab minority was still in shock from its defeat in the War of Independence, it was frightened, and its leadership was relatively weak. Only the leaders of the small Israeli Communist party spoke on its behalf. Ben-Gurion, who initially talked of full equality for Jews and Arabs in the new state, now acceded to the demand by the civil and military administrators in charge of the Arab minority to impose military government on the Arabs of Israel. Although they were granted civil rights and voted in elections to the Knesset, the authorities treated them with an iron fist: brutal searches for infiltrators, land appropriation, and restrictions on movement. Ben-Gurion did not examine this subject in depth, and despite the skepticism he displayed toward "experts" on other topics, on this issue he accepted their opinion. Even assuming that in the early 1950s there was some objective justification for imposing military government, it tarnished the image of Israeli democracy. Despite repeated pleas from the left in the governing coalition, and even from the right-wing party Herut, to rescind it, military government of the Arabs remained in place until after Ben-Gurion left office.

One of the more poignant pleas came from his old friend Manya Shochat, the founder of the Sejera collective. Sick and half-blind, she appealed to the moral sense that had inspired them in their youth: "When you worked in Sejera, a sweet boy, David Green, you dreamed about a heavenly State of Israel, and this dream, consciously or unconsciously, brought us, *with your help*, to all the victories."[8] And on behalf of that dream she asked him to erase the disgrace of the military regime. As far as we know, after the War of Independence Ben-Gurion never visited an Arab village. He scrupulously and cordially answered letters sent him by Arabs, but displayed no interest in their hardships. In Israel-Arab relations during the Ben-Gurion period, the Arabs of Israel were a marginal concern for him. He gave most of his attention to the balance of power with the Arab states and security along Israel's borders.

Ben-Gurion involved himself in matters both great and small. At the height of the War of Independence he ordered that every officer and government official representing the State of

Israel must Hebraize his name. He also repeatedly implored his colleagues to do the same, although if someone said he was the only one remaining of his family, which had perished in the Holocaust, Ben-Gurion would relent. Among his closest aides in the prime minister's office, it appears that only Teddy Kollek did not change his name—a sure sign of Kollek's independence. On the other hand, Ben-Gurion opposed forcing Hebrew on new immigrants. "Thousands of immigrants who do not speak Hebrew are coming here, and it is impossible to shut their mouths and prevent their cultural needs from being met in their own language until they learn Hebrew."[9] He opposed his education minister's attempt to close down a Yiddish theater in Israel. He also opposed a proposal put forth in the Knesset by Herut that called for prohibiting Arabs from using Arabic; he demanded that Arabic be allowed even in the Knesset.

At the height of the economic and political crises, Ben-Gurion found time to initiate an extraordinary cultural enterprise: microfilming Hebrew manuscripts from all over the world so they could be archived at the Hebrew University in Jerusalem. The idea came to him while he was vacationing in Tiberias, and he immediately wrote to Finance Minister Eliezer Kaplan requesting that he allocate fifty thousand lirot (pounds) to the project. As usual, he grounded his idea in a philosophical context. Although the three main missions of that generation were defense, immigration, and settlement, he said: "Even military history shows that the *decisive and constant* victory is that of *spiritual power*. In the final accounting, the idea and the vision are stronger than the sword and the bow, and stronger even than the atomic bomb."[10] Therefore, despite the fraught economic situation, despite the hundreds of thousands of immigrants flooding the country for whom housing, employment, and education had to be provided, the money for the microfilming project must be found "without delay." It was, Ben-Gurion declared, "the duty of the State of Israel to acquire and gather those exiles of the spirit of Israel dispersed in the Diaspora."[11] To implement the idea he set up a joint committee from the government and the Hebrew University. The enterprise took shape within only a few months and was duly launched. It was an expression of the statist concept: the state takes upon itself responsibility for the nation's spiritual treasures, and it can accomplish what individuals are unable to do.

Microfilming the Hebrew manuscripts was to be the first stage of an even more grandiose enterprise: translating all of humankind's spiritual treasures into Hebrew, from Greece and Egypt to India and China, and from antiquity to the modern era. "Everything human is not foreign to us—and everything human must be provided for in our language," he asserted. Thus was born the notion of publishing a series of "Masterworks of World Literature." Ben-Gurion did not dictate the list of works to the committee, but he did urge it to include works on Indian philosophy. Interest in this field was probably limited to only a handful of Israelis, but for Ben-Gurion it became a focus of tremendous intellectual interest and curiosity, especially with respect to Buddhism. Most of all he loved Plato and Spinoza and tried to persuade the committee to have them translated into Hebrew in full, but with only limited success. The committee members favored meticulousness and quality over fast translation, whereas he, as usual, pressed them to move the project along. The first fifty titles and authors to appear included Charles Darwin's *Origin of Species* (which Ben-Gurion suggested), the seven tragedies of Aeschylus, William James, Jacob Burckhardt, Alexis de Tocqueville, Confucius, Kant, and Montesquieu.

Affairs of state did not prevent him from attending the committee meetings, and he enjoyed the dialogue with his professorial colleagues. As early as 1949 he invited a diverse group of philosophers, writers, and other intellectuals to discuss the newly established state. This ambition to create a dialogue between the political leader and the shapers of the national culture, whom he hoped would formulate the state's intellectual foundations, was extremely naive; it seems he was captivated by the image of the philosopher-king in the vein of Marcus Aurelius. Despite the pleasure he got from the meetings, he gained no real benefit from them. It is also possible that the intellectual sparring and spiritual discussion were for him a fresh breeze, a delightful respite from tedious discussions with party representatives about the governing coalition, forming a government, and allocation of portfolios.

Ben-Gurion was a political animal, and he did not evade his responsibilities as a party leader and leader of the nation. That does not mean he did not tire of these duties as time went by and seek refuge in intellectual activities. He became a resource for researchers in the fields of philosophy and Jewish studies who had difficulty raising funds to publish their works, and he tried to help insofar as he was able, depending on what he thought of the writers.

On vacation in Greece at the end of 1950, he visited all the historical sites; his boundless energy exhausted his bodyguards. He met with Greek prime minister Sophoklis Venizelos, whose father had translated Thucydides into modern Greek, and got the impression that not much of ancient Greece was left in contemporary Greece. From Greece he went to Cambridge and Oxford, where he toured the bookshops. He preferred to talk with the philosopher Isaiah Berlin rather than meet with London dignitaries. "He is the only statesman I have ever met in my life who possesses a rich inner life, distinct from public achievements however heroic: and . . . this is something so rare, valuable and marvelous that I should like to express here, sincere and profound homage to it," Berlin wrote admiringly after their meeting, in which the talk centered on Indian mysticism, the role of elephants in Indian folklore, and Plato.[12]

Books remained his great love; every Israeli legation, from Moscow to China, located books that he asked them to purchase for him and ship to Israel. Some twenty years earlier he had stopped reading fiction and poetry, although he sometimes read new literary works published in Hebrew. He occasionally became embroiled in arguments with authors on this subject, since they were affronted by his somewhat disparaging attitude toward literature, while he was disappointed by their reluctance to present the great epic of immigration in their works.

Ever since being so moved by the Habima Theatre performance in Moscow, Ben-Gurion had kept a warm place in his heart for Hebrew theater. After seeing a performance of Sholem Aleichem's *Tevye the Milkman* at Habima Theatre in Tel Aviv with Yehoshua Bertonov in the title role, he wrote to the actor: "With your amazing talent you portrayed all the historic suffering and pride of a Jew. I have never seen or felt such a great and gifted expression of the tragic and heroic fate of the Diaspora Jew." He added: "You were not acting—you *were* the simple, innocent, loyal, proud, stiff-necked, and kindly Jew. Your performance was stunning and delicate, shocking and exciting, uplifting and brilliant." And he concluded, "It was for me one of the profoundest and most shocking experiences of my life."[13] An ardent supporter of the young Cameri Theatre, he loved its youthful spirit and freshness. He was invited to attend the opening of the Cameri's new auditorium on Nachmani Street in Tel Aviv, although he did not make the journey from Sdeh Boker in the Negev. Instead he wrote an impish letter to the theater's director, Yosef Milo, in which he both praised the theater and mentioned its only shortcoming—that "it is located in Tel Aviv, not in the Wilderness of Paran." Paraphrasing Isaiah 35:1–10, he added, "It is my hope that the day will come, and it is not far away, when water will spring forth in the desert, and streams in the wilderness, and the burning wind will become a lake, and thirst will be slaked by springs of water, and there will be a road there—and the redeemed will go and see Cameri performances in the Negev Mountains."[14]

In August 1948, Professor Shmuel Sambursky requested that Ben-Gurion revive the Board of Scientific and Industrial Research established by the British at the end of the Mandate period. Ben-Gurion responded quickly and positively. He ensured that the necessary funds were allocated to scientific work— one hundred thousand lirot, or two percent of the state budget. During the same period he became interested in nuclear research. He hoped that Israeli science would come up with solutions for water and energy shortages, and every scientist (or bizarre eccentric) who proposed a solution to these problems found an attentive ear in the prime minister. His dealings with Sambursky illuminate another aspect of his personality. Sambursky was a former member of Brit Shalom, and in the debate between that group and Ben-Gurion in 1929 had suggested that Jewish immigration be limited to four hundred thousand. When he submitted the research council proposal, Ben-Gurion asked if he would like to head the council. Sambursky said he certainly would but thought his association with Brit Shalom might disqualify him. Ben-Gurion responded that science was separate from political opinions, and Sambursky was duly appointed director of the Israeli Research Council.

The encounter between Sambursky and Ben-Gurion introduces the question of Ben-Gurion's concept of democracy. He was not a member of the multicultural generations of the 1980s and after, and he possessed a large measure of zealotry. Nevertheless he had a degree of tolerance and patience that is difficult to reconcile with his restless personality. He drew a distinction between people as individuals and as political figures. Thus although he was great friends with Ya'akov (Kuba) Riftin, an extreme leftist member of Mapam who led his party to the verge of communism, this friendship did not stop him from leveling a vituperative attack at Mapam's political concepts in a series of vicious articles, which he signed S. B. Yariv (an acronym of "Saba shel Yariv"—grandfather of Yariv, his first grandson). He greatly admired and respected Rabbi Fishman-Maimon, even though their opinions were far apart. He respected Martin Buber, although he thought Buber's pacifist views were not relevant to the time and place. In foreign affairs he respected interlocutors whose integrity he trusted and found liars insufferable. But this did not stop him from lying to the world if he believed the interests of Israel required it (for example, his denials of the Kibia operation, in which dozens of civilians were killed by the IDF, and of the existence of a nuclear reactor at Dimona). Whenever he detected a false tone in someone's speech, he would permanently exclude that person. But he was not interested in his followers' private lives, and felt, for instance, that Moshe Dayan's sexual indiscretions were none of his business. The political culture of the young nation did not comprehend Ben-Gurion's distinction between the personal and the political. After conducting a bitter dispute with an adversary from the Knesset podium, he would be surprised when the target of his barbs gave him the cold shoulder in the corridor.

The parliamentary arena was Ben-Gurion's natural battleground; he was a fiery, merciless debater. Nor were his adversaries gentle; he was the target of incessant condemnation from both left and right. The left, in thrall to the USSR, did not forgive him for disbanding the Palmach or for his pro-Western political orientation. The new state had dispossessed the left of the avant-garde roles it had played during the Yishuv period, and it felt insulted, humiliated, and rejected, especially during the four years when Mapam was not in the government and Ben-Gurion gave Mapai and himself the credit for successfully overcoming the serious crises of those years. Mapam observed his successes with frustration, a mixture of admiration and anger, and a bitterness that did not dissipate until he left the political stage, even though it was in the government after 1955.

The right did not forgive him for the "saison," for the *Altalena,* for the slogan he created in forming the coalition ("Without Herut and Maki," the Israeli Communist party), or for his opposition to the proposal that the government bring Jabotinsky's remains to Israel (he opposed doing this for any Jews except Herzl and Rothschild: "Are we to turn our country into a country of graves?" he wrote to President Yitzhak Ben-Zvi).[15] By depicting Herut and its leader, Menachem Begin, as warmongers who supported irredentism and were a constant threat to democracy, he politically delegitimized them. With respect to adversaries whom history had consigned to oblivion, however, he was prepared to forgive and forget. Thus, for example, he welcomed the publication of a book on the Bund, adding, "We should forget the Bund's failed war against Zionism, and remember with esteem its revolutionary enterprise in organizing masses of workers and its war against the Tsarist regime and against depriving Jews of their rights."[16]

The American newspaper *Forverts,* which at least until the 1920s had been Bundist and anti-Zionist, welcomed the establishment of the state, and each year, on the paper's anniversary, Ben-Gurion wrote an article in Yiddish sending greetings. While he considered the left naive and under Moscow's influence, he saw the right as dangerous and adventurist, liable to endanger Israeli democracy and even its very existence. Like the left, the right felt frustrated and helpless in the face of his political successes and leadership abilities, which captivated the immigrant masses and many veteran Israelis alike. Yet despite his scathing disputes with them, deep in their hearts even people on the right admired him. But they neither forgot nor forgave what they saw as his sins, and when he later became weakened, their retribution was swift.

To everyone—left, right, even his own party—he seemed

omnipotent, with a finger in every pie. People tended to criticize him for anything they objected to, even though he had not been involved in it. His larger-than-life image made him everybody's punching bag. The fact that he was mainly engaged in foreign policy and defense and rarely intervened in other matters, leaving them to the relevant ministers, did not relieve him of responsibility for them in the public's view. He also loved saber rattling, and the adrenaline would course through his veins when he was at the center of a battle. When a public controversy arose, as over the reparations agreement with Germany, which he formulated with Nachum Goldmann and considered vital for the Israeli economy, he joined the fight to ratify it. From then on he was attacked by both right and left for being too forgiving toward Germany. He cast a constantly growing shadow, which was to a great extent the result of the admiration and awe he evoked in the state's first decade.

If democracy means bowing to the will of the people, Ben-Gurion was no democrat. He made no bones about asserting that his role was not doing what the people wanted, but rather what he thought was best for them. He saw himself as expressing Rousseau's "general will" through his intuitive understanding of the national interest. Like a true Jacobin, he believed that democracy meant majority rule, with the rights and freedoms of the individual being limited both by the rights of other individuals and by the collective's right to defend itself. He rejected the liberal concepts of Gustav Schocken, editor of the *Ha'aretz* daily, who demanded freedom of expression for the press from the military censor, and claimed instead that the state was permitted to protect its interests by keeping its secrets undisclosed. The right of the U.S. Supreme Court to annul a law enacted by Congress seemed to him to infringe democracy, since it placed the court above the country's elected institutions. This was one reason why he did not promote the idea of a constitution; he believed there was no place in a still nascent society for a constitution, which would restrict the parliamentary government. He admired the British system and used it as an example in trying to demonstrate the advantages of not having a written constitution. Did his stance derive from a philosophical and ideological concept, or from the pragmatic needs of the man who headed Israel's largest political party? A constitution would have put a spoke in his wheel, and he wanted freedom of action.

A parliamentary democracy was created in Israel, and Ben-Gurion played by its rules: elections, coalitions, government decisions, no less freedom of the press than in much older democratic countries, freedom of speech, and freedom of assembly. He scrupulously obtained government decisions on every important matter and acted accordingly, even when they were not to his liking. In extreme cases he would resign and force the parties into new elections. Such cases mainly—perhaps entirely—involved the relation between religion and the state, collective governmental responsibility, and coalition discipline. He usually did not resign over political differences in the government, even when he found himself in the minority. Even though forming a coalition required long, debilitating negotiations, he upheld the democratic framework. His adversaries suspected him of aspiring to dictatorship, but in fact he found a different form of government inconceivable. In his diary he described Benjamin Aktzin, a political science professor with a Revisionist past who suggested that he adopt an authoritarian regime, as "a fool." He wanted to change the electoral system from proportional to majority representation in the hope that it would reduce the number of parties and thus encourage greater unity among the Jewish people, improving the conduct of political life. But once he realized that he could not get the Knesset to pass such an amendment, he stopped pushing it and postponed the proposal year after year. This failure to change the electoral system is but one proof that Ben-Gurion was not omnipotent, even in the state's first decade, when the opposition perceived him as such.

Just before the state was established, he reached agreement with the ultra-Orthodox Agudat Yisrael (Union of Israel) party on the celebrated "status quo," assuring the state's religious Jews that the marital laws would be observed as they had been during the Mandate period and that the Sabbath and festivals would be part of the national calendar. Sensitive to tradition, he granted yeshiva students exemption from military service, but soon regretted it. In total contrast with his expectation that they would disappear completely, the number of yeshiva students steadily increased. But even though he sharply criticized the exemption, he did not cancel it.

Ben-Gurion was a fierce, loyal fighter for women's equality, and he wrote to the minister of finance that the titles on official forms should read "man/woman," not "husband/wife." In the Knesset debate on the Women's Equal Rights Law, when the religious parties objected to women having equal rights regarding property and children—claiming that rabbinic authority over these matters according to religious law should not be impaired—Ben-Gurion replied succinctly that rabbis were appointed by the state and therefore their authority derived from it. If a rabbi wished to act under state authority, he had to accept the authority of the Knesset. "It is inconceivable that rabbis be granted state authority, and that authority be totally independent of state decisions."[17] He greatly esteemed the eminent Rabbi Avraham Yeshaya Karelitz, popularly known as the Chazon Ish, and visited him at his Bnei Brak home (to the delight of the rabbi's followers), but when the rabbi wrote to him requesting that he annul the "edict" conscripting girls into the army, he replied that a law of a Jewish government in its homeland was not an "edict" and that the feelings of the majority, not only of the minority, must be taken into account. He demanded that the rabbis and representatives of the religious parties accept the rule of law unquestioningly. Whenever the religious representatives in the Knesset accused him of discrimination and suppressing freedom of conscience in the education of new immigrants, or raised issues such as observing the Sabbath in public places, he relished firing back that for him Judaism did not begin and end with the dietary laws and Sabbath observance, but rather meant upholding the commandments in personal interactions: that is, speaking the truth, not insulting someone in public, and feeling love for the Jewish people. He frequently used these retorts against the religious press, which was always ready to level accusations against him, at least some of which were false.

He enjoyed conducting long theological arguments in writing with rabbis or erudite observant Jews. Ben-Gurion did not consider himself an atheist. "It is clear to me," he wrote to one of his correspondents, "that the world is not the result of a blind and random incident (albeit I cannot prove it), and that there is order and authority ('cosmos') in the world—*and perhaps* even a direction and objective. However all that is in the sphere of the intellectual ponderings of a man who recognizes the paucity of his knowledge and the limits of human knowledge; it is neither spiritual nourishment nor a guide for man's actions and behavior."[18] He thought the Bible was the greatest of all Jewish works, but it did not reveal the secret of Divinity either: "I know from the Bible what our forefathers thought about this great secret—more than that I do not know. The secret itself remains a secret."[19] He repeatedly defended Spinoza, who had been ostracized in his lifetime by ultra-Orthodox Jews and was still anathema to them. In particular he contested the closed worldview of the ultra-Orthodox, who negated secular culture, Jewish and non-Jewish alike, and extolled return to the Jewish sources, by which they meant the Talmud and the religious arbiters. By contrast Ben-Gurion depicted the Bible as the

Jewish people's work of genius, bearing both particular and universal values. But the Bible was not the only spiritual source: "We have much, very much to learn from other nations."[20] When an interlocutor claimed that he was negating himself as a Jew by engaging with Greek and Roman culture, he replied: "It is not negation. . . . As a Jew I feel it is not beneath my dignity if I see that another people has a genius in a particular field, the like of which we do not have."[21] He remained a loyal disciple of Berdyczewski, who wanted the Jews to open up to the winds of the great world, but not of Ahad Ha'am, who tended toward seclusion within the boundaries of Judaism.

But even with all his love of disputation and readiness to get into long arguments with worthy and less worthy opponents, he did not seek confrontation with the religious sector. In a 1954 letter to Moshe Sharett (formerly Shertok), then prime minister, he warned, "We must not separate religion from the state" because of the state's connection with the Jewish people. "The State of Israel and the Jewish people share a common destiny. This state cannot exist without the Jewish people, and the Jewish people cannot exist without the state. Therefore, the following three things are bound together: love of the homeland, loyalty to the state, and loyalty to the Jewish people."[22] It seems he thought that separating religion from state would cause a schism between the Jewish people and the State of Israel. Perhaps this is the source of his ambivalent stance during a debate in 1958 about whether children of mixed marriages could be registered as Jews if both parents declared their desire to do so. This debate, known as "Who Is a Jew," was an attempt to define the boundaries of the Jewish collective. Should the definition be a civil one, based on the parents' desire and their identification with the Jewish people, or a religious one, based on the mother's origins? Ben-Gurion espoused the secular-civil concept and, after a prolonged crisis, did not hesitate to disband the coalition with the religious parties. In the end, however, he

Ben-Gurion with Moshe Sharett at Sdeh Boker, 1953
(Collection of Ben-Gurion House, Tel Aviv)

sought to conciliate the religious groups by seeking the advice
of fifty religious and secular intellectuals from both the Diaspora and Israel. He supervised the choice of these "sages," and
careful study of the list proves that the outcome was a foregone
conclusion. Most of the fifty were observant Jews, who quite
naturally demanded preservation of the religious boundaries of
the Jewish collective. Ben-Gurion was determined to avoid a
Kulturkampf. "I am convinced that in our generation we must
avoid any debate that is liable to impair the common effort
toward the existence of the people and its security," he wrote to
a correspondent. "When we live in our land in safety and peace

reigns around us and in the world—we shall, perhaps, hold the great debate, and perhaps not even then."[23]

In December 1953, Ben-Gurion stunned the whole country when he announced he was resigning from the government and going to live in a new kibbutz in the middle of the Negev desert, far to the south of Beersheba, which was still a sleepy township. This move turned out to be fateful for both Ben-Gurion and the State of Israel. The news of his imminent departure fueled a rumor mill, to the effect that he had lost faith in his party and sought to change the regime, generating all kinds of baseless assumptions that the newspapers competed in circulating. His military aide Nehemiah Argov, who adored him and treated him like a beloved father, wrote in a private letter: "'The Old Man' decided to leave the government. This is a final decision and no force in the world can change it." He tried to understand Ben-Gurion's motives, but it was hopeless. Ben-Gurion gave no hints. Speculations about health reasons made no sense: "I wish for myself his health, capacity for work, and physical abilities," commented Argov.[24] Once Ben-Gurion's plans were in place he sent a long letter to the party secretary, Meir Argov, which attributed his decision to resign "for a year, two, or perhaps longer" to mental fatigue resulting from his long service in government. Six years as prime minister of Israel, preceded by fifteen as chairman of the Zionist Executive, had completely drained him, and he had decided to take a leave, since in his present state he was no longer able to fulfill his duties at the required level of dedication.

Ze'ev Scharf had been cabinet secretary since the government was formed. He worked closely with Ben-Gurion but was not part of the inner circle of "Ben-Gurion's Boys" that included Teddy Kollek, Yitzhak Navon, Ehud Avriel, Nehemiah Argov, and Haim Yisraeli, the defense minister's bureau chief. Scharf, who was not pulled into Ben-Gurion's magnetic field and can therefore be considered an objective witness, asserted that between 1947 and 1952 Ben-Gurion had not made even one mistake. This claim encompassed momentous decisions involved in directing the War of Independence, establishing the state, moving the capital to Jerusalem in 1950 in defiance of the U.N. Security Council, mass immigration, and the reparations agreement with Germany. These decisions were not all consensual. Some aroused strong opposition from both left and right (conducting the War of Independence, reparations, the shift to a pro-Western policy). Others were opposed by liberals, who thought Ben-Gurion's policies were belligerent and liable to anger the Great Powers (the decision to establish the state and moving the capital to Jerusalem). For other reasons liberals also objected to mass immigration. Scharf considered these dramatic years the zenith of Ben-Gurion's leadership.

In 1953, however, immigration dried up, a U.S. loan was granted, and Germany promised reparations. The state of emergency, which had lasted since 1939, was over. The revolution was accomplished, and after the seven days of creation came an ordinary gray day requiring incessant coalition talks with the religious parties and constant coping with government crises. The sense of spiritual uplift of the "Days of the Messiah" dissipated. In Scharf's opinion, Ben-Gurion was simply bored. He was at his best in crises. Like Churchill, he had been born for a certain time in history, and once it had passed he felt drained, wasted, and perhaps even unsuited to engage with the humdrum of everyday affairs. Moreover, despite all his achievements, it is doubtful that the state which had been born conformed to his vision. It was not the exemplary state of "the Chosen People" that he had envisaged. Just as Mao Tse-tung swam across the Yangtze River to show that he was still in possession of all his powers and remained determined to keep his people permanently fired up through constant revolution, Ben-Gurion hoped that his retirement to Sdeh Boker, the new kibbutz in the Negev, would cause a national shockwave, rouse a new wave of revolutionary zeal, and perhaps bring about the utopian state he had longed for.

A wooden cottage was made ready for him and Paula, with separate bedrooms and a large study with shelves to hold a thousand volumes, all according to Paula's instructions. In early December a convoy of ministry staff, who were to help the distinguished couple install themselves in their new home, drove down to Sdeh Boker along with a contingent of media people. Paula was not exactly happy with the idea of moving to the Negev. She had many friends in Jerusalem and Tel Aviv, and now she was supposed to accept the ascetic remoteness of the Negev expanses, in a kibbutz whose members were younger than her own children. She swiftly instituted her meticulous rules of cleanliness, insisting that visitors remove their shoes in the hallway before entering the living quarters. She considered the kibbutz kitchen not clean enough and the food not sufficiently tasty. Ben-Gurion, by contrast, accepted everything with love. He arranged to work four hours a day in the kibbutz and devote the rest of his time to reading and writing. Once he realized that hard physical work was beyond him, he helped in the sheepfold, where he enjoyed rearing the lambs. He began walking four kilometers twice a day, and Paula, as always, made him her famous "kutch-mutch"—a healthful but tasteless concoction she insisted he eat twice a day.

Israelis found the retirement of the founding father, the state's steady anchor, hard to accept. He was inundated with thousands of letters begging him not to abandon them, from young and old, dignitaries and ordinary folk. An impudent thirteen-year-old named Amos Oz, a member of the Scout movement in Jerusalem, wanted to know why he had decided to retire. This question troubled many. Ben-Gurion sidestepped the boy's question but was very impressed by his writing ability. Other youngsters consulted him about whether they should go to university or the kibbutz. At first he answered all the letters in his own hand, but quickly realized that letter writing was taking up most of his time, leaving almost none for the reading he so loved.

Moshe Sharett became the prime minister in his place, and Pinchas Lavon minister of defense. Sharett was not Ben-Gurion's choice; he felt the man was unsuited to that position, which demanded moral courage and the ability to make difficult decisions, but when Mapai chose Sharett, Ben-Gurion did not oppose the decision. Lavon was less well liked in the party. Berl Katznelson once described him as a brilliant mind in a turbid soul. Some had warned Ben-Gurion not to appoint him minister of defense, but Ben-Gurion saw the man's talents while remaining blind to his shortcomings—an example of his inability to understand people.

Theoretically Ben-Gurion was no longer involved in affairs of state. He was a member of the Knesset, but told the cabinet secretary not to send him any material that was not circulated to all the Knesset members. Theory, however, is one thing and practice another. Every now and then Sharett and Lavon came to consult him. Moshe Dayan, the chief of the General Staff, and Shimon Peres, director general of the Ministry of Defense, also visited Ben-Gurion at Sdeh Boker to air their complaints and concerns about the behavior of Lavon, whom they had thought was dovish but was now a radical, irresponsible hawk. Ben-Gurion occasionally had an idea and directly approached the people in charge, from Dayan to the officials responsible for immigrant absorption, to talk to them about it. These were usually general consultations with no specific objectives.

None of this, however, fed his burning need to inspire a new pioneering impetus, an ardor that would sweep the younger generation along and enlist them in the great national mission. Some three months after settling in at Sdeh Boker, Ben-Gurion toyed with the notion of holding a mass meeting for senior high school students that would ignite in them the sacred flame

A daily walk in the desert, Ben Gurion at Sdeh Boker, 1959 (Photo by Vered Avraham, IDF Archive)

of pioneering fervor. He examined the idea with educators, including the minister of education Ben-Zion Dinur and high school principals, and the writer S. Yizhar. He also raised it with Mapai intellectuals. Everyone praised the idea, either because it was in line with movement tradition, or because they did not wish to offend Ben-Gurion. But objections soon followed. Left and right alike viewed it as an attempt by the former prime minister to dominate the cream of the country's youth and draw them into Mapai's orbit. Within Mapai, some expressed the fear that Ben-Gurion wanted to form a new party under his leadership. The plan was in fact a product of Ben-Gurion's naïveté. The assumption that he could generate human electricity by addressing eight thousand young people was yet another example of his inability to understand people. Yet the parties built a mountain of suspicion regarding the ulterior motives of this man sitting and weaving plots in Sdeh Boker. Nothing he suggested was taken at face value. But as was his habit when locked into an idea, Ben-Gurion looked neither left nor right but plowed straight on toward his objective, undeterred by his confidants' warnings not to give the parties a pretext for attacking him by using terms like "the youth front" or "the people's front."

The open-air gathering, organized by the ministry of education, took place on 10 June 1954 at Sheikh Munis, on the site where ten years later Tel Aviv University would be built. Ben-Gurion opened his address with the rousing slogan "Mission or Career?" and from then on everything went wrong. He was suffering a bout of back pain and came to the gathering from his bed, leaning heavily on a cane. The assembled young people did not show respect for the old man standing before them. His speech was long and laborious, and the slogans he spouted contained nothing new. What was more, the sound system did not work properly and his words were carried away by the wind, so that the audience heard only part of his speech. There was also political heckling from members of Hashomer Hatzair, who had been prepped beforehand and had no compunction about badgering the founder of the state. Overall the event felt like a failure, although sharp attacks from the press of both left and right against the idea of a general pioneering movement of youth (as opposed to the separate youth movements of each party) gave him some consolation that perhaps his words had been somewhat influential.

In contrast with the Sheikh Munis debacle, a more successful gathering of several hundred young people was held in Nahalal on the initiative of the chief of the General Staff, Moshe Dayan, who was a native son. About a hundred young people from the veteran moshavim decided to leave their homes and move to immigrant moshavim. Thus began a movement, modest but nonetheless important, of aid to the immigrant moshavim in accordance with Ben-Gurion's vision. But his hope that the personal example he set by moving to Sdeh Boker would draw thousands of young people to settle the Negev desert was never realized, nor did he generate the pioneering enthusiasm he had counted on.

Meanwhile, events were unfolding in Cairo that would lead to Ben-Gurion's return from exile. They centered around a distressing enterprise that in Israeli political jargon was called "the Dirty Business." A Jewish espionage ring initiated and run by Israel sabotaged American and British targets as a provocation to induce those powers to retain their troops in the Suez Canal zone. The ring was uncovered by the Egyptian authorities, and some of its members were sentenced to death, while others were given lengthy jail sentences. The Israeli officer who commanded the cell committed suicide in jail. It later emerged that one of the ring's commanders was a double agent who blew the whistle on it to the Egyptians. As usual with such failures,

Ben-Gurion at his study in Sdeh Boker, with Plato on the wall watching (IDF Archive)

those involved tried to deny their responsibility. Binyamin Gibli, chief of Israeli intelligence, claimed that he had acted on the orders of minister of defense Lavon, whereas Lavon denied giving the order to activate the cell and claimed that Gibli had falsely extracted the order from him after the event. In any case, even if Lavon did not directly issue the order, it was he who inspired the foolhardy atmosphere that allowed such an imprudent escapade to take place.

Sharett, a weak prime minister whom Lavon despised, formed the Olshan-Dori Commission of Inquiry to examine the affair. While the trial in Cairo was ongoing, Sharett was careful not to reveal Israeli involvement. Once it was over, the commission reported that it was unable to decide whether Lavon or Gibli had given the order. Sharett should have dismissed both of them, but found it too difficult. Lavon demanded that he dismiss Shimon Peres, who had testified before the commission in camera regarding Lavon's conduct. Sharett refused, and Lavon resigned in protest. In response to Lavon's resignation and the feud within the defense establishment that had been revealed, two veteran party members, Golda Meir (formerly Meyerson) and Mordechai Namir, asked Ben-Gurion to return to the defense ministry. Ben-Gurion was moved by their plea that "the movement needs you" and concerned about the stability of the defense establishment, the apple of his eye. In February 1955 he agreed to return. In all probability he was also bored at Sdeh Boker and sought new challenges. He was sixty-nine years old.

10

————◆◈◆————

Ben-Gurion Against Ben-Gurion

DESPITE A HEARTY WELCOME from all quarters, in retrospect it seems that Ben-Gurion's return marked the end of his
great days. He was now serving as minister of defense in Sharett's
government, a situation that led to tension and conflict.

Sharett, who was minister of foreign affairs as well as prime
minister, was an extremely talented man, fluent in several languages, well educated, polished in his speech, and meticulous
in his dress and behavior. He was also overly sensitive to any
offense, real or imagined, to his dignity. Ben-Gurion was his
opposite: always ready to break with convention. He disliked
all the trappings of government and dressed casually, preferring open-necked shirts to a suit and tie. His Hebrew was excellent, but his language was functional, less flowery than that
of Sharett, who compulsively corrected other people's Hebrew.
Ben-Gurion's English was adequate but could not compare
with Sharett's command of that language. Although Ben-Gurion

enjoyed perquisites such as a car and driver, it was not their ceremonial aspect that he appreciated but the ability to get anywhere fast. While he knew his own value, he was not conceited and did not keep his distance from people. One example of the differences between the two was Sharett's refusal to attend the Rangoon Conference in December 1952 with representatives of Asian nations that were freeing themselves from the yoke of European imperialism. His reason was that the delegates would be lower in rank than foreign ministers. All of Ben-Gurion's pleas that Sharett's attendance was of paramount importance were to no avail. The foreign minister maintained his dignity.

Despite these temperamental differences, the two had collaborated for twenty years. Sharett was cautious and moderate, Ben-Gurion daring and tempestuous. They agreed on the main issues but disagreed about specific important aspects of policy. During the War of Independence, Sharett only once joined the provisional government majority, in a vote against the prime minister's proposal to exploit a Jordanian breach of the ceasefire and extend Israel's control in the West Bank, a vote Ben-Gurion called "a loss that generations will weep over." In 1950 Sharett demanded that the government honor the U.N. Security Council resolution to internationalize Jerusalem. Ben-Gurion opposed this demand and defiantly moved the country's capital there. When Sharett's prophecies of doom following this act were not fulfilled, he tendered his resignation, but Ben-Gurion rejected it, saying that anyone could err. Sharett viewed Israel's foreign relations as vitally important and sought to subordinate what Ben-Gurion saw as defense considerations to diplomatic ones. But Ben-Gurion held a sober view of Israel as a small, weak country that neither Eastern nor Western powers wanted as an ally. Instead they wooed Israel's enemies, which constantly called for its destruction. Sharett pinned his hopes on obtaining arms from the United States, whose representatives dropped constant hints that this would happen that were

Ben-Gurion and the young commander Ariel Sharon, late 1950s (IDF Archive)

never followed through. Sharett also believed that the United Nations could impose its will on Israel. But ever since the U.N. had been unable to implement the 29 November resolution, Ben-Gurion had no hopes for help from that quarter, and had no fear of the U.N. either.

Ben-Gurion was extremely sensitive about the sovereignty of the State of Israel. He worried about American attempts to behave as if the new state were its satellite. Later, when Dag Hammarskjold became U.N. secretary general, he saw Hammarskjold's policy regarding the relations between Israel and its neighbors as an attempt to impose on Israel—and only on Israel—U.N.-sponsored international rule. He accused Hammarskjold of discrimination—that is, he allowed Gamal Abdel Nasser of Egypt to breach the 1949 armistice agreement but demanded that Israel observe it in every detail. Ben-Gurion was willing to challenge the United Nations, and to a lesser degree the United States, but to both he emphasized Israel's sovereignty and its right to defend itself. Sharett, however, believed in the righteousness of the international system. His main hope was that if Israel showed moderation it would gain increased legitimacy in a world that still did not consider it a solid political fact.

In practice the discussions between them regarding these issues focused on Israel's policy of retaliation after raids by *fedayeen*, or guerrilla infiltrators, which terrorized Israeli citizens. Not all of the reprisals were successful, and Sharett argued that Israel could try to lower their human cost to the Arabs, so as not to bring down on Israel the world's rage as well as increased Arab hostility. But Ben-Gurion insisted on Israel's sovereignty over every inch of land, and was prepared to attack in force if he thought that sovereignty was breached. Regarding the scope of the reprisals, he felt that because of the nature of military actions, it was impossible to forecast how they would end and the number of casualties.

The question of who was right, Ben-Gurion or Sharett, remains unresolved. On one hand, the reprisals increased tension in the Middle East, created a cycle of bloodshed, and probably did not deter the Egyptians. On the other, at that time the Arab states were not willing to accept the existence of Israel and halt the incursions. All of Sharett's skillful, extensive political activity yielded nothing, since during those years the interests of the Great Powers did not jibe with those of Israel. The reprisals were designed, among other things, to declare the state's presence and announce: this country will not permit its territory to be reduced (something Anthony Eden, with American support, had proposed), and will robustly stand up for its rights. At the same time, Ben-Gurion was concerned that if Israel attacked Jordan, a European power, Britain, might intervene. He had no territorial aspirations: "At this stage we are not short of territory, but of Jews. And conquest of additional territory will not add Jews, but Arabs," he wrote to a young man who proposed that he take the West Bank.[1]

Ben-Gurion ascribed Sharett's moderate approach to his psychological makeup and therefore opposed his appointment as prime minister. "He does not have the courage, the foresight, and the incisive understanding of complex political situations," he asserted.[2] "There are people," he explained to Teddy Kollek, "for whom avoidance of action (even when avoidance bears grave danger) is a safe way of avoiding all the difficulties and risks, and their logic provides them with ostensibly logical reasons for this avoidance." Such people, he claimed, "are afraid when not necessary, and are not afraid when necessary. They think that no risk is involved in inaction, and they are afraid of action, as if only it involves danger."[3] When Sharett became prime minister he sought to implement a moderate policy that placed foreign policy considerations above security ones, and the majority of the cabinet supported him. Ben-Gurion was taken by surprise, for he assumed that Sharett would continue Ben-Gurion's policies. But he resigned himself to Sharett's policy and withdrew from affairs of state.

When Ben-Gurion returned as minister of defense under Sharett's premiership, he did not act against him. Having Ben-Gurion subordinate to him heightened Sharett's self-esteem, and he began to think that as prime minister he was not inferior to Ben-Gurion. In fact, though, he valued himself far more than did those around him. He did not, like everyone else, take for granted that Ben-Gurion would become prime minister again after the elections at the end of 1955. To him, Mapai's willingness to accept that Ben-Gurion would be prime minister again if he wished to was a harsh, unjustified offense.

Once Ben-Gurion did return to the prime minister's office, he persuaded Sharett to continue as foreign minister, but the tension between them became intolerable. Twice Sharett, full of newfound arrogance, organized a majority against operational proposals by Ben-Gurion: to conquer the Gaza Strip and to take control of the Straits of Tiran in order to break the Egyptian blockade of the Gulf of Eilat. Most of Sharett's supporters were ministers from the coalition parties; most Mapai ministers voted with the prime minister. Ben-Gurion felt that Sharett was obstructing his policy, which he believed represented the will of the majority of Israelis.

Meanwhile, Nasser signed an arms deal with Czechoslovakia that dramatically altered the armaments balance in the Middle East, since Israel did not yet have a source for weapons. As chief of the General Staff, Dayan pushed for a preventive war. "In my opinion," he wrote to the defense minister, "we must initiate a major clash between our forces and the Egyptian army as soon as possible."[4] While Ben-Gurion feared a war, he also feared an Egyptian attack. He felt he needed freedom of action on the political-security front, and concluded that Sharett must go. In any other country, the prime minister's decision to relieve a minister of his duties is a routine matter, but in little Israel, where the ruling party had not yet freed itself of the familial intimacy of an earlier day, it was a dramatic act. Surprisingly, Ben-Gurion suffered pangs of conscience about firing his comrade, and instead of telling Sharett straight out that he wanted him to resign because of policy differences, he searched for a more indirect pretext. He also refrained from justifying this action in public so as not to damage Sharett's image, but the result was to increase the negative perception that he sought a government with a unanimous voice.

Years later, dovish Israeli historians cloaked Sharett in the mantle of a political martyr who fought against Ben-Gurion's belligerence and consequently lost the foreign ministry. Sharett himself did everything he could to appear as a selfless public servant fighting for his truth. Forgetting his incessant bickering over control of arms procurement (with Shimon Peres and

the ministry of defense), over control of the armistice commit-
tees (with Ben-Gurion and the IDF), and his petty arguments
about who was responsible for the success of a specific procurement, he saw himself as being ousted from a post that only
he was capable of filling. Consumed with infinite bitterness, he
attributed his dismissal to Ben-Gurion's evil-mindedness and
the breakdown in their personal relationship. He was incapable
of accepting Ben-Gurion's conclusion that the good of the state
required running the foreign ministry differently. When Ben-
Gurion's time of weakness arrived some years later, Sharett
would settle the score.

In 1956, in view of increasing Soviet influence over Nasser
after the arms deal, the United States reneged on a previously
stated intention to finance construction of the Aswan Dam in
Egypt. Nasser responded by nationalizing the Suez Canal, and
the events that led to the Suez operation and the Sinai Campaign (Operation Kadesh) began to unfold. Until that summer
Ben-Gurion had been torn between pressure from his chief of
staff, who urged waging a preventive war before Egypt was able
to fully absorb its new armaments, and his own fears regarding
the eastern front and the IDF's lack of up-to-date weaponry,
plus an overall worry about going into a war, which is always
unpredictable. In July 1956, Israel and France forged a secret
agreement. France was embroiled in a bloody war in Algeria,
and the French leadership was enraged by Nasser's support of
the rebels. The agreement was unofficial, but it yielded divi-
dends in the form of arms shipments that began arriving at Israeli ports, allowing Ben-Gurion to heave a sigh of relief. He
decided to postpone the decision on attacking Egypt until the
IDF had integrated the French arms.

The story of Israel's secret collusion with the two declining imperialist powers, France and Britain, which created the
conditions for the Sinai Campaign as a pretext for the Suez operation, has been told numerous times. And Dayan's slow, per-

sistent persuading of Ben-Gurion to waive his insistence that Israel would not be the one to start the war, that the British and not just the French would take part in the operation and at the same time prevent a Jordanian-Iraqi attack, and that the operation receive America's blessing, has also been documented. In the end, Israel made the first move, which provided the British and French with grounds for seizing the Canal Zone, without the Americans being briefed beforehand. Given that the two powers supplied arms and provided air cover to protect Israeli cities from an Egyptian attack during the campaign, in the end Ben-Gurion could not resist the opportunity to try to open the Straits of Tiran.

The day before the operation was launched, Ben-Gurion briefed the cabinet. He was under no illusions and assumed that Israel would not be able to hold on to the Sinai Peninsula after taking it. "Our primary interest is the Eilat coast and the Straits," he stated. He expected that a very broad coalition against Israel would be formed, and his main concern was the position of the United States. "I fear America more than the others, America will force us to withdraw" by cutting off the loan, the funds raised through the United Jewish Appeal, and diplomatic relations. For him the main issue was freedom of navigation, and he was prepared to give up everything else. The Gaza Strip was an embarrassing subject; under Egyptian rule, it was dangerously close to Israeli centers, but ruling hundreds of thousands of refugees was also a bad option. "If I believed in miracles I would want it to be swallowed up by the sea," he said.[5]

Ben-Gurion's realistic attitude was swept away amid the waves of enthusiasm among Israelis in response to the IDF's success in taking the entire Sinai Peninsula within a week. He talked of the Third Kingdom of Israel and bestowed Hebrew names on the Gulf of Suez islands, describing them as part of ancient Jewish heritage. A threatening letter from Soviet premier Nikolai Bulganin soon arrived. Ben-Gurion also learned that Eisenhower was in a rage, since the campaign had taken the Americans by surprise and damaged their pro-Arab policy in the Middle East. Ben-Gurion hesitated only briefly before ordering the IDF to withdraw from Sinai, but he held on to the Gaza Strip, Sharm el-Sheikh, and the Red Sea coastal strip leading to it. He was ready to fight for freedom of navigation to Eilat even at the price of American sanctions.

The British public, especially the intellectuals, was enraged by its government's involvement in a failed imperialist escapade. Isaiah Berlin, however, was amazed to find that he did not share his colleagues' moral indignation. In a letter to the American historian Arthur Schlesinger, Jr., he commented ironically: "I must either be very cynical, or else so heavily biased in favour of the Israelis that I reacted differently from other good and virtuous men, with whom I long wistfully to be associated."

He added a remarkable, though exaggerated sketch of Ben-Gurion: "I have a sneaking liking for Ben Gurion, but he is a dervish of the most unbridled kind whose central image is England in 1940, who prefers desperate situations in which he is with his back to the wall, defying all the storms of the world, dying in an agony of glory and violent resistance to everything and everybody, thus cancelling many centuries of humiliating Jewish history."[6]

For four months Ben-Gurion stood firm against brutal pressure exerted by the U.N. secretary general with American support—not to mention by the Eastern Bloc, which was united against Israel. Then in March 1957 a French-Canadian proposal appeared suggesting that the maritime powers ensure free passage to Eilat. The United States was supposed to support this proposal, but did not (at least in public), so Ben-Gurion did not get the public endorsement from the maritime powers that he sought. Instead he had to accept the stationing of U.N. forces in Sharm el-Sheikh and the Gaza Strip, a solution he could not refuse because it was supported by France, Israel's loyal ally and supplier of new aircraft. He did receive a vague secret letter from President Eisenhower stating, "Israel will have no cause to regret having thus conformed to the strong sentiment of the world community."[7] This letter was later revived during "the waiting period" prior to the Six-Day War, when another American president was asked to ensure freedom of passage for the Israelis.

In the final accounting, the Sinai Campaign gave Israel ten years of relative quiet, years that were vital for the country's development. Moreover, it established Israel as a fact in the Middle East that could no longer be ignored. From then on there were no more proposals like Eden's suggestion that the Negev be divided between Egypt and Jordan. Ben-Gurion became a figure with international stature. His gnomish image with its mane of white hair appeared on the covers of numerous weeklies. It was a time of tension, prestige, and achievement alike. The people of Israel supported their leader when he spoke of the Third Kingdom of Israel, and also when he decided to withdraw. When he appeared before the IDF command and explained the rationale behind the withdrawal, the officers were so moved by his words that, contrary to military protocol, they burst into applause when he finished.

In October 1957 a mentally unbalanced Jew threw a hand grenade in the Knesset. Ben-Gurion was wounded and almost killed. While he was in hospital another very painful incident occurred. His military aide, Colonel Nehemiah Argov, hit a cyclist while driving and, convinced he had killed the man—though in fact he had not—took his own life. Newspapers printed a special issue for Ben-Gurion, just so he would not have to read about Argov's death while recuperating. When the time came, Moshe Dayan was given the task of informing "the Old Man" of Argov's death, and Ben-Gurion was devastated. Contrary to his usual custom of keeping silent at times of grief, he eulogized Argov in the Knesset. Except for that incident, however, he did not show his feelings.

Ben-Gurion had difficulty expressing painful feelings. When one of his close associates was killed in an accident, he was unable to eulogize him or console his widow. When she reproached him for his silence, he replied, "There are moments when it is impossible to speak," explaining: "We talk about what we already overcame; maybe not everyone is like this, but I cannot talk about pain that I have not yet overcome." He gave the example of his silence after the death of Berl Katznelson, whom he described as "the dearest man in my life," and said that apart from being forced to speak about him during the shiva week of mourning, he was still unable to talk about him, "because in my heart the pain is as fresh and active as ten years ago."[8] He mourned Argov in private and, except for the eulogy, did not speak of him in public.

He found a partial cure for his back pain with the help of Moshe Feldenkrais, known as the man who stood Ben-Gurion on his head. The press was delighted by the sight of the prime minister enjoying his daily workout in swimming trunks on the Herzliya beach. After a fast walk and a dip in the sea, he even managed a headstand. Ben-Gurion did not worry that it was inappropriate for the prime minister to be seen this way, and in fact it was taken as an expression of his unpretentiousness and the absence of barriers between the leader and the people.

During the period of tension that preceded the withdrawal from Sinai, he found refuge in scholarly pursuits. He read Ye-hezkiel Kaufmann's *Golah venechar* (Exile and Estrangement) and held a heated debate with him in his diary. He had a riveting correspondence with Professor Nathan Rotenstreich, who did not accept his view that the Bible was the most important of all texts that connected the distant past of the Jews in their land with the present—passing over all the Jewish spiritual creativity between those two periods, including the Zionist period. Ben-Gurion saw the First Temple period as the primary inspiration for the youth of his time, supplemented by the messianic vision, which he perceived not in the traditional way as the end of history and the coming of the Messiah, but as a constant inspiration for world reform—something the Mizrachi Jews (immigrants from Muslim countries) could relate to, instead of Zionist theory, which did not speak to them.

Ben-Gurion was not a "Canaanite" (the Canaanism movement sought to create a local Israeli identity separate from Jewish history). The connection with the Jewish people was an inseparable part of his national concept. Nor did he deny the Jewish historical past. But he thought the Bible was the most important educational text for young people growing up in Israel who had no connection to the European past that gave birth to Zionism. He described Canaanism as "one of the expressions of conceit and nihilism which some of the youth have espoused."[9] The older he got, the stronger grew his connection with Plonsk, along with the repressed pain of its destruction, a metaphor of the annihilation of the Jewish people in the Holocaust. But as with other painful feelings, he expressed it only rarely.

In October 1958 he founded a Bible study circle that he hosted every other Saturday evening at the prime minister's residence. The country's leading Bible scholars attended, and Ben-Gurion constantly raised historical theories that some scholars considered fit for serious discussion, but others thought ludicrous. He caused a furor in the country with his assertions regarding the number of Israelites in the exodus from Egypt, the origins of the Hebrew people, and similar burning issues. In June 1957 he was visited by Professor Jacob Talmon, a leading Israeli historian. "He has the face of a Polish yeshiva student," Ben-Gurion remarked in his diary. They discussed the phenomenon of totalitarian democracy, a term Talmon had coined, and afterward Talmon suggested writing a biography of Ben-Gurion as the core story of the history of the Yishuv and the state. Ben-Gurion was willing to cooperate with him on condition that he would decide which material remained classified. In the end Talmon feared taking on the task under these terms.

There was a measure of schadenfreude in Ben-Gurion's correspondence with Major-General Eric Bols, the son of Major-General Louis Bols, who had served as the chief military administrator of Palestine in 1920, before Herbert Samuel was appointed high commissioner. Bols Senior was notorious for his hostility toward Zionism. His son, who badly needed money, sought to sell the Israeli state archive a famous receipt given Bols Senior by Samuel, which stated, "Received from Major-General Sir Louis J. Bols KCB—One Palestine, complete." The irony in this request from the son of the military ruler of Palestine, a confirmed anti-Zionist, for financial support from the Jewish state was no doubt not lost on Ben-Gurion. He agreed to the purchase, but when he realized that the asking price was relatively high, he settled for a photostat copy Bols had sent him. As we have seen, Ben-Gurion did not value first edition books or historical manuscripts in themselves and was interested only in the text itself.

In 1958, Israel celebrated its tenth anniversary, observing the numerous achievements of the decade. Naturally Ben-Gurion was the principal celebrant. But the sharp-eyed could see small clouds on the horizon, which while not directly signaling a storm suggested potential danger ahead. First, the public displayed a certain weariness with his fits of heroism. In a democracy, ten years of rule, with just a short break in the middle, is a very long term of office. Once the sense of emergency that accompanied the state's early years had passed, Ben-Gurion's authoritarianism no longer seemed appropriate. He once asked whether Mapai was democratic or autocratic, and Fritz Naphtali, one of the more polite Mapai leaders, replied, "Ben-Gurion, the movement

Change of the guard: Haim Laskov (right) replacing Moshe Dayan as chief of the General Staff (IDF Archive)

accepts everything you suggest in the most democratic way."[10] How much longer could this system last?

Second, Ben-Gurion was not able to rejuvenate his party. Mapai had become a political machine, and he did not fight this corruptive trend. He was quite happy to have party activists manage elections and bring voters to the polling stations, while he exerted his tremendous prestige as the tailwind that would ensure success at the polls, meanwhile getting involved only in matters that interested him. The activists closed ranks and prevented both the Mizrachi newcomers and the country's younger generation from making their way into the leadership. Ben-Gurion had great things in mind for several of these younger people, especially Dayan, when he retired as IDF chief of staff, and Shimon Peres, director general of the ministry of defense and the architect of Israel's relations with France. Giora

Josephthal, who was of German extraction and excelled in socioeconomic issues, was third in line. Abba Eban, a talented man who played an outstanding role as Israel's ambassador to the United States, was about to complete his term of office. Ben-Gurion wanted to include them in Mapai's list of candidates for the 1959 election, but encountered fierce opposition from the party's old guard: Ziama (Zalman) Aranne, Mordechai Namir, Golda Meir, and Pinchas Lavon.

The opposition focused primarily on Dayan and Peres, two insolent young men convinced they were destined for greatness, who relied on the founding father's support. Dayan, the younger generation's leader, was dismissive toward the party activists, who in turn were fiercely hostile toward him. They were apparently afraid that Dayan, basking in the glory of his victory in the Sinai Campaign, might attempt a putsch. In December 1958, the veterans were enraged when "the youngsters" held a gathering at the Kfar Hayarok Agricultural School with the support of circles in the party that were disenchanted with its machine character. At the concluding session, attended by the party's entire leadership, Ben-Gurion chose to praise the youngsters, infuriating Golda Meir, who announced that she would refuse to assume any post whatsoever after the election. Ben-Gurion was stunned; he had never imagined a schism opening up between him and the veterans.

Still, these were just small clouds in the distance. In 1959 Mapai, which went into the election campaign for the Fourth Knesset with the slogan "Hagidu ken lazaken" (Say Yes to the Old Man), won forty-seven seats, the highest number ever. Despite her bitterness, Meir joined the government as foreign minister. On 23 May 1960 the entire nation was galvanized by Ben-Gurion's dramatic announcement to the Knesset that the Nazi war criminal Adolf Eichmann had been captured and brought to Israel to stand trial. Although the Argentine government was outraged by the kidnapping of its citizen, the vast majority of Israelis and the Jewish people saw this as an act of historic justice—a small and belated consolation for the annihilation of the Jewish people, which to that moment had never been raised as a specific issue in any international legal forum.

A few months earlier, Ben-Gurion and German chancellor Konrad Adenauer had held a historic meeting at New York's Waldorf Astoria Hotel. "It was a meeting whose like is staged by history once in hundreds of years," reported *Ma'ariv* about this encounter between the leader of the nation of the murderers and the leader of the nation of their victims.[11] Ben-Gurion sought to secure German economic and military aid to Israel after the reparations agreement ended, and Adenauer obliged. Since 1952, Ben-Gurion had promoted the concept of "a different Germany," meaning that the German people should not have to bear the Nazis' guilt forever. West Germany, which had risen from the devastation of the world war, was no longer Nazi Germany. Vainly the Israeli left fulminated against this idea, since part of their myth had been built on the heroism of the ghetto fighters and the Jewish partisans. What was more, West Germany was an ally of the West, which they loathed. So did the right, since hatred of Amalek, as the Nazis came to be known for seeking to destroy the Jewish people, was an inseparable part of their ideology.

Nevertheless Ben-Gurion continued to develop relations with West Germany. Whenever an agreement for the Germans to supply arms to Israel, or a sale of Israeli arms to the Germans, was revealed, the left would declare no-confidence in the government and cause the dissolution of the coalition. But Ben-Gurion, an inveterate pragmatist, saw Germany for what it was—a rising power in Europe—and felt that beggars like the Israelis could not afford to be choosers in their quest for armaments and other resources. As usual, he cloaked these pragmatic considerations in a mantle of ideology, and the term "a different Germany" expressed the notion that one should not

West German chancellor Konrad Adenauer (seated) visiting Ben-Gurion in Sdeh Boker, early 1960s (Collection of Ben-Gurion House, Tel Aviv)

accuse those who were not Nazis of the Nazis' crimes. His assertions sometimes went too far. "Whoever says that there is no difference between the Hitler regime and that of Adenauer or Erhard—a sense of racism rises from his words," he wrote to one of his correspondents.[12] For many who objected to his policy of conciliation with a democratic Germany, the capture and trial in Israel of Eichmann helped even the balance between pragmatism and memory.

There were Jews and non-Jews alike, in Israel and abroad, who felt that since Israel did not exist when the atrocities were committed it had no right to bring charges against Eichmann. Such people believed variously that Israel should hand him over to be tried in Germany; establish an international court and try him before all the nations that had suffered at Nazi hands; or even be merciful and pardon the murderer. Jews like Nachum

Goldmann who made such suggestions enraged Ben-Gurion. Former AJC president Justice Proskauer sent Ben-Gurion a particularly vexatious letter that revealed a profound lapse in his understanding of this issue. Proskauer worried that the trial would lead to a flare-up of anti-Semitism and hostility toward Israel in the United States, which would jeopardize the efforts to get American weapons for Israel. And in the end, he wrote, "What do you gain by it? Talking with [Israel's ambassador to the U.N. Michael] Comay the other night he spoke of the great emotional urge to try this wrongdoer. That emotional urge is not a valid reason for taking a false public relations step."[13] He proposed delivering Eichmann to the West German justice system, which was notorious for letting Nazi criminals walk free, or to an international tribunal.

Ben-Gurion answered him patiently and at length, explaining that until the establishment of Israel, there was no entity that could take legal action against murderers of the six million. Those millions were killed because they were Jews, which was also how they saw themselves; and the State of Israel, which considered itself the heir of those millions who had laid its foundations and hoped for its creation, was obliged to bring their murderers to justice. He rejected Proskauer's fears of provoking anti-Semitism. Yes, he acknowledged, there were anti-Israel politicians, such as J. William Fulbright of the U.S. Senate, or Jews who hated Israel, such as Lessing Rosenwald, the chairman of the anti-Zionist American Council for Judaism, but they did not represent the American people as a whole. In general, the people of Europe supported prosecuting Eichmann in Israel, and Germany was even helping with documentation. "You ask: what do we gain—nothing, but we do our historical duty, and our duty toward the six million of our brethren that were murdered. We are not allowed to give up this duty, otherwise we won't deserve being who we are."[14] Proskauer was unconvinced, but replied, "I recognize in your viewpoint the profound emotion which is of a kind that often overwhelms the more sharply reasoned approach that prompted my letter."[15]

The Eichmann trial was also intended to tell the story of the Holocaust to the young people who had grown up in Palestine and later Israel. The majority of the country's Jewish population did not in fact know the full story. The Jews from the Middle Eastern countries were only barely aware of it. Those from Europe were intensely aware, but many kept silent, either because it was so painful or because they felt people did not want to hear about such things. Until the trial, the Palmach generation and the younger generation thought of the Holocaust as something that had happened in another place, at another time, to other people. Thus Ben-Gurion's belief that the youth must be told the story of the Holocaust was well founded. Starting in the 1970s, when the Holocaust became one of the main components of Jewish and Israeli identity, it was turned into a weapon to attack Ben-Gurion's memory through accusations that he had not been concerned about the Jewish people during the Holocaust and had not come to its rescue. Even now such assertions occasionally resurface in Israeli popular media.

This claim first appeared in the 1940s as a general accusation by the Etzel against the Zionist Executive, but it ignored the extremely limited capacity of the Yishuv at the time and the powers at the disposal of its leadership under Mandate rule during the war. The accusation found support in Ben-Gurion's own statement that during World War II he was preoccupied with establishing the state, and that rescue was in the hands of others. Since then researchers have shown that he was in fact fully aware of every detail, action, and failure related to the question of rescue. But his public restraint on this painful topic made it easy to attack him as a man oblivious to the pain of the Jewish people.

At the same time, it was difficult to fit the Eichmann trial into this narrative. If Ben-Gurion had indeed been indifferent toward the fate of the Jews in the Holocaust, why did he want to stage a dramatic trial that would present that harsh story to the nation? Like Hannah Arendt, these critics argue that it was a show trial whose every detail was determined by Ben-Gurion, presenting the genocide against the Jews as if it were unique— even though the Nazis planned to annihilate other peoples as well. All sorts of claims like this were aimed at diverting attention from the inherent contradiction between the narrative of Ben-Gurion's indifference and the importance he attributed to the trial. His intention in bringing Eichmann to Israel and trying him publicly there was not to punish the murderer to the full extent of the law—for there was no punishment that could match the enormity of the crime—"but to unfold the canvas of the atrocities and evil plots of the Nazi regime against our people."[16] For the first time testimonies by survivors brought the story of the Holocaust into every Israeli home, making it personal, close, and intimate, a part of the Israeli national experience. The trial constituted a public trauma and catharsis, and its impact on Israeli public opinion was far greater than even Ben-Gurion had expected.

It should have been the zenith of the Ben-Gurion era. Mapai won the 1959 general election, and in March 1960 he went to the United States. Although it was not an official visit, he received an extremely warm welcome from both Congress and the presidential candidates. The Israeli press reported the visit as an unqualified success that increased Israel's prestige. Ben-Gurion's subsequent visit to Paris also added to his credit; the French loved seeing him browsing at the book stands along the Seine. Later that year, Eichmann's capture garnered headlines all over the world and won Ben-Gurion points in world opinion as the flag-bearer of historical justice.

This high standing, which seemed unassailable, was shattered in one fell swoop in October 1960, never to be restored. The story began when falsifications were discovered in certain

Ben-Gurion with French president Charles de Gaulle, 1960 (Collection of Ben-Gurion House, Tel Aviv)

documents submitted to the Olshan-Dori Commission, which had been unable to decide whether Gibli or Lavon had been responsible for "the Dirty Business" espionage fiasco. Ben-Gurion saw the whole episode as a mare's nest for which guilt could not be assigned. He supported Lavon's appointment to the very powerful position of Histadrut general secretary, and although he removed Gibli from his post as head of military intelligence, he did not demand that Gibli resign from the army. When it emerged that documents had been falsified, Lavon went to Ben-Gurion and demanded that he publicly clear his name of any wrongdoing. Ben-Gurion replied that he had not accused him, but he could not clear him since that would be construed as accusing Gibli. Only a judicial hearing could do that. For his own reasons Lavon did not want a judicial hearing. He threatened to take the matter to the Knesset's foreign affairs and defense committee, a political body whose members were party representatives, then made good on this threat at four committee sessions in the second half of October 1960. His testimony changed Israeli public discourse for all time.

Lavon painted a picture of subversion and plotting by people at the defense ministry, led by Shimon Peres, to depose him and bring Ben-Gurion back from Sdeh Boker. According to Lavon, the threads of the web ran from Sdeh Boker to the defense ministry, bypassing Lavon. Although he did not say so categorically, he created the impression that both the defense ministry and the IDF, with Ben-Gurion's knowledge and support, were engaged in adventures that Lavon, as defense minister, had not approved. The practice by various ministers and even Prime Minister Sharett of occasionally consulting Ben-Gurion in Sdeh Boker, on either his initiative or theirs—and especially the reports to Ben-Gurion by the heads of the defense establishment of their concerns regarding Lavon's conduct—now took on the sinister aspect of subversive activities by the defense establishment against Lavon. The allegation that Lavon gave the order for "the Dirty Business" was presented as part of a series of actions aimed at damaging his status and returning "the exile" from Sdeh Boker. The testimony created the impression that an innocent man was being hounded by a corrupt, bellicose establishment led by Ben-Gurion. The opposition parties had a field day. The committee's discussions were leaked to the press, the vast majority of which swiftly sided with Lavon. Some were motivated by hatred of Ben-Gurion and fear of the ambitions of those whom *Ha'olam Hazeh* labeled "Ben-Gurion's boys," while others were simply delighted by the scandal and the opportunity to watch "the twilight of the Gods."

More than anything, the behavior of Ben-Gurion and the Mapai leadership over the next few months reflects a weakening in him, a lack of resolve, and sheer amazement at what was happening around him. The opposition from the right, and even coalition members from the left, seized the moment to settle scores with Ben-Gurion. Nor did Mapai, led by Levi Eshkol, Golda Meir, and Zalman Aranne, rush to aid the besieged prime minister. Ben-Gurion responded angrily to Lavon's allegations, announced that he would refuse to sit in the same party with him, and demanded the establishment of a judicial commission of inquiry that would fully clear up both what happened in 1954 and Lavon's allegations against himself. But to the Mapai leaders such a commission seemed dangerous. Eshkol said it was "a Pandora's box," while Moshe Sharett called it "a mass grave." They feared that a judicial hearing would expose dubious acts that could be interpreted as violating the rules of governance, leaving the party open to accusations. They also liked the fact that Lavon's allegations had clipped the wings of "the youngsters," especially Dayan and Peres, by depicting Peres as duplicitous and implicating Dayan as well. They tried to persuade Ben-Gurion to forget the whole thing, go back to business as usual, and hope that the media frenzy would abate.

But Ben-Gurion refused. He had been accused of undermining proper governance while in Sdeh Boker, and of adventurous escapades while still in office. The defense establishment and the IDF, Ben-Gurion's crowning achievement and very dear to him, were being publicly defamed and scorned. Although he was not afraid of a judicial commission of inquiry, just to be on the safe side he checked whether there might be anything whose exposure Dayan feared. The only thing Dayan said he could be accused of was having approached Ben-Gurion directly, bypassing Prime Minister Sharett, when he was concerned about Lavon's adventurism. But he had already testified about this to the Olshan-Dori Commission, and had no further skeletons in his closet.

To ease the tension Eshkol, the party conciliator, proposed a seven-man ministerial committee to examine whether a judicial commission was necessary. Ben-Gurion opposed this proposal but did not veto it. His line was that he wanted no part of this business. It was a weak position that greatly embarrassed his supporters in the party, while reinforcing Eshkol and his colleagues who thought the Old Man would accept the committee's findings. Perhaps he might have, if the committee's conclusions had not completely exonerated Lavon. Given this finding, and the fact that the committee had not hesitated to hand down a verdict in a judicial matter, Ben-Gurion announced that he was taking a vacation, and that when he returned on 13 January 1961, he would resign.

He did not resign on the spot for two reasons: the Zionist Congress was being held in Jerusalem, and there was a crisis in Israel-U.S. relations because the Eisenhower administration had published information about Israel's development of a nuclear capability. In December 1960 the administration realized that the large facility under construction in the Negev, not far from Dimona, was apparently a secret nuclear reactor that Israel was building in addition to the research reactor intended for peaceful uses that was under construction, with U.S. support, in Nahal Soreq.

Ever since the establishment of the state, Ben-Gurion had been interested in nuclear energy. The vast population gap between Israel and its neighbors, together with their constant threats, led him to believe that only by maintaining a scientific and technological advantage over them could the imbalance be redressed. The first stage in developing Israel's nuclear program was to send talented young people to study nuclear physics at prestigious research centers in the United States and Europe. The second stage came with a one-time opportunity, after the Sinai Campaign, to collaborate with the French, who provided the know-how and technology to bring the reactor being built in Dimona to nuclear capability. This close cooperation ended with Charles de Gaulle's rise to power in 1958. He did, however, permit French firms to continue providing the Israelis with equipment according to existing contracts, making it possible to complete the reactor. Only a few ministers, including Sharett and the minister of finance, were privy to the project, which apparently was not discussed by the cabinet. The project was partly financed by the defense ministry budget, and largely by funds that Ben-Gurion raised using the Sonneborn Foundation method.

Now, at the height of the Lavon Affair, Israel's nuclear capability became a serious bone of contention with the U.S. administration, which was resolved not to allow the proliferation of nuclear weapons. In the second half of December 1960 the United States demanded explanations from Ben-Gurion about the reactor that had been discovered in the Negev. On 21 December he made a statement in the Knesset about the reactor, explaining that its objectives were research for development of the Negev, water desalination, inexpensive energy, and so forth. Ben-Gurion, the flag bearer for ethics and integrity in the state's internal relations, did not bat an eyelid over lying for "raisons d'état." The Israeli press published items about the project, but far fewer than expected, since it and the public were preoccupied by the Lavon Affair. There had been a temporary respite while the ministerial committee deliberated, leading to hopes that the affair would soon disappear from the public agenda. However, once the Zionist Congress ended, and the U.S. administration shifted to quiet diplomacy, so that Israel's nuclear capability was no longer in the headlines, Ben-Gurion announced his resignation in reaction to the government's unprincipled approval of the findings of the ministerial committee, which had no authority to rule on a judicial matter.

At this point events spun out of control. The public perceived Ben-Gurion's resignation as blackmail designed to impose his will on his colleagues, who were loath to bend to it. The media depicted Lavon as a martyr being hounded by Ben-Gurion, a lone figure fighting for the rightness of his cause against the regime and the army. A large group of eminent professors at the Hebrew University signed a letter of protest against Ben-Gurion, whom they saw as a man with dictatorial tendencies who forced his government colleagues to do his will.

The resignation was depicted as an unfair weapon in the political struggle. One journalist wrote in vain that it was Ben-Gurion's prerogative to use this weapon, and the prerogative of his government colleagues, if they were not satisfied with him, to accept his resignation. This position was rejected on the grounds that it ignored Ben-Gurion's special status. Martin Buber explained that in his capacity as a great historical figure, Ben-Gurion should humbly accept his opponents' opinion. Buber, Rotenstreich, and Talmon, Ben-Gurion's erstwhile interlocutors, now joined ranks against him. He always claimed that neither praise nor denigration had any effect on him; Golda Meir remarked that he gave his colleagues the feeling that he did not need any of them. But in truth he was extremely hurt by the vicious attacks in the press on him and his confidants, and even more so by the manifestos and letters by academics that had a powerful effect on public opinion. He clipped the articles attacking him, and if their writers were important to him, he responded. Thus while he ignored the defamatory articles published in *Ha'olam Hazeh*, the positions of Buber, Efraim Elimelech Auerbach (an eminent professor of Jewish studies), and their colleagues struck at the very foundation of his self-image. He retaliated by telling Buber that he was resigning from the Committee for the Translation of World Masterworks into

Hebrew, a pathetic reaction that shows the distance between the actual man and the menacing image of a dictator that was being propagated.

The members of his party, his government, his supporters and admirers, began sending him pleas to get down from his high horse of resignation and allow the affair to sink into the recesses of national memory. But Ben-Gurion could not do so. Even Lavon's dismissal from his position in the Histadrut, at Eshkol's initiative, which whipped up a storm in Israel generally and in the party in particular—intensifying hostility toward Ben-Gurion—did not pacify him. The country went to the polls again, and in November 1961 Ben-Gurion formed his last government, with the Mapai seats in the Knesset down from forty-seven to forty-two. He continued to demand a judicial commission of inquiry, claiming that it was impossible to clear one party without a judicial hearing, since that meant automatically finding the other party guilty, and that the government had encroached unforgivably on the judicial branch.

The vote by the Mapai Central Committee to dismiss Lavon from his Histadrut post showed that approximately a third of the party leadership supported Lavon, including a large group of intellectuals. Some truly believed that an innocent man who had set out to clear his name had been treated unjustly; others were angry with Ben-Gurion for disregarding the party's needs and being prepared to bring it to the brink of a split; still others were irked by his intention to promote "the youngsters," the doers, at the expense of the idealistic ideologues of days gone by. Against Ben-Gurion's wishes, they sought to strengthen the socialist-workers camp at the expense of the "étatists," who prioritized the state over the social institutions within it.

As in his struggle against Weizmann during World War II, he was right on the issues, but the struggle was destructive. Just as getting rid of Weizmann during the war could only result in setting all his comrades against him, even though his claims were justified, now his obsession with setting up a judicial commission of inquiry increasingly isolated him both in his party and in the government. He also lost prestige among broad segments of the public. His struggle with Weizmann had been arrested by his party comrades, led by Berl Katznelson. Now there was no one whose authority Ben-Gurion was willing to accept, and he dragged himself, his party, his government, and the people into dizzying, unbridled confusion. All of the qualities that had made him a leader—his resolve, stubbornness, polemic ability, ability to stand on principles, and total identification of his personal interests with those of the nation—now hardened into obsessiveness. The Israeli people had had enough of reading about the Lavon Affair, which interested only a few. But Ben-Gurion, who had been sensitive to the people's feelings, was now suddenly impervious to voices from the grassroots, to requests from dignitaries and simple folk alike who sent him hundreds, if not thousands, of letters begging him to let go of this business that they were sick and tired of. All in vain. Like Michael Kohlhaas in Heinrich von Kleist's nineteenth-century novella, who in his quest for justice destroyed an entire country, Ben-Gurion paid no heed to what he was bringing down in his attempt to achieve justice.

During his last eighteen months in office he went to meet President John F. Kennedy (not on an official state visit, something not granted to an Israeli prime minister until the Johnson administration). When in 1963 he tried to meet with Kennedy again, the president politely but firmly refused. The American president had harassed him with demands for full transparency on the Dimona nuclear reactor, but Ben-Gurion somehow managed to allow American representatives to visit the site while concealing from them what was actually happening there in order to prevent a deterioration in relations with the United States.

On 15 June 1963, Ben-Gurion announced his final resignation from the office of prime minister. He was going to Sdeh Boker to write the history of the establishment of the state so that young people would learn about the past and not think of the State of Israel as a self-evident phenomenon. This time his retirement to Sdeh Boker did not create a public storm. In fact, the public felt the time had come to replace him. Still, in certain circles, tears were shed. At a farewell party held in the general staff garden by the IDF high command, Ben-Gurion responded to the parting speeches in a voice trembling with emotion. One of the officers present wrote in a letter, "I was sitting with arch-cynics from Arik [Ariel] Sharon's band . . . I swear to you that every last one of those manly men was choked with tears. . . . I saw how that little man grew in stature as a giant of the spirit and emotions, and how all the rest, without exception, were dwarfed by him."[17] In one of his final acts he informed his successor, Eshkol, that he had promised to appoint Yitzhak Rabin chief of the general staff. He also asked Rabin to give a second chance to Sharon, a brilliant field officer whose promotion had been put on hold. That was his swan song.

11

Decline

For a leader, longevity is not a blessing. The peak of his achievement is behind him, and before him are only days of decline. On a personal level, the last decade of Ben-Gurion's life was one of pitiful deterioration as old age, increasing loneliness, sickness, and feebleness all set in. In the public realm, this formerly all-powerful figure was reduced to a symbol, important but without political clout, like Weizmann in the twilight of his life.

Levi Eshkol, who replaced Ben-Gurion as prime minister, instituted a policy designed to calm and conciliate the nation after the stormy Ben-Gurion years. He sought first to restore unity in Mapai by appeasing the Min Hayesod (Back to Basics) faction. These were Lavon supporters who had remained in Mapai but founded their own journal and had their own intra-party group, which threatened a split unless their leader was somehow rehabilitated. Eshkol drafted a personal letter to the

Min Hayesod group announcing that Lavon's dismissal was a thing of the past, and he could now return to party activity. In addition, as a first step toward bringing Akhdut Ha'avoda back into the fold and reuniting the party with the faction that had left it in 1944, he founded the Ma'arach (Alignment). In order to do this, he removed from the Mapai agenda one of the issues closest to Ben-Gurion's heart: changing the electoral system to majority representation, which Akhdut Ha'avoda feared would damage it in elections. Akhdut Ha'avoda and the Lavon supporters belonged to different cultural and political milieus. The first was right-wing in politics and left-wing on social and economic issues, while the second were dovish politically and tended toward free-market policies economically. Their common ground was resentment of Ben-Gurion and opposition to the advancement of his protégés.

The alliance between Lavon's followers and Akhdut Ha'avoda was perceived as blocking the advancement of the "youngsters," so Ben-Gurion embarked on a new battle. Disregarding the appeals of his trusted comrades and confidants, he set a course for a head-on collision with his successor. The vast majority of the population supported Eshkol and saw Ben-Gurion as an embittered old man who could not accept his own retirement. A memorable cartoon by Dosh (Kariel Gardosh), which portrayed Ben-Gurion smashing his own monument, expressed how he was destroying his public image.

Before the general election for the Sixth Knesset on 2 November 1965, the Mapai tribunal (the party's internal judicial body) charged Ben-Gurion with making defamatory remarks against the party and its leaders. He thereupon left Mapai and formed a new party, Reshimat Poalei Yisrael (Israel Workers List, known by its Hebrew acronym, Rafi). He and his comrades were attacked as "neo-fascists"—a deadly insult at the time, usually reserved for Begin and other right-wingers. Rafi won ten seats in the Knesset, while the Ma'arach won forty-five, since the majority of Mapai voters remained loyal to the party. For the founder of the state and its undisputed leader, this was a stinging slap in the face.

The next few years were not good for Ben-Gurion. He did not stop trying to defame Eshkol, and in the end his old comrades broke off relations with him. He tried but failed to reestablish a dialogue with Golda Meir—she was not the forgiving kind. He sat in Sdeh Boker trying to write his version of the history of the establishment of the state. On his desk lay the memoirs of Churchill and of de Gaulle, a statesman Ben-Gurion had come to admire for his courageous policy on Algeria. But he was incapable of writing a story. Apart from memories of his Plonsk days and of the Second Aliya, about which he had already spoken and written several times, he did not weave a narrative but simply collected random documents he found in his archive and inserted them in his text without explanation or evaluation. He hoped that through this book, which he called *Memoirs*, he could bring the saga of the establishment of the state to the younger generation, but in fact there was absolutely no chance that those young people would read it. Ben-Gurion lacked the literary talent to write a memoir. Two biographers he cooperated with, Michael Bar-Zohar and Shabtai Teveth, did work far superior to his. Their books are required reading for research on Ben-Gurion to this day.

In order to write his memoirs, Ben-Gurion approached Golda Meir, who at the time was general secretary of the party, and asked her permission to go through the minutes of the Mapai institutions from the 1930s to the 1950s. She agreed only to let him study the parts of the minutes that quoted him, but not his comrades. It was as if the present hostility between him and Mapai was projected into the past. He also asked his old love Miriam Taub (formerly Cohen), with whom he still corresponded, to locate for him in the Zionist Archive in New York those documents that touched upon his activity in the United

States. She eagerly consented, while expressing the hope that "purely personal letters have been destroyed, so that they do not fall into the wrong hands at any point."[1] Their correspondence over the years included ritual statements whereby her husband sent his regards to Ben-Gurion, and Miriam sent her greetings to Paula. But in one letter she explained that "letters leave so much more unsaid than said, that sometimes I think one should write them only when very young—before one has learned all the things not to say."[2]

In 1966, Ben-Gurion turned eighty, and a group of his followers sought to mark the event with a celebration in Sdeh Boker that would be worthy of the founder of the state. Oved Ben-Ami, a right-winger who built the city of Netanya and was a great admirer of Ben-Gurion, undertook to organize the main event. He asked President Zalman Shazar to head the anniversary committee, and Shazar agreed. Then the petty arm-twisting began. The defense ministry, headed by Eshkol, would not help organize the ceremony. Eshkol and Meir pressured Shazar to withdraw as chairman of the committee, and Shazar acquiesced. Only after a concerted effort did Ben-Ami persuade him to continue in the position, but on condition that the ceremony would be private and he would not have to deliver an address. On the eve of the ceremony the defense ministry refused to put a helicopter at the president's disposal to fly him to Sdeh Boker. According to Ben-Ami, only after he threatened to give the story to the press did the ministry relent. Knowing nothing of all these machinations, Ben-Gurion went out in 104-degree heat to welcome the president. The ceremony was modest, with about fifty people present who waxed nostalgic and drank a toast. The prime minister did not attend.

In contrast with the leadership's peevishness toward "the Old Man's" eightieth birthday, it was marked by popular celebrations all over the country. Ben-Gurion and the professors who had battled him were reconciled. Professor S. H. Bergmann sent a warm letter reminiscing about the publication of the masterworks. Ben-Gurion replied cordially, expressing his sorrow over Buber's passing: "I did not always accept his opinions, but always admired him for his spirit that embraced the entire world."[3] He corresponded with Gershom Scholem and discussed "the heroes of history." Ben-Gurion held—or so he said—that history was made as a collective enterprise by multitudes, not by individuals. He thought that Kabbalah was a "mixture of nonsense and lofty ideas," but looked forward to reading the next volume of Scholem's biography of Shabtai Zvi.[4] He also maintained a friendly correspondence with Jacob Talmon and invited him to visit him in Sdeh Boker, an invitation Talmon accepted gladly.[5]

The eve of the Six-Day War seemed to offer "the Old Man" a brief comeback. Chief of the General Staff Rabin, torn between a dithering cabinet and a general staff spoiling for a fight, came to consult him. But instead of encouraging Rabin, Ben-Gurion sharply reprimanded him for mobilizing the reserves and putting Israel in a critical situation in which it would be forced to go to war without an ally. During "the waiting period," articles appeared in the press—including *Ma'ariv*, a daily that had openly supported Lavon—calling for Ben-Gurion's return to government. His arch-rival Menachem Begin came to see him in secret and proposed that he return to the premiership. This historic reconciliation did not return Ben-Gurion to the government, but it changed the face of Israeli politics by legitimizing the Likud party, which Begin founded. At a critical moment people needed the sense of security imparted by the little man with the metallic voice, who was always ready to throw down the gauntlet to all of Israel's enemies. But the eighty-one-year-old Ben-Gurion was no longer that man. He was pleased when Dayan was invited to serve as minister of defense, but he no longer had anything to say on these matters. In Michael

Bar-Zohar's view, the Six-Day War in 1967 marked the end of the Ben-Gurion era.

After the swift Israeli victory in the war, he called for rapid settlement of Jerusalem's environs, and after touring the Golan Heights and observing the Jordan Valley from them, he said they too should be annexed to Israel. Except for Jerusalem and the Golan Heights, though, he was ready to return the rest of the occupied territories in exchange for peace. Because he wanted to preserve Israel's character as a Jewish state and feared that the country would be inundated by Arab workers, he consistently opposed annexation of territories. Although he sometimes deviated from this line—he talked about Jewish settlement in Hebron, for example, though not about annexing it—his position was, and remained, that peace was more important than territory, and his principal concern was maintaining a massive Jewish majority in the country. Since the establishment of the state, and perhaps even since the 1930s, Ben-Gurion had not believed in the possibility of Jewish-Arab peace in his time. But now he felt that the Jews had something to offer the Arabs in exchange for peace, and therefore peace must be Israel's strategic objective.

Paula passed away in 1968, and a huge void opened up in his life. She was neither an intellectual nor even an emotional partner for him; her interests were those of a middle-class housewife, a caring mother raising her children and zealously protecting her husband while keeping troublesome people away from him, including any she did not like. She had a sharp eye and a far greater understanding of people than her husband, who dwelt in other spheres. Her vocation was taking care of Ben-Gurion: ensuring that he ate healthy food, got a good night's sleep, and was neatly dressed. He needed her presence, but it is extremely doubtful that they had much to talk about. Whenever she traveled to Tel Aviv from Sdeh Boker, he sent her telegrams filled with yearning and wishing for her return. Her death left the wooden cottage feeling empty. He sank into depression and spoke little, except to his bodyguards, his secretary, and Yehoshua Cohen, a kibbutz member and former terrorist (member of Lehi) with whom he became friendly. His inability to make small talk was now more notable than ever—he could not chat with people he met in the kibbutz dining hall. When his grandson asked why he continued to eat Paula's tasteless "kutch-mutch," he replied that it was out of respect for her memory. He was very moved when the Beersheba School of Nursing was named after her, seeing this as a mark of esteem for her noble act of following him to the wilderness, to a land not sown.

As his loneliness became harder to bear, he tried to persuade Miriam Taub to come for a visit, even though she explained that her husband was sick and unable to travel to Israel. In rather wooden English, he wrote, "I need not thank you for a letter—I keep it."[6] Occasionally he talked of the three friends he had had in his life, though their identities tended to change. The only constant one was Berl Katznelson. The others were Shlomo Lavie from Plonsk, Shmuel Yavne'eli, and Yitzhak Ben-Zvi, all members of the Second Aliya who died before 1964. He sought to revive his friendship with Shlomo Zemach, who was not one of his admirers and had opposed the Biltmore Program and even the establishment of the state. "There can be no doubt that the comradeship and youthful love like that between David and me are never lost. On the contrary, in old age one returns to them and holds onto them heart and soul," Zemach wrote in his diary.[7] Over the next few years their relationship had its ups and downs, but the connecting thread remained unbroken. Their memories of Plonsk were the glue between them, and Ben-Gurion persuaded Zemach to write a chapter for the town's commemorative volume. Zemach explained that he found it hard to write about Plonsk, because his grief over his three sisters, who had been incinerated, would not leave him until his dying day. He also told Ben-Gurion that he dreamed a great deal about the town, the Jewish school, and his father's house, but whereas in the past he had dreamed about them in Hebrew, since the Holocaust all the people in his dreams spoke Yiddish.[8]

This story brings to light some of the hidden pain borne by the founding fathers' generation, who yearned for the home, family, and town they had left behind, of which nothing remained. In the end Zemach did write about Plonsk, and *The Book of Plonsk* was published in a handsome edition. The aristocratic Zemach's ambivalence toward the son of the *Winkeladvokat* from Goat Alley who rose to greatness did not dissipate in his old age. Ben-Gurion, on the other hand, old, forlorn, and seeking human warmth, enjoyed spending hours with Zemach. When Paula died he wrote to Rachel Beit-Halakhmi that now only two people close to him remained in the world: herself and Shlomo Zemach.

Ben-Gurion's last years were marked by reconciliation. This was possibly an expression of the lost power of his personality: who was Ben-Gurion without the constant assaults on barricades and the incessant struggle? It was also perhaps an effect of the ennui that follows love or hate, when energy is spent and acceptance of reality dawns. By now Eshkol and Lavon had died. The old hostilities were over. Ben-Gurion's eighty-fifth birthday was celebrated with splendor in 1971, with all the state leaders participating, in celebratory sessions of the Knesset, the Jewish Agency, and the Histadrut—the three institutions to which he had devoted large parts of his life. In her address to a festive meeting of the party secretariat, Prime Minister Golda Meir opened with greetings to the celebrant, and concluded with a warm invitation to him to come back to his old party. She described Ben-Gurion as a man who made difficult decisions,

The grand old man, tired (IDF Archive)

knowing the risks they involved—not because he was unafraid, but despite being afraid. True courage, she affirmed, lay in being afraid yet doing what must be done in spite of the fear.

To mark the twenty-fifth anniversary of the State of Israel, a few months before the outbreak of the Yom Kippur War in 1973, the IDF radio station broadcast a discussion of the founding father, Ben-Gurion. He spoke first, about the nation's duty to protect and preserve the three principles for which Jewish independence had been renewed: ingathering of the exiles, making the wilderness bloom, and the constant aspiration to become "the Chosen People" and "a light unto the nations." It was a pathetic Ben-Gurionesque speech that emphasized the Prophet Isaiah's vision of peace, but said nothing about the challenges that faced Israel at twenty-five.

There are conflicting opinions about Ben-Gurion's clarity of mind in the final year of his life. At times he was as lucid and sharp as in the past, at others he was vague, did not recognize people who spoke to him, and repeated the same things over and over. The IDF radio station apparently made an effort to avoid any embarrassing scenes, and once Ben-Gurion had finished, other speakers took over the discussion.

When the Yom Kippur War broke out, he was alone and forgotten. The loyal Haim Yisraeli updated him on events, but it is doubtful if he was aware of what was happening. In December 1973, a short time after the cease-fire, the founding father passed away. The State of Israel was still in shock from the war, mourning the numerous dead. The cease-fire had not yet guaranteed quiet, and no one gave a thought to Ben-Gurion's passing. He was buried in the place he had chosen on the escarpment of Wadi Zin, next to Paula. As he had instructed, Ben-Gurion's tombstone was inscribed simply with the dates of his birth and death and the date of his immigration to Palestine. The rest would be recounted in the history of Israel.

Epilogue

IN 1960 Richard Lichtheim, a veteran Revisionist, wrote to Ben-Gurion wishing him a long duration for his life and work and saying, "You have what Bismarck called 'Civil Courage'—the courage to do or fight for things which are not to the majority's liking, or even plain unpopular." He concluded, "That is the true mark of the statesman who is not only a politician but a leader."[1] This definition pinpoints a crucial quality that made Ben-Gurion Ben-Gurion. His other qualities were a sense of historical timing and opportunity, resolve, tenaciousness, and a willingness to take calculated risks. His recognition that the establishment of the Jewish state would require a bloody war and his readiness to bear the brunt of responsibility for it—which in retrospect seem almost self-evident—were, at the time, stunning intuitions leading to decisive actions, unprecedented in Jewish history. Sending young people into battle knowing that they might not return was a type of decision Jews had not made since the Bar-Kokhva revolt in the second century. Yet Ben-Gurion was prepared to gamble on the fate of the Yishuv and the lives of thousands. It is doubtful if among the leadership of the Yishuv or of the Jewish people as a whole there was anyone else capable of making such a decision. From this standpoint Berl Katznelson was right when he described Ben-Gurion as "history's gift to the Jewish people."

Even as he was ready to gamble on the nation's future, he was also extremely cautious. He favored cooperation with Britain when his colleagues and the majority of the Yishuv were bitterly opposed to British authority. He took care not to push the British into disbanding the Jewish defense force because he could already see on the horizon the clouds of a war with the Arabs. He knew how to throw down the gauntlet to the United Nations and the Great Powers, but except for the War of Independence he was careful about going to war without the support of an allied power. His withdrawal from the Sinai Peninsula in 1957 was designed to end Israel's isolation, which he viewed as an existential danger. He aspired to enter the American sphere of influence, seeing that democratic power as Israel's long-term rock of support. That did not prevent him from building the nuclear reactor at Dimona in the teeth of American opposition. As much as he wanted an ally, he was equally jealous of his tiny country's independence, and when it faced an existential threat, no one was more resolute in protecting its interests.

Ben-Gurion's greatest years were between 1942 and 1953. It seems that his whole life was but a prelude to this period, when he manifested his extraordinary ability to foresee political developments, formulate the tools for responding to them, and enlist forces from within the Jewish people to seize the opportunities that presented themselves. When asked how he made these fateful decisions, he claimed that he used two kinds of decision making. The first was simple, direct, and ordinary. The other was more complicated and applied to the most important decisions. In such cases, he struggled, felt restless, and could not make up his mind. And then suddenly, he *knew:* the right decision came to him. Those who heard this felt their hair stand on end, as if in the presence of history.

Some crowned him a prophet who predicted the future and the visionary showing his people their path. Ben-Gurion was no prophet, and did not claim to foretell the future. When asked once by the media to forecast what would occur by the turn of the century, he hedged, saying he was expressing his hopes, rather than prophesying. He predicted that the United States would become a welfare state with a planned economy—which did not happen—but also that the USSR would become democratized as a result of pressure from its growing intelligentsia. He hoped that Western and Eastern Europe would become federations of democratic socialist states, which happened in part. He viewed China and India as two future great powers and thought that nurturing relations with China was extremely important; he was highly critical of the United States for its hostile policy toward this vast country. In the spirit of his faith in science, he believed that the secret of cold fusion would be discovered and provide inexpensive energy, raising the standard of living throughout the world. He floated the idea of an injection that could change one's skin from white to black and vice versa and thereby solve the problem of race relations in the United States. He thought a cure for cancer would be found and predicted that the average lifespan would reach a hundred years. Finally, he forecast that peace between Israel and the Arabs would be achieved by the end of the twentieth century.

This mélange of prophecy and nonsense shows that Ben-Gurion was not always right, and when called upon to address developments outside his sphere of knowledge, he understood no more than any sagacious journalist. But the fact that this question was put to him demonstrates not only his standing in

Israeli society, but also among the Jewish people, and perhaps even in twentieth-century history. In a single decade a man who in the early 1940s was hardly known outside the borders of the small Jewish community in Palestine joined the list of the twentieth century's greatest leaders, those "great monsters of history" whose acts and failings shaped reality.

Ben-Gurion became his nation's leader during a time of unparalleled trauma. His paternalistic leadership gave a sense of security and direction to a nation that found itself in the greatest crisis in its history after the destruction of European Jewry. Could he have been a leader during a different period? Churchill, the greatest leader of World War II, had previously been a political failure, and afterward became an aging, declining figure. Would Ben-Gurion's tempestuous personality, his constant search for fresh challenges, have been acceptable during normal times, in a peaceful, democratic country? It is true that Israel has never really been peaceful. Yet once the Zionist revolution became routinized, the great chapter of Ben-Gurion's leadership ended. The charisma he acquired in the War of Independence continued to act upon great and small alike. But this was a result more of inertia than of a renewed belief in his powers. The greatest decision he made after the Declaration of Independence was on mass immigration. But when it came to coping with the task of molding a nation from masses of immigrants—a need he recognized and viewed as his mission— he failed. The question of what will be the content and the goal of life after all the material questions were solved worldwide— this question haunted him, with respect both to his own people and to all nations.[2]

Ben-Gurion liked to argue that history is made by the masses, not individuals. But just as Lenin brought the Bolshevik Revolution into the world and Churchill delivered a fighting Britain, so with Ben-Gurion and the Jewish state. He knew how to create and exploit the circumstances that made its birth possible.

At the critical moment in a delivery, the role of the midwife is decisive. This was Ben-Gurion's role. One can always play the game of "what would have happened if . . ." Perhaps the State of Israel would not have been established if not for Ben-Gurion. Perhaps. Perhaps those who proposed postponing the decision, or giving up on the idea of a Jewish nation-state and establishing a bi-national state, were right. These are hypothetical possibilities that will remain in the sphere of intellectual speculation. The determining factor was Ben-Gurion's presence at the helm at the decisive moment; he was the one who brought the Zionist dream to fruition.

NOTES

Chapter 1. Plonsk

1. Ben-Gurion to Rivka Shachar, Jerusalem, 22.7.1962, Israel Defense Forces Archives (hereinafter IDFA), 3649-890/73.

2. Ibid.

3. Avigdor Grün's letter to Herzl, 1901, *Zikhronot Ben-Gurion* [Ben-Gurion's Memoirs, hereinafter *Zikhronot*] (Hebrew).

4. Ben-Gurion to Haim Yisraeli, Jerusalem, 27.10.1953, Ben-Gurion Archive, Sdeh Boker (BGA).

5. Ben-Gurion to Golda Meir, 28.8.1952, BGA.

6. Shlomo Zemach, *Sippur hayyai* [The Story of My Life], recorded by Ada Zemach (Tel Aviv and Jerusalem: Dvir, 1983), 25.

7. Ben-Gurion to Shmuel Fuchs, 16.7.1904, *Igrot Ben-Gurion* [Ben-Gurion's Correspondence, hereinafter *Igrot*], Yehuda Erez, ed. (Am Oved and Tel Aviv University, 1971), 22.

8. Ben-Gurion to Fuchs, 14.2.1905, ibid., 50.

Chapter 2. "I Found the Homeland Landscape"

1. Ben-Gurion to his father, Petach Tikva, 1.10.1906, *Igrot*, vol. 1, 1904–1919, 75.
2. Ben-Gurion to his father, Petach Tikva, 8.11.1906, *Igrot*, ibid., 82–83.
3. The Ramla Platform, in Yitzhak Ben-Zvi, *Poalei Zion ba-aliya hashniya* [Poalei Zion in the Second Aliya] (Tel Aviv: Mapai Publishing, 1950), 209 (Hebrew).
4. David Ben-Gurion, *Zikhronot*, vol. 1 (Tel Aviv: Am Oved, 1971), 34–35 (Hebrew).
5. Zemach, *Sippur hayyai*, 72.
6. Ben-Gurion to his father, Sejera, 30.6.1909, *Igrot*, vol. 1, 136.
7. Ben-Gurion to his father, Zikhron Ya'akov, 21.1.1910, ibid., 149.
8. Israel Shochat to Ben-Gurion, 12.4.1957, IDFA, 890/73-2145.
9. Ben-Gurion to Yitzhak Molcho, Sdeh Boker, 13.6.1968, IDFA, 890/73-618/.
10. Ben-Gurion to his father, Istanbul, 23.4.1913, *Igrot*, 269.
11. Ben-Gurion to his father, Istanbul, 29.12.1913, ibid., 293.

Chapter 3. Exile and Return

1. Shabtai Teveth, *Kin'at David* [David's Zeal] (Jerusalem and Tel Aviv: Schocken, 1976), 362 (Hebrew).
2. *Zikhronot*, vol. 1, 95–96.
3. Ibid., 98.
4. Ben-Gurion to Paula, Windsor, 25.6.1918, ibid., 103.
5. Ben-Gurion to Paula, Windsor, 3.6.1918, *Igrot*, vol. 1, 351.
6. Ben-Gurion to Paula, Ramla, 8.5.1919, ibid., 418–419.
7. Ben-Gurion to Paula, Windsor, 14.6.1918, ibid., 355.
8. Ben-Gurion to Paula, 1.6.1918, ibid., 349.
9. Ben-Gurion to Paula, 23.9.1918, ibid., 391.
10. Ben-Gurion to Paula, Jaffa, 3.3.1919, ibid., 414.
11. Berl Katznelson, *Akhdut Ha'avoda*, collection, 18 (Hebrew).

12. Union proposal, Akhdut Ha'avoda Book, vol. 1 (Tel Aviv: Akhdut Ha'avoda Publishing, 1929), 2 (Hebrew).

13. *Zikhronot*, vol. 1, 121.

Chapter 4. Labor Leader

1. Ben-Gurion, "Hatafkid hamishki shel histadrut hapoalim" [The Economic Role of the Histadrut], *Mima'amad le'am* [From Class to Nation] (Tel Aviv: Davar, 1933), 124 (Hebrew).

2. *Zikhronot*, vol. 1, Moscow, 24.9.1923, 235.

3. Ibid., Moscow, 18.11.1923, 262.

4. Ibid., Moscow, 11.10.1923, 251.

5. Ibid., Moscow, 16.12.1923, 268.

6. Ibid., Moscow, 27.10.1923, 254–255.

7. Ibid., 16.12.1923, 268.

8. Ibid., 25.8.1923, 225.

9. Ben-Gurion, "Hayi'ud haleumi shel ma'amad hapoalim" [The National Mission of the Working Class], *Mima'amad le'am*, 232.

10. Ibid., 233–234.

11. Ben-Gurion, "Hamashber batsionut utnuat hapoalim" [The Crisis in Zionism and the Labor Movement], *Mima'amad le'am*, 299.

Chapter 5. From Labor Leader to National Leader

1. Ben-Gurion, "She'elat hamishtar veyahasei shekhenim" [The Question of Regime and Relations with Neighbors], Akhdut Ha'avoda Conference in Ein Harod, *We and Our Neighbors* (Tel Aviv: Davar Publishing, 1931), 74 (Hebrew).

2. Ben-Gurion, Minutes of the Fourth Akhdut Ha'avoda Conference, 1924 (Tel Aviv, 1926), p. 30 (Hebrew).

3. Arthur Ruppin, from a letter to Dr. Jacobson, Jerusalem, 3.12.1931, *Pirkei hayyai* [My Life Story], vol. 3 (Tel Aviv: Am Oved, 1968), 203 (Hebrew).

4. The Joint Akhdut Ha'avoda and Hapoel Hatzair Secretariat, October 1929, Labor Party Archive (LPA), Bulletin no. 1 (Hebrew).

5. Ben-Gurion, Diary, 10.7.1930, *Zikhronot*, vol. 1, 417.

6. Ben-Gurion at the Mapai Council, 25.10.1930, LPA (Hebrew).

7. Chaim Arlosoroff to Chaim Weizmann, 30.6.1932, IDFA, 890/73-3342 (Hebrew).

8. Ben-Gurion, *Pegishot im manhigim aravim* [Meetings with Arab Leaders] (Tel Aviv: Am Oved, 1967), 19–20 (Hebrew).

9. Ben-Gurion to Jabotinsky, 38.10.1934, IDFA, 890/73-3549 (Hebrew).

10. Jabotinsky to Ben-Gurion, Paris, 29.10.1934, IDFA, 890/73-3549 (Hebrew).

11. Ben-Gurion, Trogen, Switzerland, 14.9.1935, *Zikhronot*, vol. 2, 436.

12. Ben-Gurion, Lucerne, 5.9.1935, ibid., 411.

13. Ben-Gurion, ibid., 437.

Chapter 6. Days of Hope, Days of Despair

1. Quoted by Norman Rose, *Lewis Namier and Zionism* (Oxford: Clarendon Press, 1980), 42.

2. Doris May to Ben-Gurion, Lancing, 1.10.1946, BGA.

3. Ben-Gurion at the Mapai Central Committee, 5–6.2.1937, *Zikhronot*, vol. 4 (Tel Aviv: Am Oved, 1974), 64.

4. Ben-Gurion, meeting of the Jewish Agency Executive, Fall 1936, IDFA, 890/73-3155.

5. Ben-Gurion to the Mapai Central Committee, London, 1.7.1937, *Zikhronot*, vol. 4, 257.

6. Ben-Gurion to Amos Ben-Gurion, London, 5.10.1937, letters to Paula and the children (Tel Aviv: Am Oved, 1968), 210.

7. Ben-Gurion at the Mapai Central Committee, 10.4.1937, *Zikhronot*, vol. 4, 151.

8. Ben-Gurion to Paula, letters to Paula and the children, 215.

9. Ben-Gurion to Weizmann, 22.8.1935, IDFA, 890/73-1958.

10. Ben-Gurion to Brodetzky, 4.1.1938, IDFA, 890/73-4157/.

11. *Baffy: The Diaries of Blanche Dugdale, 1936–1947*, 18.9.1938 (London: Vallentine Mitchell, 1973), 99.

12. Ben-Gurion to Eliezer (Kaplan), London, 21.12.1938, IDFA, 890/73-3005.

13. The 21st Zionist Congress, 233.

14. Ben-Gurion at the Mapai Central Committee, 12.9.1939, *Bama'arakha*, vol. 3 (Tel Aviv: Mapai Publishing House, 1950), 18.

15. Ben-Gurion to Paula, London, 31.5.1940, IDFA, 890/73-4079.

16. Ibid., 1.7.1940, ibid.

17. Ibid.

18. Ibid., 8.7.1940, ibid.

19. Ibid., 21.8.1940, ibid.

20. Ibid., 8.9.1940, IDFA, 890/73-3546.

21. Ben-Gurion, minutes of the Jewish Agency Executive, 16.2.1941.

22. Ibid. My thanks to Dr. Zohar Segev, who drew my attention to this matter.

23. Minutes of the Special Meeting of the Office Committee of the Emergency Committee, 17.9.1942, IDFA, 890/73-1471.

24. Ben-Gurion to Renana, Washington, 18.2.1942.

25. Weizmann to Blanche Dugdale, London, New York, 8.1.1943, *The Letters and Papers of Chaim Weizmann*, vol. 20, Michael J. Cohen, ed. (Jerusalem: Israel Universities Press, 1979), 387.

26. Ben-Gurion to Doris May, Washington, 18.2.1942, BGA.

27. Ben-Gurion to Miriam Cohen, Jerusalem, 15.2.1943, BGA.

28. Ibid., 35.1.1944.

29. Miriam Cohen to Ben-Gurion, 18.4.1944, IDFA, 890/73-3515.

30. Minutes of the Jewish Agency Executive, Jerusalem, 4.10.1942, IDFA, 890/73-1471.

31. Meeting of Mapai activists, 8.12.1942, IDFA, 890/73-1471.

32. Ben-Gurion to Miriam Cohen, Jerusalem, 20.9.1944, BGA.

33. Ben-Gurion to Dov Yosef, London, 14.4.1945, IDFA, 890/73-95.

34. Ben-Gurion's diary, 7–8 May 1945. The verse is from Hosea 9:1. Quoted by Tuvia Friling, *Hetz ba'arafel: Ben-Gurion, hanhagat hayishuv venisyonot hatsala bashoah* [Arrow in the Dark:

David Ben-Gurion, the Yishuv Leadership, and Rescue Attempts in the Holocaust] (Jerusalem: Ben Gurion University and the Institute for Contemporary Judaism, The Hebrew University of Jerusalem, 1998), 944 (Hebrew).

Chapter 7. On the Verge of Statehood

1. Dugdale, *Baffy*, 30.4.1946, p. 236.
2. Judah Nadich, *Eisenhower and the Jews* (New York: Twayne Publishers, 1953), 232.
3. Ben-Gurion to Goldmann, 21.7.1954, BGA.
4. Ben-Gurion to Weizmann, Paris, 28.10.1946, IDFA, 890/73-2002.
5. Ben-Gurion to Mr. Rudolf G. Sonneborn, Sdeh Boker, 1.2.1967.
6. Ben-Gurion to Paula, London, 10.2.1946, IDFA, 890/73-3546.
7. Ben-Gurion to Paula, London, 19.6.1946, IDFA, 890/73-3476.

Chapter 8. "We Hereby Declare . . ."

1. Ben-Gurion to Moshe (Shertok) and Golda (Meyerson), Tel Aviv, 3.3.1948, IDFA, 890/73-3598.
2. Ben-Gurion to Shaul (Avigur), Tel Aviv, 5.4.1948, IDFA, 890/73-3598.
3. Ben-Gurion to the women's organizations, 29.3.1948, IDFA, 890/73-4093.
4. Ben-Gurion to Golda (Meyerson) and Moshe (Shertok), Tel Aviv, 3.3.1948, IDFA, 890/73-89.
5. Ben-Gurion to Ehud Avriel, 4.3.1948, IDFA, 890/73-9093.
6. Ben-Gurion, *Yoman milkhama, 1948–1949* [War Diary, 1948–1949], Gershon Rivlin and Dr. Elhanan Oren, eds. (Tel Aviv: Ministry of Defense, 1982), vol. 1, 416 (Hebrew).
7. Ben-Gurion to Galili, 21.6.1948, IDFA, 890/73-4277.

Chapter 9. Helmsman of the State

1. Ben-Gurion to Ziama (Zalman) Aranne, Tel Aviv, 6.1.1951, IDFA, 890/73-1808.

2. David Ben-Gurion, *Netzach Yisrael* [Eternal Israel], Government Yearbook, 1957, "Like Stars and Dust" (Ramat Gan: Masada, 1976), 147 (Hebrew).

3. Ben-Gurion to Abba Eban, 2.1.1951, IDFA, 890/73-1808.

4. Ben-Gurion to the Knesset Constitution, Law, and Justice Committee, 13.7.1949.

5. Ben-Gurion to Yitzhak Gruenbaum, Jerusalem, 28.3.1950, BGA.

6. Ben-Gurion to the Eighth Agricultural Conference, 9.10.1955, IDFA, 890/73-2085.

7. Ben-Gurion to a meeting of the general staff, 16.3.1961, IDFA, 890/73-3875.

8. Manya Shochat to Ben-Gurion, Jerusalem, 2.3.1959. I have not been able to find an answer from him to her letter.

9. Ben-Gurion in the Knesset plenum, 10.8.1952, IDFA, 890/73-2095.

10. Ben-Gurion to Eliezer Kaplan, Tiberias, 5.3.1950, BGA.

11. The Government-University Committee for the collection of Jewish manuscripts throughout the world, 6.6.1950, IDFA, 890/73-4103.

12. Isaiah Berlin to the prime minister of Israel's private secretary, New College, 8.12.1950, *Letters*, Henry Hardy and Jennifer Holmes, eds. (London: Chatto and Windus, 2009), 204–205.

13. Ben-Gurion to Yehoshua Bertonov, Jerusalem, 28.8.1950, BGA.

14. Ben-Gurion to Yosef Milo, Sdeh Boker, 30.11.1954, BGA.

15. Ben-Gurion to Ben-Zvi, Jerusalem, 3.8.1956, BGA.

16. Ben-Gurion to A. S. Stein, Jerusalem, 27.6.1955, BGA.

17. Prime Minister Ben-Gurion, Knesset Plenary Session 91, 2.7.1951, IDFA, 890/73-4105.

18. Ben-Gurion to Dr. Joseph Schechter, Jerusalem, 2.9.1957, IDFA, 890/73-1304.

19. Ben-Gurion to Yitzhak Damiel (Schweiger), Mount Carmel, 13.4.1953, BGA.

20. Ben-Gurion to David Glass, the Kirya, 26.2.1953, BGA.

21. Ben-Gurion to Dr. Yehoshua Brand, Jerusalem, 15.6.1952, BGA.

22. Ben-Gurion to Sharett, 21.6.1954, IDFA, 890/73-4099.

23. Ben-Gurion to Rabbi S. B. Orbach, Sdeh Boker, 14.7.1954, IDFA, 890/73-2096.

24. Nehemiah Argov to Efraim Evron, Tel Aviv, 21.10.1953, Nehemiah Argov, Publication of friends, 1959, p. 144.

Chapter 10. Ben-Gurion Against Ben-Gurion

1. Ben-Gurion to Nathan Yellin-Mor, Sdeh Boker, 2.9.1954, BGA.

2. Ben-Gurion, "Leparashat hilufei gavra bemisrad hachutz" [On the question of a foreign ministry reshuffle], Jerusalem, 28.6.1956, IDFA, 890/73-2023.

3. Ben-Gurion to Teddy Kollek, Sdeh Boker, 16.4.1954, BGA.

4. Moshe Dayan to the minister of defense, 13.11.1955, IDFA, 890/73-2184.

5. Ben-Gurion at the cabinet meeting, 28.10.1956, IDFA, 205/73-532.

6. Isaiah Berlin to Arthur Schlesinger, beginning–mid November 1956, Letters, p. 554.

7. Eisenhower to Ben-Gurion, undated, IDFA, 890/73-502.

8. Vera Shomroni to Ben-Gurion, 30.8.1954, IDFA 890/73-2535; Ben-Gurion to Vera Shomroni, Sdeh Boker, 30.8.1954, BGA.

9. Ben-Gurion to Shimshon Zelniker, Sdeh Boker, 14.1.1954, IDFA, 890/73-2103.

10. Golda Meir, at a festive Mapai secretariat meeting, 30.9.1971, IDFA, 890/73-89.

11. "Pegisha she'ein doma la" [An Unparalleled Meeting], Ma'ariv, 15.3.1960.

12. Ben-Gurion to attorney Leon Eli, Sdeh Boker, 6.6.1966, IDFA, 890/73-3660.

13. Joseph M. Proskauer to Ben-Gurion, 31.5.1960, BGA.

14. Ben-Gurion to Judge Proskauer, Tel Aviv, 8.7.1960, BGA.

15. Judge Joseph Proskauer to Ben-Gurion, New York, 17.7.1960, BGA.

16. Ben-Gurion to Dr. Nachum Goldmann, the Kirya, 2.6.1960, BGA.

17. Mordechai (Morele) Bar-On, *Ben hame'ah she'avra* [A Son of the Last Century], an autobiography (Jerusalem: Carmel, 2011), 278 (Hebrew).

Chapter 11. Decline

1. Miriam Taub to Ben-Gurion, New York, 25.3.1964, IDFA, 890/73-747.

2. Miriam Taub, New York, to Ben-Gurion, 1.5.1952, BGA.

3. Ben-Gurion to S. H. Bergmann, Tel Aviv, 14.10.1966, IDFA, 890/73-2010.

4. Ben-Gurion to Gershom Scholem, Haifa, 2.11.1966, ibid.

5. Jacob Talmon to Ben-Gurion, 6.12.1970, IDFA, 890/73-120.

6. Ben-Gurion to Miriam Taub, 14.11.1971, IDFA, 890/73-3005.

7. Shlomo Zemach, *Pinkasei reshimot 1962–1973* [Notes] (Tel Aviv: Am Oved, 1996), 28 (Hebrew).

8. Shlomo Zemach to Ben-Gurion, 5.6.1966, IDFA, 890/73-631.

Epilogue

1. Richard Lichtheim to Ben-Gurion, Jerusalem, 18.2.1960, BGA.

2. Ben-Gurion to Rabbi Morris N. Izendart, apparently in 1960, BGA.

ACKNOWLEDGMENTS

THE IDEA OF WRITING about David Ben-Gurion came to me as a result of my involvement in the Jewish Lives series, a collection of short biographies illuminating the diverse Jewish contributions to the human creation over the past three millennia, sponsored by Leon Black. My friend and colleague in the editorial team of the series, Steve Zipperstein, encouraged me to embark on this intellectual adventure, and so did Ileene Smith, the editor of the series on behalf of Yale University Press. The Leon D. Black Foundation generously supported this endeavor. Linda Kurz smoothed the administrative edges of our team's cooperation.

The Ben-Gurion Archive at Sdeh Boker was most generous in making the labyrinth of Ben-Gurion's papers accessible. The late Haim Yisraeli opened the Israel Defense Forces Archive for me, and Ms. Ilana Allon, the director of the archive, gave the needed push to have the files declassified on time. Ms. Hanni

Hermolin of the Beit Ben-Gurion Association was most helpful in helping me locate the necessary photos, and so did the people of the Labor archive at the Lavon Institute.

My favorite translator, Anthony Berris, translated this book and as usual did a great job. Stephanie Golden made it more colloquial and accessible to the American reader. Sylvia Fuks-Fried read the manuscript and made important comments. John Palmer was very helpful in advancing the manuscript at Yale University Press, and Phillip King gave it the final polish. I am thankful to all of them for their encouragement and professionalism.

My favorite assistant and friend, Dr. Nurit Levinovsky-Cohen, was a great help in locating materials, checking details, and guarding me from any mischief. I am most grateful to her for her help and friendship.

This book was written during the last year of my late husband's life, and it will always be associated with painful memories, but also with the fact that he read most of it and was satisfied with my work. I will always miss his criticism and encouragement.

INDEX

Abdullah (king of Transjordan), 160
Adenauer, Konrad, 218, 219
Aeschylus, 183
Agricultural Union, 67
Agricultural workers: associations of,
    54, 55; Ben-Gurion as, 18, 25, 26,
    30; Ben-Gurion on, 18, 26, 27, 57;
    conference of, 56; and Hapoel
    Hatzair, 19, 21; Jews as, 24; and
    Second Aliya, 26, 42
Agudat Yisrael (Union of Israel) party,
    191
Ahad Ha'am (Asher Ginzberg), 6, 10,
    193
Aizik, Simcha, 16
Akhdut Ha'avoda (Zionist-Socialist
    Union of Jewish Workers in
    Palestine), 65, 67, 98, 233; formation
    of, 58–60, 63; and Hebrew language,
    59; and Mapam, 168
Aktzin, Benjamin, 190
Alami, Musa, 93–95

Algeria, 209, 234
Aliya: Third Aliya, 64–67; Fourth
    Aliya, 72, 73, 74; Fifth Aliya, 92, 95;
    Aliya Gimmel, 139; Youth Aliya, 178.
    See also Second Aliya
Aliya Hadasha (New Aliya) party, 150
Allon, Yigal, 167, 168–169, 171, 173
Altalena affair, 164–166, 188
American Council for Judaism, 220
American Jewish Committee (AJC),
    44, 123, 220
American Jewish Congress, 128
American Jewry: Ben-Gurion's
    attempts to mobilize, 113, 116, 120,
    121, 122–123, 125, 126, 128, 131,
    143–144; and displaced persons
    problem, 142; public opinion of,
    134, 137, 142
Anarchists and anarchism, 56, 169
Der Anfang (The Beginning), 29–30
Anglo-American Committee, 143
Ansky, S., The Dybbuk, 69–70

Anti-Semitism: and Eichmann trial, 220; of Nazi party, 80, 86. *See also* Holocaust and Holocaust survivors
Arab federation, 93–95
Arabic language, 182
Arab-Jewish tension: and Arab intellectuals, 41; and Arab opposition to Jewish settlement, 82, 84, 85, 86, 136–137, 142–143; and Arab riots (1929), 86; and balance of power, 113; and establishment of Jewish state, 148, 149, 150; lack of solution for, 153; and Palestine partition plan, 113–114; and Poalei Zion conference in Sejera, 28, 29; and Young Turks' revolution, 27–28
Arab League states, 143
Arab Legion, 160, 163, 164, 173
Arab Liberation Army, 159–160
Arab nationalism: Ben-Gurion's experience with, 41, 82, 86; Ben-Gurion's talks with Arab leaders, 93–95; and opposition to Jewish settlement, 82, 84, 85, 86; rise of, 60
Arab Revolt (1936), 102, 105, 106, 109, 115, 137
Arab states: and establishment of Jewish state, 148, 149, 150, 160; Israel's balance of power with, 181; and Israel's sovereignty, 206; and World War II, 118–119
Arafat, Yasser, 166
Aranne, Ziama (Zalman), 217, 225
Arazi, Yehuda, 149
Arendt, Hannah, 222
Argov, Meir, 195
Argov, Nehemiah, *152*, 195, 212–213
Arlosoroff, Chaim, 78–81, 90–92
Armenians, Turkish persecution of, 40
Armistice agreements (1949), 172, 173, 205, 209
Aswan Dam, 209
Atlee, Clement, 136
Auerbach, Efraim Elimelech, 228
Avriel, Ehud, 139, 149, 177, 195

Balfour Declaration, 48–49, 50, 60, 62, 76, 82, 118, 119
Balkan War (First), 34–35, 38
Barak, Ehud, 166
Bar-Giora (clandestine organization), 27, 28, 29
Bar-Kokhva revolt, 243
Bar-Zohar, Michael, 234, 237
Basel Program, 124
Battle of Britain, 117
Begin, Menachem, 97, 137–138, 164–165, 188, 233, 236
Beit-Halakhmi, Rachel, 9, 11, 16, 20, 60, 239
Beit-Halakhmi, Yechezkel, 20
Ben-Ami, Oved, 235
Ben-Eliezer, Yariv, *152*
Ben-Gurion, Amos, 63, 100–101, 109, 120, 150–153
Ben-Gurion, David: birth and youth of, 2, 3–14; celebrations for birthdays of, 235–236, 239; death and grave of, 17, 241; decision making of, 243–244; education of, 4–5, 11, 12–13, 31–36; essential qualities of, 242; family background of, 2–4; finances of, 5, 35, 65, 66; health of, 9, 18–19, 35, 36, 48, 213; hidden fervor cloaked with deliberate rationalism, 67; and law studies in Istanbul, 27, 31–36, 55; library of, 65–66, 70, 105, 116, 185; and literature, 55, 105; marriage of, 47–48, 64, 100, 237–238; old age of, 232–239, 240, 241; personality of, 8–10, 24, 47, 54, 60–61, 66, 89, 104, 115, 127, 129, 130, 132, 140, 155, 160, 170, 178, 186, 213, 239, 245; photographs of, 12, 39, 47, 59, 63, 94, 101, 128, 152, 161, 172, 179, 194, 199, 201, 205, 216, 219, 223, 240; predictions of future developments, 244–245; relationship and correspondence with Miriam Taub, 129–130, 133; self-mythology of, 25, 29
Ben-Gurion, Galia, *152*
Ben-Gurion, Geula, 53, 62–63, 100–101, *152*

Ben-Gurion, Mary Callow, 150–153
Ben-Gurion, Paula: Ben-Gurion's correspondence with, 52, 53, 58, 64, 117, 150–151, 170, 237–238; and Ben-Gurion's declaiming the Declaration of Independence, 162; and Ben-Gurion's joining Jewish Legion, 51–52; children of, 51, 52, 53, 63, 64; courtship with Ben-Gurion, 46–47; death of, 237–238; finances of, 66; "kutch-mutch" of, 197, 238; marriage of, 47–48, 64, 100, 237–238; in Palestine, 62–63; photographs of, 47, 63, 152; relationship with Ben-Gurion's family, 64; and retirement to Negev desert, 197; on Weizmann, 110
Ben-Gurion-Leshem, Renana, 63, 64, 126, 152
Ben-Yehuda, Eliezer, 7
Ben-Zvi, Rachel, 29, 30
Ben-Zvi, Yitzhak, 24, 27, 28, 29, 40–41, 43, 44, 45, 46, 49, 52, 58; Ben-Gurion's relations with, 24, 29–30, 60, 188, 238; law studies in Istanbul, 31, 32, 35, 36; and Poalei Zion, 38, 39, 43; return to Palestine, 36–37
Berdyczewski, Micha Yosef, 6, 10, 15, 193
Bergen-Belsen, 136
Berlin, Isaiah, 184, 211
Bermann, S. H., 235–236
Bertonov, Yehoshua, 185
Betar (Brit Trumpeldor youth movement), 77, 80, 97, 99, 137
Bevin, Ernest, 89, 142, 143, 153
Bialik, Hayim Nachman, 6, 69
Bible, 192–193, 213, 214–215
Bichovsky, Shimon, 70
"Black Saturday" (Operation Agatha), 144, 147
Bols, Eric, 215
Bols, Louis, 215
Bolshevik Revolution, 49, 50, 57, 58, 68
Borochov, Ber, 14, 22, 23, 24
Brandeis, Louis D., 46, 49

Brenner, Yosef Haim, 19, 30–31, 54, 70
British Empire: Ben-Gurion on, 89, 104, 126; colonial racism of, 130–131; effects of World War II on, 126; and Weizmann, 124, 126
British Expeditionary Force, 117
Brit Shalom (Peace Alliance), 84–85, 150, 186
Brod, Max, 159
Buber, Martin, 46, 187, 228–229, 236
Buchenwald (Germany), 136
Buddhism, 183
Bulganin, Nikolai, 210
Bulgaria, 34, 35, 140, 175
Bund (Jewish Workers' Party in Poland, Lithuania, and Russia), 4, 15, 44, 57, 188
Burckhardt, Jacob, 183

Cahan, Abraham "Abe," 44
Cameri Theatre, 185–186
Canaanism movement, 214
Central Europe, 43
Central Powers, 37, 38–40
Chamberlain, Neville, 116
China, 244
Chosen People, Spinoza's concept of, 10
Churchill, Winston S., 116–119, 133, 166, 170, 196, 234, 245
Cohen, Miriam. See Taub, Miriam
Cohen, Yehoshua, 238
Cold War, 157
Comay, Michael, 220
Committee for the Translation of World Masterworks into Hebrew, 228–229
Communist party, 68, 69, 180–181
Communists and communism: competition with Zionism, 68, 69, 70, 71; and Soviet Union, 66
Confucius, 183
Conservative party (Britain), 95–96
Coupland, Reginald, 105
Cyprus, British-controlled detention camps in, 141, 175
Czechoslovakia, 111, 112, 155, 208

Dachau, 136
Darwin, Charles R., 183
Dayan, Moshe, 217, 236; Ben-Gurion's
    relations with, 187, 198, 209–210, 212,
    225–226; as chief of General Staff,
    198, 200, 208, 216
Declaration of Independence, 147–148,
    160–161
De Gaulle, Charles, 223, 227, 234
Diaspora, 14–15, 21, 57, 60, 77, 98
Dimona nuclear reactor, 187, 226, 227,
    230, 243
Dinur, Ben-Zion, 199
Displaced persons (DP), 136, 139,
    140; camps, 136, 137, 140–141, 142,
    143–144, 145–146, 175; transfer of
    displaced Jews to Palestine, 120–121,
    122, 123, 124–125, 140, 143, 145–146
Dosh (Kariel Gardosh), 233
Dostoevsky, Fyodor, 6
Dubnow, Simon, 4
Dugdale, Blanche, 103, 104, 107, 110,
    112, 126, 140

Eastern bloc, 211
Eastern Europe, 4, 43, 48, 57, 77, 171;
    and immigration to Palestine, 72,
    136, 140, 143; Zionists of, 8, 79–80
Eban, Abba, 172, 217
Eden, Anthony, 13, 206, 212
Effendi, Yahya, 41
Egypt, 127, 160, 162, 172–173, 206, 208,
    212
Eichmann, Adolf, 217–222
Eisenhower, Dwight D., 136, 211, 212,
    226
El-Arish, 172
Entente Powers, 38–40, 49
Erhard, Ludwig, 219
Eshkol, Levi, 225, 226, 229, 231, 232,
    234, 235, 239
Etzion Bloc, 160
European Jewry: Ben-Gurion on,
    176–177; World War II annihilation
    of, 1, 124, 131, 245. See also Holocaust
    and Holocaust survivors
Ezra association, 5, 7, 9–10, 15

Faisal (Hashemite king), 82
February Revolution, 49
Feldenkrais, Moshe, 213
Feuerberg, Mordecai, 6
Fishman-Maimon, Rabbi Judah, 162,
    187
Forverts, 44, 188
France, 216; Ben-Gurion and, 117, 139,
    144, 222; and Israel's nuclear
    technology, 227; and Suez crisis,
    209–212
From Class to Nation (Ben-Gurion), 66
Fuchs, Shlomo, 5–6, 7, 8, 10, 13, 24
Fulbright, J. William, 220

Galili, Israel, 160, 164–170
Gaza Strip, 208, 210, 211
Gedud Ha'avoda (The Joseph
    Trumpeldor Labor Battalion), 65
General Zionists party, 73, 75, 76, 146,
    147
Germany: aggressive policies of, 111,
    112; displaced persons camps in, 140,
    143, 145–146, 175; economic and
    military aid to Israel, 218–219;
    invasion of Low Countries, 116;
    Nazi party's power in, 77, 80, 86,
    92; reparations agreement with, 145,
    189, 196, 218; threat of invasion of
    Palestine, 122–123, 127, 131
Gibli, Binyamin, 202, 223, 224
Golan Heights, 237
Goldman, Emma, 48
Goldmann, Nachum, 145, 189,
    219–220
Gordon, Aharon David, 55
Gordon, Judah Leib, 6
Grady, Henry F., 145
Great Britain, 68, 118, 143; Ben-Gurion
    and, 147, 173, 190, 243; Jews from
    Palestine fighting World War II
    under, 119–120; and Palestine par-
    tition plan, 105–111, 113–114, 133, 138;
    proposed evacuation of Palestine,
    154, 158; public opinion in, 110, 112,
    114, 117, 118; and rule of Palestine,
    57; secret agreement with Israel,

209–210; and Sinai Campaign, 211;
Weizmann's pro-Zionist lobby in
London, 39, 49, 89, 103–104, 124,
125–126; and World War II, 116–120,
122
Greece, 34, 184
Green, Abraham, 4
Green, Avigdor, *63;* arms cached at
house of, 15; Ben-Gurion's corre-
spondence with, 17, 20, 27, 33–34,
35–36; and Ben-Gurion's law studies
in Istanbul, 32–36; Paula Ben-
Gurion staying with, 64; as father,
9; as Hibbat Zion member, 4;
occupation, 2–3, 5; and plan to
immigrate to Palestine, 63–64
Green, Feigeleh (Zipporah), 32–33, 64
Green, Rivka, 32, 35
Green, Sheindel, 2–3, 8, 9
Greenberg, Chaim, 109
Green Line, 173
Gruenbaum, Yitzhak, 176
Gulf of Suez islands, 210
Gur, Rabbi of, 3

Ha'akhdut (Unity; Poalei Zion
journal), 26, 30–31, 33, 40
Ha'aretz, 176, 180
Habima Theatre, 69–70, 185
Haboker, 176
Haganah, 113, 144, 158; Ben-Gurion
and, 114, 115, 116, 148, 155, 156, 167;
and Irgun, 137, 138–139; and Mapam
members, 168; military traditions of,
163–164; and provisional govern-
ment of Jewish state, 160
Haganah National Command, 115, 138
Haile Selassie (emperor of Ethiopia),
112
Hakibbutz Hameuhad, 98, 100, 131,
168
al-Halamiya, Egypt, Jewish Legion
camp in, 55, 56
Halifax, E. F. L. Wood, Lord, 125
Hamashbir (cooperative), 55
Hamizrachi party, 73, 90, 100, 107, 147
Hammarskjold, Dag, 205, 211

Ha'olam Hazeh, 224–225, 228
Hapoel Hatzair (The Young Worker)
party, 19, 21–22, 54, 56, 57–58, 65, 91
Hapoel Hatzair (journal), 21
Harrison, Earl G., 136
Harrison Report, 136, 140
Hashomer (The Watchman)
organization, 28, 29, 31, 45, 46, 56
Hashomer Hatzair (SSSR), 69, 70
Hashomer Hatzair (Young Guard), 65,
150, 168, 200
Hasidism, 3–4
Haskala (Jewish enlightenment), 2, 3
Hazit Ha'am, 80
Hebrew culture, 6, 53, 54
Hebrew language, 59; Ben-Gurion
and, 5–7, 22, 30, 33, 99, 182, 183, 185,
203; Israel and, 159, 182, 183; in
Palestine, 18, 21–22, 30, 37, 42
Hebrew Language Committee, 159
Hebrew literature, 6, 10
Hebrew Resistance Movement, 138,
144
Hebrew University, Jerusalem, 84,
182–183, 228
Hebron, 237
Hechalutz, 52, 69, 71, 79, 98; Ben-
Gurion's organization of, 42, 44
Herut party, 181, 182, 188
Herzl, Theodor, 4, 5, 7–8, 10–11, 50,
71, 124
Herzliya Gymnasium, Tel Aviv, 7, 40,
92
Heshin, Alexander, 45, 51
Hibbat Zion (Lovers of Zion)
movement, 4
Histadrut (General Federation of
Jewish Workers in Palestine), 75;
and Arab workers, 84; and Ben-
Gurion as representative to agri-
cultural exhibition in Moscow,
68–70; Ben-Gurion as secretary
general of, 65, 66, 81, 84, 92–93,
99, 100; and Ben-Gurion's agreements with Jabotinsky, 98; and
Ben-Gurion's ambition for centralist
regime, 67, 68; and Ben-Gurion's

Histadrut (*continued*)
eighty-fifth birthday celebrations,
239; and Ben-Gurion's proposal of
general commune of all workers,
67; British arrests of leaders, 144;
clashes with Betarists, 97, 99; as
confederation, 67–68; employment
bureau of, 175; employment exchange
of, 77; formation of, 62, 64; Lavon
as general secretary of, 223, 229
Histadrut Conference, 67
Hitler, Adolf, 111, 114–115, 117–118, 120,
130, 141, 219
Ho Chi Minh, 144
Holocaust and Holocaust survivors:
and American Jewry, 142; annihilation of Jewish people, 124, 131, 133,
214, 218, 220; Ben-Gurion's public
restraint on, 221–222; and changes
in Jewish people, 146; in displaced
persons camps, 137, 140–141, 146;
and Eichmann trial, 217–222; and
Jewish Brigade, 120; and Jewish
immigration to Palestine, 143, 146,
159; revelations of, 131–132, 136;
testimony of survivors, 222
Hoover, Herbert C., 124–125
Hungarian Jewry, 133
Hussein bin Ali (Hashemite Arab ruler
of Arabia), 111, 118
al-Husseini, Haj Amin (mufti of
Jerusalem), 93, *94*, 153
"Hypotheses for a State Regime in
Palestine" (Ben-Gurion), 87–88

Ibn Saud (king of Saudi Arabia), 103,
134
India, 171, 184, 244
Inter-community war, 157–160
International Socialist Congress, 23
Iraq, 105, 119, 160, 173, 175
Irgun Tsva'i Leumi (National Military
Organization; Etzel), 137–138, 139,
144, 164, 165, 166, 221
Israel: Arab minority in, 180–181, 207,
237; Ben-Gurion as defense minister,

203–207, 224; Ben-Gurion's leadership and, 188–189, 191, 196, 245–246;
Ben-Gurion on national identity,
174, 214; Ben-Gurion and Olshan-
Dori Commission, 222–230; Ben-
Gurion as prime minister, 1, 9,
174–180, 181, 182–183, 185–186,
188–195, 207–222, 225; Ben-Gurion's
resignation as prime minister,
195–197, 226–231; Ben-Gurion's
return from retirement, 202, 224;
Ben-Gurion's role in building of,
149, 173, 174–180, 196; Ben-Gurion
on sovereignty of, 205–206; birthday
celebrations for Ben-Gurion in,
235–236, 239; and cultural development, 185–186; and democracy, 181,
186–187, 188, 189–191, 243; economic
development of, 175, 180, 182, 189;
and Eichmann trial, 217–222; and
fedayeen raids, 206–207; and Gaza
Strip, 208, 210, 211; and Germany
postwar, 218–219; and Hebrew language, 159, 182–184; and immigrant
absorption, 176, 177–180, 182; Jewish
population growth in, 175–177, 182,
196, 206–207, 245; lack of constitution, 189–190; and nuclear energy,
187, 226–228; public opinion in, 222,
228; and religion/state relation, 190,
191, 192–195; and scientific development, 186; Sharett as minister of
foreign affairs, 203, 204, 207,
208–209; Sharett as prime minister,
198, 202, 203, 206, 207, 224, 226;
sovereignty of, 205–206; state
archive of, 215; and Straits of Tiran,
208, 210; and Suez Canal zone, 201;
and terrorist incursions, 180, 206;
twenty-fifth anniversary of, 241;
Weizmann as president of, 147; and
women's rights, 191–192
Israel Defense Forces (IDF), 224, 225,
241; Ben-Gurion and, 166–169, 172,
173, 212, 231; killing of civilians, 187;
Seventh Brigade, 163; in Sinai

Campaign, 209, 210–211, 212; in War of Independence, 164–165, 166, 171–172, 173
Israeli Research Council, 186
Israel Military Industries, 149
Istanbul, Turkey, Ben-Gurion's law studies in, 27, 31–36, 55
Italy, 77, 111, 112

Jabotinsky, Vladimir (Ze'ev): Ben-Gurion and, 96–99, 111, 188; and Jewish Legion, 39; as leader of Revisionist movement, 73, 75–76, 77, 78, 80, 90; and New Zionist Organization, 99, 139
Jaffa, 18, 19, 70, 103
Jamal Pasha, 37, 38, 40
James, William, 183
Jerusalem, 72, 144, 157–158, 163–164; capital moved to, 204
Jewish Agency Executive, 79, 90, 107, 108, 138, 239; Ben-Gurion as chairman of, 103, 108, 113–114, 116, 139; Ben-Gurion as head of political department, 81, 95; Ben-Gurion's resignation as chairman of, 132–133
Jewish Brigade, 120, 133, 138, 140, 156, 157, 163, 164
Jewish Colonization Association (JCA), 27
Jewish immigration to Palestine: and absorption in Jewish economy, 73, 96, 105, 106; and Anglo-American Committee, 143–144; Arab demands for cessation of, 102; Ben-Gurion on immigration as core Zionist policy, 103, 112; Ben-Gurion's proposal of defense of immigrants, 114; and Biltmore Program, 123–124, 125; British curtailment of, 108, 109, 112; and Brit Shalom, 186; from Germany, 150; illegal immigration, 113, 114, 115, 139, 141–142, 144, 148; and labor movement, 59, 72–75; and MacDonald Letter, 87; and reality of life in Palestine, 19–20; Weizmann

on, 104, 124; and White Paper (1939), 114, 136–137, 142–143; and Yishuv, 72, 91, 92, 106, 109, 112; and Zionist Executive, 103; and Zionist propaganda, 23
Jewish intelligentsia, 21, 84, 92, 176, 180
Jewish Joint Distribution Committee (JDC), 142
Jewish Labor Committee, 123
Jewish Legion, 48, 49, 50, 51–53, 55–56, 156
Jewish National Fund, 37, 66
Jewish philanthropic associations, 73
Jewish Socialists, 45
Jewish state, establishment of:
  armistice borders, 173; Ben-Gurion's leadership and, 93, 96, 106, 158–159, 160, 165–166, 170; Ben-Gurion's vision for, 60, 84, 106–109, 110, 111, 120–121, 122, 123, 125, 135–136, 146, 147, 148–149, 154, 242–243; Declaration of Independence, 147–148, 160–162; Herzl's vision of, 10, 124; U.N. partition plan and, 154, 157, 158, 161, 171; Weizmann's vision of, 123, 125. See also Israel; Palestine
Johnson, Lyndon B., 230
Jordan, 212
Josephthal, Giora, 216–217
Josephus, Flavius, 17

Kabbalah, 236
Kant, Immanuel, 183
Kaplan, Eliezer, 182
Karelitz, Rabbi Avraham Yeshaya, 191–192
Katznelson, Berl: and Akhdut Ha'avoda, 58, 59; on Ben-Gurion as history's gift to the Jewish people, 243; Ben-Gurion's alliance with, 53, 56–57, 58, 59, 60–61, 75, 97, 98; on Ben-Gurion's proposal of general commune of workers, 67; Ben-Gurion's relationship with, 132, 133,

Katznelson, Berl (*continued*)
170, 213, 238; charisma of, 66; death
of, 133, 170, 213; and illegal Jewish
immigration, 113; and Jewish Legion,
56; on Lavon, 198; and Nonpartisan
party, 54, 55, 56, 57–58; and partition
plan, 106–107, 108, 111; on party
factions, 131; political background
of, 54–55; resignation from Mapai
Central Committee, 77; and
Weizmann, 103, 230
Kaufman, Yehezkiel, 213
Kennedy, John F., 230
Kenya, 138
Kfar Hayarok Agricultural School,
217
Kibbutzim, 75, 100, 144, 178
Kibia operation, 187
Kishinev pogrom, 7, 28
Knesset Israel (Israeli parliament), 181,
182, 187, 190, 191, 192, 198, 212, 213,
217, 224, 227, 229, 233, 239
Kollek, Teddy, 139, 182, 195, 207
Kupat Holim sickness fund, 55

Labor movement: alliance with
religious Zionism, 100; anarchistic
elements of, 169; and Arab workers,
83–84, 85; Ben-Gurion as leader
of, 62, 65, 66, 67, 68–70, 77, 81, 99,
100; and Ben-Gurion's class war in
Palestine, 73–74, 100; Ben-Gurion's
move toward hegemony of, 75–77;
and Ben-Gurion's stance on political
violence, 77–78, 99; Ben-Gurion
working toward majority in Zionist
Congress, 78–81; and Jewish immigration to Palestine, 59, 72–75; and
partition plan, 107; political activity
of, 87; and Ramla Platform, 22–23;
and Second Aliya, 41, 81; transfer
of power to state, 175; and Zionist
Executive, 76–77, 78, 81; and Zionist
organization, 78–80
Labour party (Britain), 63, 83, 89,
116–117, 133–134, 135
Ladino language, 32, 33

The Land of Israel Past and Present
(Ben-Gurion and Ben-Zvi), 46, 83
Laskov, Haim, 216
Latrun, battles for, 163–164, 168
Lavie, Shlomo, 60, 238
Lavon, Pinchas: allegations against
Ben-Gurion, 224–226, 227, 228, 229,
230, 236; death of, 239; and "the
Dirty Business" espionage ring, 202,
223–224, 227; and Eshkol, 232–233;
and Mapai election (1959), 217; as
minister of defense, 198, 202, 224;
and Olshan-Dori Commission,
223–224
League of Nations, 60; Permanent
Mandates Commission, 87
the Left: and *Altalena* affair, 166; and
Ben-Gurion, 187, 188, 189, 196, 199,
200, 225; and Bolshevik Revolution,
58, 68; and Bund, 57; European left,
77; and Mapam, 164; and Palmach,
169; and Russian polemical
literature, 14
Left Poalei Zion party, 68
Lehi (Lohamei Herut Yisrael; the
Stern Gang), 133, 137, 138, 238
Lenin, Vladimir Ilyich: Ben-Gurion's
admiration of, 71–72, 85, 108, 118;
legacy of, 245; realism of, 86
Levantine culture, 176
Libya, 175
Lichtheim, Richard, 242
Likud party, 236
Lydda, 170–171

Ma'arach (Alignment), 233–234
Ma'ariv, 218, 236
MacDonald, Malcolm, 89, 111–116,
119, 120
MacDonald, Ramsay, 87, 89, 90
MacDonald Letter, 87, 90
McMahon, Henry, 111
Maghreb, 176
Magnes, Judah, 150
Makleff, Mordechai, 167, 168
Malaria, 18–19, 25, 36
Mao Tse-tung, 196

Mapai (Mifleget Poalei Eretz Yisrael; Workers' Party of the Land of Israel), 78–79, 98, 146, 147, 225; Ben-Gurion's leadership of, 75, 78, 87–89, 99, 132, 159, 187, 207, 215–217, 229–230; and Ben-Gurion's memoirs, 234–235; and Ben-Gurion's partition plan, 106, 109–110; charges against Ben-Gurion for defamatory remarks, 233–234; Eshkol's leadership of, 232–233; and Faction B, 131, 168; and Jewish state, 150, 159, 162, 164; Katznelson's resignation from, 77; Min Hayesod faction, 232–233
Mapam party, 164, 168, 173, 186–188
Mapu, Abraham, 6
Marcus, David "Mickey," 159, 163
Marcus Aurelius, 184
Marshall, George C., 160
Marxism, 14, 19, 21, 22–23, 57, 66
Masaryk, Jan, 112
May, Doris, 104–105, 129
Meir, Golda, 106, 155–156, 160; Ben-Gurion's correspondence with, 9; as foreign minister, 217; relations with Ben-Gurion, 159, 162, 202, 217, 225, 228, 234, 235, 239, 241
Memoirs (Ben-Gurion), 234
Meyerson, Golda. See Meir, Golda
Middle East, 175–176, 208, 211
Milo, Yosef, 185
Mitnagdim, 3
Mizrachi Jews, 76, 214, 216
Molotov-Ribbentrop Pact, 115
Montenegro, 34
Montesquieu, Charles-Louis de Secondat, Baron de, 183
Montgomery, Bernard, 131
Montor, Henry, 148
Morgenthau, Henry, 38
Morocco, 176
Morrison, Herbert, 145
Morrison-Grady Plan, 145, 146
Moshavim (cooperative agricultural settlements), 179–180, 200–201
Moshavot (colonies), 18, 24–25, 74
Mossad for Illegal Immigration, 148

Mount Hermon, 25
Moyne, Walter Guinness, Lord, 133, 138
Munbaz, Benia, 152
Munich crisis (1938), 111
Mussolini, Benito, 77

Nadich, Rabbi Judah, 140–141
Namier, Lewis, 103, 104, 113–114
Namir, Mordechai, 202, 217
Naphtali, Fritz, 215–216
Nasser, Gamal Abdel, 205, 208, 209
National Committee, 158
National Library, Jerusalem, 70
"The National Mission of the Working Class" (Ben-Gurion), 73
Navon, Yitzhak, 195
Nazi party: collaboration of non-Jew displaced persons with, 136; rise of, 77, 80, 86, 92. See also Holocaust and Holocaust survivors
Negev desert: Ben-Gurion living in kibbutz in, 195, 196–201, 202, 224, 225, 231, 234; Eden's proposal for division of, 212; fighting in, 172; and nuclear technology, 187, 226, 227, 230, 243
Nelkin, Rachel. See Beit Halachmi, Rachel
Netanya, 163
New Zionist Organization, 99, 138–139
Nietzsche, Friedrich, 10, 11
Nonpartisan party, 54, 55, 56, 57, 58
Nuclear energy, 186, 187, 226–228, 243

Olshan-Dori Commission of Inquiry, 202, 222–226
Operation Agatha ("Black Saturday"), 144, 147
Operation Danny, 168, 170–172
Operation Horev, 172
Operation Kadesh, 209–210
Operation Yoav, 169
Ottoman Empire: Ben-Gurion's attitude toward, 38, 40; and

Ottoman Empire (*continued*)
Capitulations, 37; and democracy,
31; and First Balkan War, 34; and
Palestine, 18, 23, 37, 45
Oz, Amos, 197

Palcor news agency, 107
Pale of Settlement, 2, 4, 7–8, 16
Palestine: Arab opposition to Jewish
settlement, 82, 83, 86, 102, 115; and
Balfour Declaration, 48–49, 60,
62, 76, 82, 118, 119; Ben-Gurion
and Ben-Zvi's book on, 46; Ben-
Gurion's class war in, 73–74; Ben-
Gurion's deportation from, 40–41,
53, 82; Ben-Gurion's descriptions
of, 20; Ben-Gurion's immigration
to, 6, 8, 11, 13, 14, 16, 17–19; Ben-
Gurion's partition plan, 106–109;
Ben-Gurion's vision of Jewish
majority in, 50; bi-national proposal,
84, 85, 246; British proposed evacuation of, 154; capitalism in, 72, 73;
Coupland's partition plan, 105–106,
107; Herzl's defining Jewish state
in Palestine, 10, 124; Jamal Pasha's
deportation of foreign subjects
from, 37, 38, 40–41, 49; Jewish
economic and social foundations in,
76; and Jewish land purchase, 87,
102, 112, 114, 116; Jewish majority
needed in, 54, 60, 62, 83, 84, 85, 88,
90, 95; and Jewish public opinion,
77; Jewish sovereignty in, 84, 85,
95, 106; landscape of, 18, 25; Mandatory government, 57, 60, 62, 74, 76,
79, 82, 86–88, 93, 102, 106, 108,
109–110, 112, 116, 133, 139, 146, 175;
and Morrison-Grady Plan, 145;
partition plans, 105–111, 113–114, 133,
138, 145, 154, 157, 158; and Passfield
White Paper, 86–87, 89; political
violence in, 77–78; proposal for
autonomous areas of, 84, 145; and
territorial contiguity of Jewish
settlement, 84, 88; transfer of
displaced Jews to, 120–121, 122, 123,
124–125, 140, 143, 145–146; White
Paper (1939), 114–116, 119–120, 126,
134–137, 142–143; and World War II,
122–123; Shlomo Zemach's immigration to, 13–14, 16. *See also* Jewish
immigration to Palestine; Yishuv
Palestine Lands Transfer Regulations,
116
Palestine Royal Commission, 105
Palmach, 144, 163, 169; and *Altalena*
affair, 165–166; Ben-Gurion's
disbanding of, 187; Ben-Gurion's
lack of trust in, 156, 167, 168, 169;
and Ben-Gurion's preparation for
war, 148, 155; flexibility of, 156, 157;
and knowledge of Holocaust, 221;
and Mapam members, 168
Pan-Arab Movement, 94
Passfield, Sidney Webb, Lord, 86
Passfield White Paper, 86–87, 89
Pearl Harbor attack, 122
Peel, William Robert, Lord, 105
Peel Commission, 106, 107, 108
People's Council, 147–148
Peres, Shimon, 198, 202, 208, 216, 217,
224, 225
Petach Tikva, 18, 32
Petty-bourgeois society, and Fourth
Aliya, 72, 73
Philby, Harry St. John, 103
Phony War, 116
Pioneering ethos, 42, 175, 176, 198–201
Plato, 105, 129, 183, 184
Plonsk, Poland, 4, 13–14, 15, 159;
Ben-Gurion's connection with, 1–2,
214, 234, 238–239; Ben-Gurion's
return visits to, 26, 35, 36; Paula
Ben-Gurion with Green family in,
64; education in, 3, 4–5; Jews of,
1, 2, 3–4, 9
Poalei Zion (Workers of Zion) party:
and Akhdut Ha'avoda, 59; in
America, 24, 65; and Arab workers,
83; and Bar-Giora, 27; Ben-Gurion
as member of, 14–16, 20–24, 29, 38,
39, 43, 55, 57; and Bolshevik Revolution, 68; exile of leaders of, 54;

and Jewish Legion, 56; and language issue, 21–22; in New York, 44; Ottomanization of, 38, 40; in Palestine, 20, 21–24, 57, 58; Palestinocentrist trends in, 22; political vision of, 31, 32; and Ramla Platform, 22; in Russia, 14, 24; and Zionism, 14, 23–24, 57, 58

Pogroms, 7, 15, 28, 57, 68

Poland: Ben-Gurion's attempts to visit, 140; Jewish immigration to Israel from, 175, 176; and Palestine partition plan, 108; and Zionist Congress elections, 79, 80. *See also* Plonsk, Poland

Polish language, 6

Proskauer, Joseph, 123, 220–221

Rabin, Yitzhak, 171, 231, 236

Rafi (Reshimat Poalei Yisrael; Israel Workers List), 233–234

Ramla Platform, 22–23

Rangoon Conference (December 1952), 204

Revisionist party: and Arlosoroff, 80; and Ben-Gurion, 78, 79; and Betarists, 77; Jabotinsky as leader of, 73, 75–76, 78, 80; and labor movement, 77; and partition plan, 107; secession from Zionist Organization, 99; and Seventeenth Zionist Congress, 90

Riftin, Ya'akov (Kuba), 186–187

the Right: and *Altalena* affair, 166, 188; and Ben-Gurion, 173, 188, 189, 196, 199, 200, 218, 225; and General Zionists, 73; and Zionism, 57

Romania, 140, 175

Rommel, Erwin, 127, 131

Roosevelt, Franklin D., 113, 121, 133, 134

Rosenwald, Lessing, 220

Rotenstreich, Nathan, 213, 228

Rothberg, Meir, 68

Rothschild, Edmond de, 25, 48, 73

Rousseau, Jean-Jacques, 189

Royal Navy, and illegal Jewish immigration to Palestine, 141

Ruppin, Arthur, 81, 85, 95

Ruskin, Lewis, 113, 114

Russia: civil war in, 57, 67, 68; ideology of social democracy, 4; New Economic Policy in, 71; tsarist rule in, 40, 45, 49, 188

Russian "Go to the People" movement, 7, 21

Russian language, 22

Russian Revolution, 14, 15

Rutenberg, Pinchas, 49, 50, 96

Sa'id, Nuri, 103, 104

Salonika, 32, 33

Sambursky, Shmuel, 186

Samuel, Herbert, first viscount, 215

Saudi Arabia, 105

Scharf, Ze'ev, 195–196

Schlesinger, Arthur, Jr., 211

Schocken, Gustav, 189

Scholem, Gershom, 46, 236

Sdeh Boker, 185, 196–201, 202, 224, 225, 231, 234

Second Aliya: and agricultural labor, 26, 42; Ben-Gurion's memories of, 234, 238; and cooperative settlements, 53–54; and Galilee, 24, 25; and individual immigration, 191; internal coalescence of, 53–55; and mission of Zionism, 11, 23–24, 41–42; opposition to declarative Zionism of Zionist Congresses, 50; and Palestine labor movement, 41, 81; and reality of Palestine, 19–20, 24; and "shortcut" bypassing capitalism, 66, 72; Third Aliya's relationship with, 65; and Yizkor Book, 46; and Shlomo Zemach, 13

Secular socialist-oriented schools, 175

Sejera, 25, 26, 27, 28, 29

Serbia, 34

Shamir, Shlomo, 163

Sharett, Moshe (Shertok), 92, *194*, 227; Ben-Gurion's correspondence with, 193; and Ben-Gurion's preparations for war, 156; Ben-Gurion's relationship with, 132, 203–204, 206,

Sharett, Moshe (Shertok) (*continued*)
207–209, 225; and Declaration
of Independence, 160, 161; and
partition plan, 107, 110; as prime
minister, 198, 202, 203, 206, 207,
224, 226; recruiting American Jews
for Jewish army, 159
Sharm el-Sheikh, 211
Sharon, Ariel, 205, 231
Shazar, Zalman, 235
Sheikh Munis, 200
Shertok, Moshe. *See* Sharett, Moshe
Shiloah, Reuven, 139
Shochat, Israel, 22, 27, 28, 29, 35
Shochat, Manya, 27, 35, 181
Sholem Aleichem (Shalom Rabino-
wich), 185
Silver, Rabbi Abba Hillel, 128, 142,
146–147
Sinai Campaign, 209–212, 217, 227,
243
Sinai Peninsula, 172
Six-Day War (1967), 164, 180, 212,
236, 237
Sneh, Moshe, 138–139, 144
Socialist International, 45, 59
Socialists and socialism, 34, 58, 107,
175, 180; Poalei Zion and, 14, 15,
22–23, 24; and Zionism, 15, 50–51, 57
Social Revolutionary (SR) party, 49
Sokolov, Nachum, 7
Solel Boneh, 67, 75
Sonneborn, Rudolf G., 149
Sonneborn Foundation, 149, 227
Soviet Union, 66, 209; agricultural
exhibition in, 68–70; and Zionism,
70–72, 157
Spinoza, Baruch, 10, 183, 192
Stavsky, Avraham, 80–81
Stern, Abraham, 137
Stern Gang (Lehi), 133, 137, 138, 238
Strumsa, Joseph, 32
Suez Canal: Israeli "Dirty Business"
espionage ring, 201–202, 223–225;
nationalization crisis, 209–211
Syria, 160, 163

Tabenkin, Yitzhak, 14, 66, 97, 98, 100,
131, 169
Talmon, Jacob, 214–215, 228, 236
Taub, Eddie, 130
Taub, Miriam (Cohen), 129–130, 133,
234–235, 238
Tchernichovsky, Saul, 6
Tel Aviv, 37, 59, 103, 165, 166; Herzliya
Gymnasium, 7, 40, 92; Jewish
immigration to, 72, 74
Tel Aviv Museum, 162
Tel Aviv University, 200
Territorialism, 4, 54
Teveth, Shabtai, 22, 25, 129, 151, 234
Thucydides, 184
Tocqueville, Alexis de, 183
Tolstoy, Leo, 6
Transjordan, 93, 105, 159, 160, 172
Truman, Harry S., 133, 136–137, 140,
142–143, 145, 172
Trumpeldor, Joseph, 39
Tse'irei Zion (the Young of Zion)
party, 58
Turgenev, Ivan, 6
Turkey, 37. *See also* Ottoman Empire
Turkish language, Ben-Gurion's study
of, 32, 33

Uganda Program, 7–8
Ukraine, 2, 29, 68, 69
United Jewish Appeal, 148, 210
United Nations: Ben-Gurion and,
205–206; British transfer of Palestine problem to, 153, 154; General
Assembly's vote for partition, 154,
157, 161; Hammarskjold's imposing
international rule for Israel, 205, 211
United Nations Security Council, 196,
204
United Nations Special Committee
on Palestine (UNSCOP), 154, 161
United States: arms for Israel
promised by, 204–205; Ben-Gurion's
activity in, 41, 43–46, 120, 121, 126,
128–129, 131, 147, 234–235; and Ben-
Gurion's concept of democracy, 189;

Ben-Gurion's relations with, 173, 205–206, 222, 243; and Israel's development of nuclear capability, 226, 227, 230, 243; loan to Israel, 196, 210; and Meir's raising funds for arms, 155; public opinion in, 121, 122, 134, 142; and Sinai Campaign, 210–211; support for reduction of Israel's territory, 206; and U.N. General Assembly resolution for partition of Palestine, 157, 158; Weizmann's activity in, 127, 132; and World War I, 45, 49–50; and World War II, 122, 124–125. See also American Jewry

U.S. State Department, 121

Venizelos, Sophoklis, 184
Vienna, Austria: Ben-Gurion's visits to, 26, 35, 40; World Federation of Poalei Zion conference in, 26, 35
Von Kleist, Heinrich, 230

Wadi Zin gravesite, 17, 241
War Communism, 67, 71
War of Independence: Arab defeat in, 180; and Ben-Gurion's agents, 139; and Ben-Gurion's authority, 170, 196, 243, 245; and Hebraization of names, 181–182; and Sharett, 204; truce and armistice agreements, 164–165, 172, 173, 205, 209
Warsaw, Poland, Ben-Gurion's move to, 11–13
Warsaw Mechanical-Technical School, 11, 12–13
Wauchope, Arthur, 90–91, 92, 95, 107
Wawelberg, Hyppolite, 11, 12
Webb, Beatrice, Baroness Passfield, 87
Weizmann, Chaim, 91, 128; Ben-Gurion compared to, 121, 122, 125–126, 145; Ben-Gurion's relationship with, 110, 116, 127–128, 132, 146, 147–148, 229–230; Ben-Gurion's restoration to presidency of Zionist Organization, 99–100; and Biltmore

Program, 123, 124, 125, 127; on British Empire, 126; and Conservative party of Britain, 95–96; and Coupland partition plan, 107; decline of, 232; on Fourth Aliya, 72; gradualism and moderation of, 76, 90, 125, 145; and Palestine partition plan, 110, 111, 112, 133; and Palestine Royal Commission, 105; and Passfield White Paper, 87; and Twenty-first Zionist Congress, 115; and Twenty-second Zionist Congress, 146, 147; United States visit of, 122; on violence against British, 144; and World War II, 118, 119; and Zionist activity in London, 39, 49, 89, 103–104, 124, 125–126

Weizmann-Faisal Agreement of 1919, 94
We and Our Neighbors (Ben-Gurion), 66
West Bank, 173, 204, 207
Western Europe, 40, 86; World War II and, 116, 124–125, 126
White Paper (1939), 114–116, 119–120, 126, 134–137, 142–143
Wilson, Woodrow, 49–50
Wise, Stephen, 118
Women's Equal Rights Law, 191
Woodhead Commission, 111, 113
Workers' Councils, 67
World Federation of Poalei Zion, 21, 26, 59, 63, 65
World War I, 36, 37–40, 45, 71, 111, 118, 119
World War II, 1, 116–121, 122, 133

Yadin, Yigael, 160, 163, 164, 167, 168, 180
Yalta conference, 134
Yavne'eli, Shmuel, 238
Yemen, 105, 175
Yiddish language, 21–22, 29–30, 43, 99, 141
Yishuv: Ben-Gurion as leader of, 93, 95, 96–97, 99, 107, 114, 117, 121, 127,

Yishuv (*continued*)
137, 138, 139–140, 143, 146, 147, 153,
155, 162, 215, 243; and Declaration of
Independence, 162; defense forces
of, 27, 28, 29, 112, 117, 137, 148,
155–156, 162; development of, 83, 91,
92; and Holocaust, 221; and immigration, 72, 91, 92, 106, 109, 112, 115,
141, 144, 176; and inter-community
war, 157; and the left, 187; and partition plan, 108, 109, 111; and policy
of restraint, 137; public opinion in,
107; and Russian language, 6; and
transition to Jewish state, 158–159,
166, 167, 177, 178; and voluntarism,
175, 178; and White Paper (1939),
114, 115; and World War II, 119
Yisraeli, Haim, 195, 241
Yizhar, S. (Izhar Smilansky), 199
Yizkor Book, Ben-Gurion's expanded
edition of, 45–46
Yom Kippur War, 241
Young Turks revolution (1908), 27, 31
Youth Aliya, 178

Zeilsheim, Germany, displaced persons
camp in, 140
Zemach, Shlomo, 10, 26; Ben-Gurion's
friendship with, 3, 5–6, 7, 13, 14, 20,
60, 238–239; immigration to
Palestine, 13–14, 16
Zerubavel, Jacob, 30–31, 45, 51
Zikhron Ya'akov, 26, 30
Zionism: American Zionism, 43,
123–124, 128, 129, 134, 142, 146; Arab
opposition to, 76, 82–83; Ben-Gurion
as leader of, 99–100, 101, 121, 246;
and Ben-Gurion on secessionist
organizations, 137–139; Ben-Gurion's
"fighting Zionism," 115, 116, 118, 137,
139, 145, 154–155; Ben-Gurion's
Zionist ideals, 51–52, 74, 125, 126;
and Berdyczewski's concept of will,
15; and Biltmore Program, 123–124,
125, 127, 131, 149–150, 238; Borochov
on, 23; competition with communism, 68, 69, 70, 71; and crisis of

faith, 74–75; and egalitarianism, 54;
and Faction B, 131, 168; and Herzl,
4, 10–11, 50; and Histadrut, 65;
ideology of, 4; and Jewish Legion,
55; and Jews' right to establish
independent entity in Palestine,
62; Joint Emergency Council, 123,
128; and Katznelson, 54; labor
movement's alliance with religious
Zionism, 100; and MacDonald
Letter, 87; Ottoman Empire's
opposition to, 37; and partition
debate, 106–108; and Poalei Zion,
14, 23–24, 57, 58; and public opinion,
97, 98, 141; and Rutenberg, 49; and
"shortcut" bypassing capitalism, 66,
72, 73–74; and socialism, 15, 50–51,
57; talks between Ben-Gurion and
Jabotinsky on, 96, 97; and transfer
of displaced Jews to Palestine, 121,
122, 123, 136; and United Nations
partition plan, 154; and World
War II, 118–120, 123
Zionist Actions Committee, 145, 147,
148, 149
Zionist Archive, New York, 234–235
Zionist Congress, 23, 41, 50, 73; First
(Basel, 1897), 4; Sixth (Basel, 1903),
7–8, 16; Eighth (The Hague, 1907),
24; Eleventh (Vienna, 1913), 35–36;
Seventeenth (Basel, 1931), 75–76,
89–90; Eighteenth (Prague, 1933),
78, 79, 80, 92, 98; Nineteenth
(Lucerne, 1935), 98, 99–100, 101;
Twentieth (Basel, 1937), 108, 110;
Twenty-first (Geneva, 1939), 115;
Twenty-second (Basel, 1946),
145–147; Twenty-fifth (Jerusalem,
1960–1961), 226, 227; and Ben-
Gurion's national leadership, 99–101;
labor movement majority in, 78–80;
and Palestine partition plan, 109–110
Zionist Executive: and Arab Revolt
(1936), 102; Ben-Gurion as chairman
of, 100, 116, 127, 131, 147, 153, 195;
Ben-Gurion and defense portfolio
of, 148; Ben-Gurion's work in, 66,

81, 92; and Ben-Gurion/Weizmann cooperation, 132–133; British arrests of members, 144; coalition of, 76–77; as governing body, 75; Irgun's claims against, 221; and Jerusalem-Biltmore Program, 131; and Jewish Agency Executive, 79; and Palestine partition plan, 110; and policy of restraint, 102; Silver as head of in United States, 147; Weizmann's resignation from, 87. *See also* Jewish Agency Executive

Zionist Organization: Ben-Gurion's restoration of Weizmann to presidency of, 99–100; funding of, 72, 73, 75, 76, 79; Herzl as president of, 5,

7–8; and labor movement, 78–80; and national capital, 54, 59, 66; and nationally owned land, 54, 59, 66; neutrality during World War I, 38–39; and Palestine partition plan, 110; and provisional state council for Jewish state, 158–159; and secessionist organizations, 137–138; Sokolov as president of, 7; Weizmann's representation to British and American governments, 125, 127, 128, 132; Weizmann's threats to resign as president, 144

Zion Mule Corps, Egypt, 39

ZS, the Zionist-Socialist party, 69, 70

Zvi, Shabtai, 236

JEWISH LIVES is a major series of interpretive
biography designed to illuminate the imprint of Jewish
figures upon literature, religion, philosophy, politics, cultural and
economic life, and the arts and sciences. Subjects are paired with
authors to elicit lively, deeply informed books that explore the
range and depth of Jewish experience
from antiquity through the present.

Jewish Lives is a partnership of Yale University Press
and the Leon D. Black Foundation.

Ileene Smith is editorial director.
Anita Shapira and Steven J. Zipperstein are series editors.

PUBLISHED TITLES INCLUDE:

Bernard Berenson: A Life in the Picture Trade, by Rachel Cohen
Sarah: The Life of Sarah Bernhardt, by Robert Gottlieb
Leonard Bernstein, by Allen Shawn
David: The Divided Heart, by David Wolpe
Moshe Dayan: Israel's Controversial Hero, by Mordechai Bar-On
Becoming Freud: The Making of a Psychoanalyst, by Adam Phillips
Emma Goldman: Revolution as a Way of Life, by Vivian Gornick
Hank Greenberg: The Hero Who Didn't Want to Be One,
    by Mark Kurlansky
Lillian Hellman: An Imperious Life, by Dorothy Gallagher
Jabotinsky: A Life, by Hillel Halkin
Jacob: Unexpected Patriarch, by Yair Zakovitch
Franz Kafka: The Poet of Shame and Guilt, by Saul Friedländer
Rav Kook: Mystic in a Time of Revolution, by Yehudah Mirsky
Primo Levi: The Matter of a Life, by Berel Lang
Moses Mendelssohn: Sage of Modernity, by Shmuel Feiner
Walter Rathenau: Weimar's Fallen Statesman, by Shulamit Volkov
Solomon: The Lure of Wisdom, by Steven Weitzman
Leon Trotsky: A Revolutionary's Life, by Joshua Rubenstein

FORTHCOMING TITLES INCLUDE:

Rabbi Akiva, by Barry Holtz
Irving Berlin, by James Kaplan

Hayim Nahman Bialik, by Avner Holtzman

Léon Blum, by Pierre Birnbaum

Louis Brandeis, by Jeffrey Rosen

Martin Buber, by Paul Mendes-Flohr

Benjamin Disraeli, by David Cesarani

Bob Dylan, by Ron Rosenbaum

Albert Einstein, by Steven Gimbel

George Gershwin, by Gary Giddins

Allen Ginsberg, by Edward Hirsch

Peggy Guggenheim, by Francine Prose

Ben Hecht, by Adina Hoffman

Heinrich Heine, by Fritz Stern

Theodor Herzl, by Derek Penslar

Louis Kahn, by Wendy Lesser

Groucho Marx, by Lee Siegel

J. Robert Oppenheimer, by David Rieff

Marcel Proust, by Benjamin Taylor

Julius Rosenwald, by Hasia Diner

Mark Rothko, by Annie Cohen-Solal

Jonas Salk, by David Margolick

Steven Spielberg, by Molly Haskell

The Warner Brothers, by David Thomson

Ludwig Wittgenstein, by Anthony Gottlieb